Praise for *Unleash Your Authentic Self!*

"If you are serious about transforming your life and tapping into your true potential, *Unleash Your Authentic Self* can be the doorway to a brand new world of possibility." Christopher Howard, No. 1 Best-selling Author and Lifestyle & Wealth Strategist.

"*Unleash Your Authentic Self* is filled with truth after truth. When you read it, get a highlighter because you will want to make note of the truths that resonate with you the most and apply them to your life." Lisa Garr, host of the *Aware Show.*

UNLEASH
YOUR
AUTHENTIC
SELF!

UNLEASH
YOUR
AUTHENTIC
SELF!

Your Inner Truth Sets You Free

ELAINE MC GUINNESS

BALBOA.
PRESS
A DIVISION OF HAY HOUSE

Balboa Press books may be ordered through booksellers or by contacting:

Balboa Press
A Division of Hay House
1663 Liberty Drive
Bloomington, IN 47403
www.balboapress.com
1 (877) 407-4847

Because of the dynamic nature of the Internet, any web addresses or links contained in this book may have changed since publication and may no longer be valid. The views expressed in this work are solely those of the author and do not necessarily reflect the views of the publisher, and the publisher hereby disclaims any responsibility for them.

The author of this book does not dispense medical advice or prescribe the use of any technique as a form of treatment for physical, emotional, or medical problems without the advice of a physician, either directly or indirectly. The intent of the author is only to offer information of a general nature to help you in your quest for emotional and spiritual well-being. In the event you use any of the information in this book for yourself, which is your constitutional right, the author and the publisher assume no responsibility for your actions.

Certain stock imagery © Thinkstock.
Any people depicted in stock imagery provided by Thinkstock are models, and such images are being used for illustrative purposes only.

Print information available on the last page.

Library of Congress Control Number: 2015900487

ISBN: 978-1-5043-2654-4 (sc)
ISBN: 978-1-5043-2655-1 (hc)
ISBN: 978-1-5043-2653-7 (e)

Balboa Press rev. date: 2/23/2015

For Fran

The world can teach no images of you unless you want to learn them. There will come a time when images have all gone by, and you will see you know not what you are. It is to this unsealed and open mind that truth returns, unhindered and unbound. Where concepts of the self have been laid by is truth revealed exactly as it is. When every concept has been raised to doubt and question, and been recognized as made on no assumptions that will stand the light, then is the truth left free to enter in its sanctuary, clean and free of guilt. There is no statement that the world is more afraid to hear than this:

I do not know the thing I am, and therefore do not know what I am doing, where I am, or how to look upon the world or myself. Yet in this learning is salvation born. And what you are will tell you of itself.

(Helen Schucman and William N. Thetford, *A Course in Miracles*)

CONTENTS

FOREWORD

Expressing your authentic self is what sets you free. Expressing your truth comes from standing in your own power of who you truly are. You can reset the compass of your mind now to steer you in this direction. In this way, you come to know the truth of who you really are, and thus you can detach from who you thought you were. You can take aim now towards aligning with and expressing your authentic self, no matter what your circumstances. Expressing your true self is natural in reality. Your true self seeks to express love and compassion. Your authentic self looks for the good and seeks to help, support, and guide you and others, when appropriate. It is possible to detach yourself from others' opinions. You can learn to view challenges as opportunities to learn, and when you learn, everything is as it should be. Learning is continuous, enabling you to be a better person than ever before, in all areas of life. By moving towards your authentic self at your core, you become aware of the beauty, inner peace, belonging, *being*, *is*, and *I am* that are always there. With this connection to your true source, your perception of everything on the outside becomes transformed also. You can now see beauty, love, abundance, and harmony in your daily experiences on a grander scale. It is your perception that creates your experiences, and your perception comes from who you think you are. As you move closer to your core, you become self-actualized. With this self-actualization, you have fewer assumptions or judgements about other people, while at the same time there is less noise or talk inside your head. When aligned with your authentic self, you can rise above issues that arise, while remaining neutral and non-judgemental at the same time. This is because you know your true power lies within, and you don't need anything from the outside. When you are "in-powered", you don't need approval or acceptance from anybody else, because you already approve of and accept yourself fully from the place of your authentic self. Because of this, you can accept and interact directly with everything around you, without letting your thoughts get in the way.

By spending more time in silence, you can sit with yourself in peace and feel your inner awareness growing. In this way, through self-reflection you can learn more about yourself and others. You can realize that through your challenges and suffering, you have gained strength and awareness. Nothing has been wasted, and everything has been useful. You have no regrets. You learn to recognize yourself in how you perceive others around you. You may also come to realize how the *I* and *me* exist within. *I* is that spiritual aspect of your inner being – that is, your authentic self. *I* connects with the source of the universal mind, through which all things come into creation. The *me* is your self-concept of who you think you are now. Your concept of yourself changes over time, as do the outside conditions of your life. In reality, the *I* never changes. It is that infinite, all-knowing, and all-powerful aspect of your true divinity. The *I* observes the *me* in your daily activities. The *I* is that subjective part of you and is not caught up directly with emotions. *I* is not the ego mind, and therefore *I* can remain detached and free in good and bad times, no matter what. While you become aware of this perspective of the *I* and *me* in this book, you will also learn about the conscious and the subconscious mind. By unlearning and shedding the layers of conditioning and self-defeating beliefs you may be carrying, you free yourself gradually to express yourself fully. In this way, you drop the former illusion of who you thought you were. By casting off this illusion, you reveal the real you that interacts directly with the world from the inside out. When you have compassion and empathy for those who suffer, you are living through love and with love. Love conquers all fear. Negativity is replaced by love, like light in a dark room. Love is the answer to all of life's problems. Love conquers hatred, and light banishes darkness.

Your power lies in the now. Now is eternity. You can learn to live in the now and so avoid ruminating about the past or worrying about the future. Your body gives you access to the inner body, which lies between you and your source. All is well in the here and now, where space and time do not exist. You can learn to listen to the stillness in the gaps around you. By being aware of the silence without, you become aware of the silence within, where the soul resides in stillness. Peace and joy co-exist with the spirit. Only the ego gets in the way and blocks your path to this serenity. You cannot fight the ego, but you can accept and overcome it by being constantly aware of it in your presence of mind. This practise becomes easier with repetition. By tapping into your own inner power, you can handle the challenges life sets for you. You realize that everything is as it should be. Everything that happens is in divine order. Accepting all that is in the moment, without resistance, allows abundance into your life to flow like a river. When you are in the flow, you know, feel, and believe that anything is possible. With belief, you can participate in creating your reality on the outside from where you are on the inside. In this way, you become a co-creator with the universe for your own reality. You deserve the best. You deserve to give yourself the best and allow good things to come into your life now. At times, life can be a struggle, but in the process, it strengthens you and teaches you valuable lessons about the power of the human spirit. Live in the power! Live in the now! I would like to be of service to you in helping you to bring these things into focus for yourself. In this way you become empowered to bring about balance in your own life. In the process you learn to flow with the good and learn from the perceived bad. You become stronger for it and understand so that it won't be a problem again. You can become more focused on what you want out of life. Now you can stand back from the dramas of life and not become hooked by them or the opinions of others.

Know that you do your best always. No matter what dramas may unfold, you can learn to view them objectively and not to get caught up in them; to stand back, so to speak. Your way of letting go is through self-knowledge, acceptance, and mindfulness. Your inner state of being can be unaffected by events that happen around you, when you are grounded in who you really are. In the process of self-discovery, you can condense your learning into something you can relate to, be aware of, or do something about through action and so become free. Your alignment with your authentic self is what gives you balance in life. Once your empowerment from within is ignited, it takes on a life of its own. Realize the importance of asking the right questions and the manner in which they are asked. There is a skill in asking questions as well as in listening. Your authentic self does the right thing while honouring your values. With self-realization, you will find that you react much less, if at all, to certain situations going on around you. You will tend not to judge people as much and, instead, become curious about them. You will be much less likely to get offended and take things personally. You will have compassion and empathy for what might have been considered irritating before. Your thoughts will become less in number while you look at things from others' perspectives also. You will put yourself in their shoes, which leads you to feel compassion for them instead. Your feelings do not need to be connected to others' feelings. Letting go means that you can still care about others while being free to live your life as you are meant to, with a fully rounded wheel of life that feels smooth in its flow. In expressing your authentic self, you come to realize that you have an obligation to live a happy, full life in peace, harmony, and joy with yourself and others. Are you ready for this change in your life? You can make the commitment to yourself now on paper that you can and will make the change, and it will start or continue from now in the moment.

We are all one. We are not separate. We are all part of the energy field. Quantum physics is showing this to be the case. What you do individually affects the energy in the field, and likewise, you are affected in the same way. Stay grounded. Be impeccable with your word. You can learn to control the "monkey mind." When you do so, your thoughts become pure, and in this way, your vibration energy becomes raised to a higher level of being on the earth plane. The words you use and the thoughts you think should be in constant awareness. If you forget what you're saying or thinking, you lose connection with your true self. Freedom allows expression of your real self. To be free is to be true to your essential self, your very nature. Being free means you can express yourself fully. Being true to yourself means you can just be yourself. When you allow this to happen, you are surrendering by letting go and trusting in all that is, in all that you are. When you focus on joy, peace, serenity, and bliss, you are at home in yourself, in your heart. Truth for you is not the same truth for someone else. You do not need to change yourself to agree with someone else's truth or to validate their truth. You cannot change other people. You can change only yourself. Often attributed to Mahatma Gandhi are the words, "Be the change you wish to see in the world." You are who you are in body, mind, and spirit. You don't need to pretend to be what or who you are not. When you are aligned with your authentic self, how you are on the inside is how you are on the outside. Who do you think you are? Is who you think you are the real you, or is it the self-concept that was imposed on you from the outside through your conditioning in life? Is it time to shed the layers of conditioning now to reveal the real you? Do you know now why you weren't fulfilled before? My intention is that this book will help you to find your own answers in life by tapping into your authentic self and in so doing set yourself free. In expressing your authentic self, you free yourself to experience the abundance and prosperity in life that were always your birthright. Your freedom to manifest abundance in your life comes through being aligned with your authentic self.

PREFACE

Through this book, my aim is to give back to life and be in service to you. My intention is to assist you in gaining self-knowledge and insight into your life. With this self-awareness, you can set yourself free from the suffering, pain, and struggle you may be experiencing at present in your life, through expressing your authentic self. Your own truth is what sets you free from physical and emotional pain. By being true to yourself, you can promote your own healing of the body, mind and spirit.

Unleashing your authentic self is a journey of self-discovery, self-awareness, self-knowledge, and self-empowerment to live your life with freedom. In this way, I can help you to learn to unlearn from the inside out. What you have learned so far in life provides you with so many more opportunities to develop and evolve personally. Your experience of life, no matter what it is, can actually be the foundation for you to unshackle the chains of illusion and trapped emotions that you felt compelled to put up with until now. Your understanding of your experience, once expressed, is what frees you from your former slave-master of guilt, fear, and anger. Self-expression is made possible by means of your own self-realization. You can express that which you know only in the context of how you know yourself. Your belief about who you are is your reference point from which you express yourself. In this way, my aim is to help you to live your life on purpose by inspiring and empowering you towards awareness and self-understanding. In this way, you become compelled and propelled on the path towards self-actualization in expressing your authentic self. This is how you can create your own destiny and live the life of your dreams.

In expressing your authentic self, you become one with the universe as a co-creator for your reality. Empowerment comes from within. Know and believe that you have this untapped power within you at the source of your being. Your true power is linked with your heart connection to the universal realm, where anything is possible. When you open up your heart to what is possible, the universe bestows upon you everything you need: the right people at the right time, the right opportunities at the right time, and being in the right place at the right time. Synchronicity, or non-accidental coincidences, begins to increase in frequency in your life when you tune into the path you are meant to follow. After becoming fully aligned with who you truly are on the inside, there are fewer obstacles on the outside that can prevent you from moving forward. Obstacles can be perceived as challenges you can overcome to get to your destination. Each challenge brings with it a strength that you take on board in surmounting it. As you move closer to your real self at your core, your life on the outside moves automatically towards purpose and fulfilment. This happens through developing self-awareness.

When you develop awareness or self-realization, your life takes on a whole new meaning, as well as the possibilities therein. As you become fully aligned with your authentic self, you get to see things in a different light. You will notice that the light gets brighter all the while, shining brighter upon your reflections and insights of yourself as you take part in your own personal journey to your core. When you can express who you truly are at your core, you are in alignment with your authentic self. When you express your authentic self, you bring forth those aspects of yourself that arise from your divinity. By being true to your self, you transform yourself, your life, other people, and the world. It is this truth that sets you free. By freeing yourself, you allow others to free themselves also. This book aims to show you how to understand, access, and express your authentic self in the world. It takes a leap of faith and courage along the way, for it means a journey of transition to your own personal transformation. As you align with your authentic self, everything you desire flows to you with ease and grace. When you harmonize with your authentic self, your life on the outside becomes harmonized with your heart's desires at the same time. Your inner conditions determine your outer conditions in life. By connecting with your inner power, you realize your ability to co-create with the universe, which is ever abundant. That which is in you is what you are and have already. You have everything you already need in your true essence; that is your authentic self. You can be, do, or have anything your heart desires in reality. Create that vision of what you want for yourself and get to know your authentic self on the inside. By merging the two, you become unstoppable!

Namaste,
Elaine

PART 1:
SELF-UNDERSTANDING

The great masters tell us that the most important question in the world is: "Who am I?" Or rather: "What is I?" What is this thing I call "I"? What is this thing I call self? You mean you understand everything else in the world and you didn't understand this?

—Anthony De Mello

CHAPTER 1

WHO ARE YOU?

If somebody asked you, "Who are you?" what would your answer be? Could you tell him or her in one sentence? If so, how would you describe yourself? Are you defined by your personality, mind, body, or the roles you play? How do you see yourself? You are so used to looking outward to the world in order to make sense of it because this is how you have been taught to learn and gain information. Therefore, you have become conditioned to this way of being and so have forgotten that there is another way to perceive things. We use our five senses of sight, hearing, touch, taste, and smell to make sense of the world. The paradox is that unless you first understand yourself on the inside, you will not fully understand yourself in relation to what is on the outside of you in the world, especially in relation to other people.

What you see on the outside comes from what is already on the inside. You always get what you look for. Otherwise, you would not be seeing it. Also, what you see is what you recognize in yourself. Otherwise, you would not know it. This self I refer to is part of the personality. You are not your personality. You are not your body. You are not your mind. Who you really are at your core is the essence of your being. It remains constant and always has. It is the deepest part of you that lies at your core, hidden from your conscious mind and state of being. Your higher self, your authentic self, gives rise to the knowingness you have that seeps into consciousness at times. Your personality is shaped by the experiences and memories you've had in this lifetime, which gave rise to your habits, mannerisms, and behaviour in general. Your authentic self just is, and it is the real you.

Your journey through life is always moving towards self-actualization, which is the point at which you come to know your self. Challenges in life give rise to lessons to be learned. Every obstacle in life is an opportunity to learn who you really are. There is no such thing as mistakes; there is only feedback. We all learn from our mistakes, which in reality are feedback we can use to become better. The more you learn about yourself, the more you move towards your authentic self. Some people take longer for self-realization, as they believe they must take the path of suffering by holding on to get to where they need to go. Others take the path of self-understanding and awareness without much effort by just letting go and accepting. In this way, they move with steady momentum towards their source, where true self-empowerment lies at the core. Integrating with your true self, in this sense, allows you to live your life with freedom, joy, peace, love, and happiness. Living life in bliss like this is possible. When you see it, you believe it, the saying goes. Well, when you believe it, you see it. Belief is everything. What you believe creates your reality, your idea of who you think you are, and your concept of your self.

What Is Self-Concept?

According to Carl Jung, self-concept is an innate blueprint that represents wholeness and is the central balancing agent within every human. For Jung, individuation is the continual process of striving towards psychological maturity and self-fulfilment to spiritual enlightenment of this self. This is achieved by integrating the conscious and the unconscious aspects of the personality. The process of individuation allows you to see yourself ultimately as an individual person in your own right. In attaining this insight, you can interact with autonomy both in the external world and internally, with yourself. In learning through self-insight how you were compelled to distort personality, you can let go of repression, resolve inner conflicts or traumas, and rely more on messages from the subconscious. In balancing opposing elements of your personality, you allow yourself to achieve the integration of your conscious and unconscious mind. This in turn leads to psychic (mind) wholeness and unity.

According to Jung, you develop psychically in such a way that your best functions are enhanced along with social or educational pressures, inducing conformity. In this way, certain aspects of your personality are distorted because you actually believe you are who you appear to be when you wear the social mask. Your protective social mask is the persona you adopt in society, while your shadow is the unacceptable traits of your character you fear to acknowledge. According to Jung, your self-concept develops when you perceive conditions of self-worth from parents or other caretakers during childhood. By trying to fit in or comply with social expectations, you unconsciously repress or distort elements of the personality for approval or acceptance. The result is a distorted personality; you are incongruent with your true self by becoming a conforming people-pleaser for acceptance in society.

According to Abraham Maslow, the goal of identity (self-actualization, or authenticity) seems to be an end goal in itself while also a rite of passage as you step along the path to the transcendence of your identity. For Maslow, self-actualization is a continuing goal that humans strive towards. Maslow devised a pyramid of needs to illustrate how, once your survival needs are met, you move from satiated-deficiency needs (D-needs) to being needs (B-needs). Once your D-needs of safety, love, respect, self-esteem, and belonging are fulfilled, you turn to B-needs, which motivate you towards self-actualization.

Abraham Maslow's Hierarchy of Needs

Self-actualization empowers you towards autonomy and individuation in restoring your true self. In this way, by having positive self-regard, you can relieve tensions and conflict, thus allowing you to be creative and resourceful in attaining life goals to fulfil your potential. Exerting free will and choice thus allows you to have peak experiences, according to Maslow. In moving towards self-actualization, you move towards unity, individuality, and a search for personal freedom and spontaneous expression.

When freeing yourself of the past, you can then find your natural self through a process of seeking self-realization, insight, and self-fulfilment. Introspection, or looking inward, is invaluable in facilitating this process of self-discovery once all basic needs have been met. This process of self-discovery is self-directional; you strive to achieve a purpose, realize potential, attain ambitions, expand horizons, and improve life circumstances along a constructive growth path towards change and wholeness.

Your true self is the underlying essence of your authentic self, where psychological freedom resides with positive self-regard and where there is congruence with the experiences of life. Carl Rogers describes people who are becoming more actualized as having "(1) An openness to experience (2) A trust in themselves (3) An internal source of evaluation, and (4) A willingness to continue growing."(Morison 2004: 86). Self-actualization is the most important item on the hierarchy of needs. The fulfilment of all the other needs is for the purpose of self-actualization. Without aspiring to self-actualization, life can be wasted. Self-actualization is brought about by integration of all the parts to a unified whole.

Who Are You Really?

Your sense of self determines how and who you are in the world. You are what you think you are, though your thoughts may not reflect the real essence of who you truly are. Sometimes you can sacrifice yourself for the sake of others. You can be so engaged having compassion for everyone else in your life that you leave none for yourself. By giving yourself compassion, you find balance in your life. Having compassion for others can mean saying no and not always saying yes. This allows others to be coactive in their own lives and not codependent on those around them. If you enable others too much, they can become codependent on you and thus fail to learn to do things for themselves. When you respect your own needs, others will respect you also. Being authentic to your real self means doing what's best for everybody, including yourself. You may have felt guilty before at the thought of saying no to people's requests. By saying no sometimes, you let others go and allow them to learn to grow and evolve for themselves. Otherwise, they will never learn and so you are not doing them a favour. Know that you can now say no without feeling guilty. When you do so, you feel stronger inside and are able to speak up for yourself, using your sense of humour for this purpose if necessary.

In achieving saying no, you also allow your self to catch up on what you have put off or sacrificed before for the sake of others. You don't need to be a martyr to be a good person. It is important to take care of your own needs first. This is not selfish. What is right for you is right for others ultimately. If you sacrifice who you are, you are depriving others of the gifts that you can truly offer to the world as your real self. You know what your needs are at your core. When you nourish and cultivate your authentic self, your real self emerges into your being of who you are now in the world. You integrate all aspects of your self as one, living in a state of clarity, peace, harmony, focus, and self-empowerment. Your authentic self emerges as it grows into you. When this happens, and when all the blocks and walls have been removed, you attract abundance and wealth into your life. You are truly open to re-ceiving all that the universe has to offer. You draw prosperity and abundance in wealth and loving relationships to you like a magnet when you are being authentic. This means you are in true alignment with who you really are and that you are at one with all in the universe.

Sometimes people can take you for granted. No matter how much you give, it never seems to be enough in their eyes. Have you ever felt that life just happens to you? Sometimes it may feel this way because you think you have no control over your destiny. You can create your destiny from the way you think in the now. All your actions follow from how you think and intend things to be. You co-create with the universe in manifesting things or events in this world into being. To bring about change, steps must be taken. The more steps that are taken, the easier it is for you to break away from the old path. This world really has a lot of insane distractions if you get sucked in or hooked by them, according to the ego mind. By identifying with your real self, you can be free and unrestrained to experience the natural beauty and abundance that are always around you, even in the midst of chaos. These things are always there even when you choose not to see them. What you focus on, you see. What you see comes from your line of thinking, or your perception. Things in themselves are neutral. It is we who put a perspective on them. You write the story of your life. It is not written for you. Your past does not determine your future. Your true power to change anything lies in the now. You can change the direction any time you want to get to where you already are in reality outside of time. You always have a choice over what you do or what you don't do, no matter how things may seem. You always have a choice as to how you think about a situation, person, or place. When your control comes from the inside, you can consciously choose automatically. When your control comes from the outside, self-understanding and awareness are needed to realize that this is an illusion or delusion that was conditioned into your learning by others. Your true power lies within and not outside of you.

According to Buddhism, the mind is like a monkey and it is often referred to as the 'monkey-mind. Like a monkey the mind can be all over the place, but know that now you have everything you need already! In this moment of now, you can tap into the power of the subconscious by first working on understanding the nature of the conscious mind.

We each have about sixty thousand to ninety thousand thoughts daily. Many of these daily thoughts are the same and familiar. As such, they could be called habits. These habits can consist of thoughts or beliefs that are self-limiting. For example, when a person says, "I am stupid", that person is identifying his or her self-concept with stupidity instead of the feeling of being stupid. There is a difference. Saying "I am [this or that]" repetitively can lead to a self-limiting belief that is not necessarily true. All learning takes place at the subconscious level. This example starts off with a conscious thought that, through repetition, becomes a self-limiting belief in the sub-conscious mind. This belief, like any belief, becomes reinforced each time it is said. This self-limiting belief can then form part of your self-concept, and as a result, you live in the illusion of who you think you are as a finite, limited being. What you recognize as familiar can also be considered safe by the mind, and that is why this happens without you realizing it. The way you view yourself affects the way you are in the world and in turn affects what you create around you. You create your reality. Reality doesn't just happen by itself. You are an active participant in your reality through what you do and what you don't do. Life doesn't just happen to you; it happens through you! All beliefs are in the subconscious mind and affect your behaviour automatically without conscious thought – like autopilot, so to speak. Your reality then becomes the one you create, because you cannot see outside of what you are looking for in the world to fit your view of your self, which is distorted. Your subconscious is responsible for 95 per cent of your behaviour.

You will always find what you are looking for. Whatever you focus on grows. Where your attention goes, that's where your energy goes. Thoughts carry energy and affect the actual workings of the brain, in terms of chemicals, such as neuropeptides and the hormones produced in the body. The brain is a tool which the mind uses to carry out tasks, and not the other way around. The mind does not control you either. However, the monkey mind may make you think so at times, when you have all these thoughts in your head at the one time, one jumping to another all over the place. You have everything you need already in your authentic self, where peace, joy and love are constantly present. When you reach this state of oneness with your true self, there are no blocks to all the abundance and happiness you desire. Desire is of the Father, and what you desire in life is linked with your soul's mission and purpose towards your destiny of what you truly want to do with your life. To move towards your destiny, you need to have a vision that you can visualize in your mind's eye. Living your life on purpose is what brings you true fulfilment. This can only be achieved through self-discovery by looking in, instead of looking outside of ourselves as we are so accustomed to. Self-discovery means moving towards, becoming aware, and understanding who you really are in the deepest part of you.

When you live your life according to your authentic self, you are at one with your self and the universe. This is where the source lies for your inspiration or being "in spirit" in life. This is the source of your essence, your energy, and your unlimited potential. It is by stretching beyond the familiar boundaries of the mind that we go into unknown territory, and this takes courage. Feel the fear and do it anyway. When you have conquered your fear, what you do becomes normal as you continue to stretch your boundaries of reality. Your life becomes more expanded, as do the possibilities in life. As Wayne Dyer says, "When you change the way you look at things, the things you look at will change." Your goals are signposts to your "destiny-ation." Your values fuel the journey. When obstacles arise, you can choose to view them as opportunities to learn. You decide where you go; how you think; what you focus on; how you feel; what you hear; what you see, smell, and taste; and the language you use. You decide how you experience everything around you and how you internalize it as your experience of your reality. You decide what is real for you, as well as your own truth. Only then can you close the gap between where you are right now and what you want. What you want is within your reach, one goal at a time. Anything is possible. Aim for outside the boundaries in the realm of limitless possibilities. There is no box other than the one you surround yourself with when you are not free to express who you really are. This box exists because of a constricted way of thinking which you take for reality. Reality is whatever you think it is. As you think, so are you. You live within the boundary conditions of your thinking. By having situational awareness, you train your eyes to see what you are focused on. In life, you get what you expect. For this reason, expect the best for your self and dream big. Where energy goes, energy flows, leading to results. A synchronicity of events can lead you to see possibilities which before were not as clear.

You know now that you can achieve these possibilities through action, by taking one step at a time. You now realize that you have more choices in your life and that you can work towards whatever you set your mind to. When you think outside of the box, you can see more of all that is. You can see other people in their boxes. Your intuition is sharper. You understand more. You are content and at peace with your self. Everything is as it should be. All is well. You are enjoying the journey and evolving along the way from the lessons you learn. Bring it on! You can choose your state of being, the way you perceive the world, and the meanings you ascribe to all your experiences. All meaning is related to the context, not to the content therein. Knowing this makes you feel in control. You always have more to learn, and it is good to be learning for the rest of your life. In this way, you continue to grow and evolve in mind, body, and spirit. In doing so, you empower yourself and you can learn to love learning, because you're doing what you love. When you love what you do, it is effortless and easy, thus bringing more of the same. All successful people have one thing in common – they continue to learn actively on a daily basis. What's the next lesson? What's the next learning? Onwards and upwards!

You empower your self from within. The world is a reflection of your consciousness, and this affects what happens on every level of experience. Perception is projection. What you perceive in the outside world comes from what you project onto it. People cannot behave towards you in any other way than you project them to be. When you truly know this, you can avoid becoming entangled with them. In the past, you may have procrastinated about making decisions because of things other people said, such as when they gave advice or told you what they thought was best. It is up to you to commit to taking the right action for you and where you want to go in life. It's how you manage the playing field of life that counts. Who you are determines what you perceive in this life. Your values, beliefs, decisions, and learning from challenges are all inextricably linked with the reality of your being. The world is a big mirror that reflects what you project onto it. Every situation is neutral in itself. It is we who give meaning to situations that affect our individual emotional states, which in turn affect our physiology and behaviour. Beliefs determine actions and, therefore, results. We create everything that comes into effect in our lives. External events are neutral; they don't in themselves produce happiness. It's the consciousness with which we participate in activities that makes the difference. When you start paying attention to the riches inside, the riches start manifesting outside because you start exuding the happiness you want to attract. True happiness emerges from within. It is always present on the inside. When you know this, you may realize then that you have not been living according to your full capacity. You have blocked your self in the past with your self-defeating beliefs through conditioning when you listened and took into account other people's opinions of you. In relationships, you may have been conditioned to think of others and so forgot your real self. That was your responsibility, but not your fault. Now you understand, with expanding awareness, why this was so. With this awareness and understanding comes responsibility to act in your best interests in alignment with your authentic self. In the past, you compromised your self in favour of others to win their approval or to feel accepted. You need to accept your self first; otherwise, nothing will change. Your relationship with your self can change in this way, and because of this, everything on the outside is much better. Being true to your authentic self is all it takes.

What other people think is a reflection on them and not on you. Whatever they have to say about you, good or bad, does not change who *you really are*. You know who you are. Your knowingness is always there in your gut feeling and intuition. When you tune into this knowingness on the inside, you can interact with others according to your true self. In this way, you set yourself free from old ways of being or doing. You can be free to have and share joy with others. "The Truth shall set you free" is carved on a stone tablet in an Italian church beside a mountain on the edge of the Alps. I was there in 2007 during a paragliding trip through the Alps with Mike (the pilot). He is a very spiritual paraglider and can fly like a bird in the sky. Synchronicity brought him into my life at the right time. He taught me about the power of belief. I never doubted in him or my self when we flew in seemingly impossible conditions! I wondered since then what this truth was that would set me free. I know now that it's my own truth, the truth that lies in my authentic self. By living my own truth, according to my ideals and in alignment with my values, I can radically change my life, live where I want to live, and be where I want to be. You can do this too! We all can. Life is too short to be doing what we "ought to", "should", or "must" do, according to others' standards. You have been "shoulding" on your self for too long.

While you can learn from other people, you can live your dream and not dream the dream of what they think is best for you. You either create your reality or allow someone else to create it for you. You can be you in an authentic sense, free from negative emotions tied to other people's feelings and states of being. Your free will gives you the choice to no longer feel responsible for how others are. You have been walking in a trance of disempowerment for long enough. Now you are awake and empowering yourself, and that's why you are reading this book. It is time to seriously act, and not just act serious any more. Instead of looking to others to hold you to a high standard, you can now hold yourself to a higher standard of accountability. You raise the bar on your life and will do whatever it takes to reach it. Beyond mastery lies artistry. Everything is about the artistry of living. You can create your wonderful masterpiece in the tapestry of life itself. You are your own work of already existing art that is waiting to be released and revealed to the world. Your authentic self already exists. The world is waiting to witness your authentic self, as only then can you offer the true gift of who you really are in your place in the universe. It's time now to take your place and shine your light so that you can allow others to shine theirs too. When you shine your light on who you really are, you are expressing your authentic self in every form for others to see. Your truth is who you are, and others recognize this also, because their authentic self is waiting to come out too. Imagine what the world would be like if everyone lived as their authentic selves; there would be total integrity, honesty, cooperation, harmony, and peace in the whole which is one. We are all individual sparks of the one light. We recognize that spark in each other, as we all share the same essence within. We are all connected as one. Your authentic self is an individual expression of the whole. The paradox is that while it appears separate, it is not so in reality. This is the illusion that we live in. In the same way, your subconscious is linked to the collective consciousness. The whole is not the sum of its parts. It is more than that. This is how the universe operates.

Dreams will remain dreams unless you have the courage to act. Courage is the ability to act in spite of the fear. There is no failure, only feedback. Feedback leads to growth. Challenges are opportunities to learn. You can clear the space in the past that makes way for the present. Then you can feel focused, as you are not distracted by the same things you previously used your energies up on. You can now have more energy and scope of vision. You can surround your self with like-minded people who will elevate you, and you them. You can have adventures in life, and effortless access to the same. What's important to you is what you have to give to the world around you. The future belongs to those who believe and act on the beauty of their dreams.

Life is like the ocean. The tide washes in (sometimes like a tidal wave!) and the tide washes out. The next day brings a new tide. It's all in how you look at it and how you play the game of life. You can make excuses instead of expanding and playing big. Have belief in your self. Incongruence within your self can only lead to you being stuck and in conflict ... sounds like limbo! To be free from this state, you can detach from others' opinions, assumptions, and judgements of you. This is what they think from their own reference point of what is true for them – their truth. It is not the truth in reality, even though you may see some elements of your truth in what they say. It is not the truth in totality for you. You know who you really are and how you really are. As Milton Erickson says, "Ambiguity causes trance." You have been in a trance long enough in this waking dream of your life because you have been worried about what other people think of you. Wake up now! While you can accept what other people think or say, you don't have to take on board their views by incorporating them into your sense of self. You are your self, not what others say you are or should be. They are entitled to their opinions, assumptions, and judgements. You know who *I am*.

While you were growing up, your life may have revolved around pleasing others. Doing what was asked of you and doing what you believed may have been expected of you. Realize that the love you received in this way was conditional. You learned to expect a reward of love in the form of comfort or praise for a task you'd performed. Maybe you became upset and offended when that reward was not freely forthcoming. You did not feel accepted or loved and learned to identify with your responsiveness towards others. You felt responsible for other people's feelings and always felt a need to seek their approval in your own self-validation. Therefore, your self-concept was reliant on the opinions of others. In this case, your locus of control was external and not internal. You were at the mercy of others' opinions, assumptions, and judgements. Through gaining these insights into yourself, you can free yourself to have peak experiences of self-actualization on a more frequent basis. Then you won't blame your self any more for how others choose to feel. It is not your responsibility to try to make them feel better. That's their responsibility. Your journey in life will have then changed direction towards self-actualization with increased momentum. You can then have peak ex-periences that some would describe as esoteric. You can be fascinated, in-trigued, and excited about what else you have to learn. Your whole life makes sense now. Everything that happened, happened for a reason. It's all good!

Awareness and Understanding of Self

Awareness is the first step to understanding the self. The second step is change. Understand what you intend to change and the reasons behind the change. Knowledge brings awareness; therefore, knowledge is power. Change is a process and is a constant transition towards your inner self. All change takes place from the inside and not from the outside. Life is a learning ground for you to become all you can be. Learning new things can be a challenge physically, mentally, emotionally, and spiritually. Before, you may have been offended at times or might have felt responsible for other people's feelings. You may also have been a fixer of other people's problems. Now, realize that everybody is responsible for his of her own feelings, both good and bad. Any negativity on a person's part comes from inside him or her and not from the outside. Now you can detach and observe while having empathy for others' inner turmoil. You can be fun-loving and spontaneous, have a good belly-laugh, and enjoy bringing a smile to people's faces. You may have put your self second sometimes in the past, with regard to others' needs, but now you can focus more on your own agenda without getting drained. Remind your self that everybody has access to the same power within, where they can find solutions to their problems, though they may need a bit of help in the form of guidance at times. You can be optimistic and look on the bright side of things. Communicating well with people is important. You can learn the skills of having good rapport skills with other people. Challenges in life may not be pleasant, but you know that the good side of them is that after coming through them, your character is stronger than before. You can consider your self adventurous and not afraid to get outside your comfort zone. This is why I took up paragliding. At first my heart would thump in my chest before I ran off a mountain; then it became normal and I had no fear at all. I always landed on a high. While flying, I would look down, thinking of all the people going about their daily business and worrying about things that don't really matter at the end of the day. If they stopped to look at the beauty around them, to really see it, that would change their perspective about what is important in life. Accept who you are. Know that you are changing constantly and have changed a lot, especially since your childhood. You are right where you are meant to be. You may have worried before about what other people thought, but now you know that what you think is your responsibility and what they think is theirs. The only way to change things in your world around you is to change your self within. The outer world is a reflection of your inner world. You can have more clarity and peace of mind in your present reality. You can look back on the past from this present moment and understand how you became who you are through your conditioning.

During your first few months of life, the nature of your relationships that you develop with your caretakers can fundamentally affect your interpersonal relationships with others in adult life. These patterns of interaction with primary carers that have been set up in childhood will consequently be repeated later on in life as you search for a relationship that replicates your childhood experiences. If you view others consciously or subconsciously as objects for the satisfaction of your wants, you attach to others in an immature subject-object relationship. The I-it attitude will be taken when you, as the subject, view the other person as an object for the satisfaction of your personal needs when the relationship is developed. In this case, the other person is regarded as an impersonal being. If you respect the other person as a separate individual, then you will form a mature subject-subject relationship. The subject-subject relationship adopts the I-thou stance where you, as the subject, views the other person in a relationship as an independent being whose personality is worthy of respect. In this way, you achieve individuation and mature separation from your primary carers. This is achieved by working through your feelings of loss that accompany personal growth and separation from primary carers, as well as by increasing your self-awareness of reality in helping you to come to terms with the conflicting elements of love and hatred. When you have achieved separation, you can understand how certain people may have acted within the constraints of their own conditioning because of the illusion that they had of the cause of their pain.

Without awareness and self-understanding, you may have been under this illusion of the ego mind, which is competitive, wants to be right, is judgemental, and is always trying to change things on the outside. The ego mind is consumed by its own self-importance, and so it is totally focused on its own needs, while others' are excluded. This can lead to an emptiness and isolation from others. When there is a breakdown in awareness, desensitization from situations can occur when you shut off from your reactions to internal stimuli or external threats. This can occur in the form of numbing yourself and denying the experience by diluting, diffusing, or disregarding your thought patterns, emotional responses, and sensory impressions. When this happens, meaningful interaction with others can be lacking if you avoid sensation or meaningful impact. Without movement in the right direction, introjection can then lead you to a lack of self-direction and self-regulation. Introjection is what occurs when others' attributes and values are absorbed into your own personality. Action is avoided. The ego's desire for control leads to a lack of spontaneity and participation in life. A dysfunctional closeness and overdependence on others may develop as well. The emotional blurring of boundaries in relationships means that some of your identity is lost in the desire to merge with others. Loss of identity may affect your decision-making and self-sufficiency. At this stage, the ego mind can project your feelings onto others. You then may attribute to others the qualities that you cannot recognize within yourself, either positive or negative. A negative projection can confine you to restrictive behaviour in yourself towards others. This is when you do things for others, usually of a caring nature, that you would like done for yourself. When you care for others in an overly sacrificial manner, you can be caught up by the inconvenience of their needs being put before your own needs. You are helping others without helping yourself first. While helping others is good, it is important to take care of your own needs first. It is only good for you to derive pleasure from the fulfilment of your own needs, and this gives you gratification from living a full life, even while helping others. Now that you have woken up, you can be at peace within your self. Everybody has a purpose in life, part of which is to discover his or her real self, the divine within, aside from the ego and its cravings. You can feel, at last, that you are on the right path to your purpose in life and your self-actualization, evolving with momentum towards your real self. With this awareness comes the understanding needed to help others to do the same and become truly free also. This truth sets you free.

Humility is a valuable tool to protect against the ego's way of thinking, as it enables you to see the power of spirit in other people, no matter what their circumstances. This power can be seen as your potential to awaken to your authentic self if you so choose. The other option is to continue to sleep and dream in the illusion of the everyday world and its human affairs. Relative reality is how you perceive it on the outside, whereas real reality emanates from within into surroundings that reflect back what is inside. For this reason, you can intend to follow your intuition in discovering who you really are by using your gut instinct and synchronicity wherever they may take you. Trust in the process of change by having faith and belief. Being authentic means you are who you are meant to be. In emerging as your authentic self, you can let go of the old, conditioned ego-self and its ways of thinking. Now you can become identified with the real you as separate from your ego. As Marcus Aurelius said, "It is in our power to have no opinion about a thing, and not to be disturbed in our soul, for things themselves have no natural power to form our judgements." Over the temple ruins at Delphi are inscribed two words which, when translated, say, "Know thyself". It reminds me of Shakespeare's words "To thine own self be true, then it must follow as night the day, thou can't be false to any man." By being true to yourself, you can be honest with yourself first, and then other people. This truth is what sets you free.

Duality of Appearances

I see people as spiritual beings having a human experience, and I see that the real self is divine in its nature. Thinking outside the ego mind means detaching, while looking on as an observer, without becoming offended, angry, or upset by other people. In this way, you can have compassion and empathy for those people instead. Ego thinks of itself as separate from others. When you see yourself in other people is when you really start getting to know your real self. Everybody and everything around you is connected and not physically separate, as it appears. Things as they appear are not necessarily as they are in themselves. Appearances can be deceptive. We are conditioned to perceive in a certain way, through the duality of things, using the five senses. Without light, there is darkness. This duality of experience is how things appear to be. In reality, they exist as one unit in everything. There is no duality, only unity.

I used to wonder what quantum physics was all about. Having met Masaru Emoto (who studied water crystals and vibratory affects on healing) and other people in the field, I realized there is so much to learn about this in relation to healing. There is so much potential if one knows how to tap into it. Quantum physics has demonstrated that a light photon can exist either as a particle or wavelength, depending on the observer in any moment of time. Current science has already proved this to be so. According to quantum physics, we are all made up of energy at a subatomic level – energy which vibrates at different levels, or waveforms, for each person.

The spiritual field of energy is present everywhere. It is infinite potential with regard to your physical and non-physical appearance on earth. Even though you emanate and manifest from this infinite source that is everywhere, during creation you become present in time and space in form on earth. The source is still a part of you and can be tuned into by raising your levels of awareness to new possibilities that before may have seemed impossible. I believe you can tune out of this source too, if you believe it is separate from you and exists on the outside rather than the inside. You can follow your destiny to a large degree by taking charge of your inner resources once you discover what and where they are in the source of your being. Things don't just happen to us; we let them happen to us in the ordinary world.

By using the power of the subconscious, you can learn how to think about and deal with yourself in relation to the world, and not the other way around. By becoming heart-centred, you remove yourself from the thoughts in your head. You are not only in the world, the world is in you. Extraordinary living can be possible when you raise your awareness in this way. By taking charge of your life in this way, you live it on your own terms and not everybody else's. You do not compromise who you are meant to be for the sake of other people's opinions and beliefs. You should not concern yourself with what other people think. Ego beliefs do not define who you are, but only who you think you are – that's the illusion. These ego-self beliefs are based on material possessions, achievements, reputation (in terms of what others think of you), separateness from other people, and separateness from God. Sometimes these beliefs can be self-defeating. You may not be aware of them consciously. When you realize that your mind does not define your authentic self, you begin to let go of these former beliefs and wake up to who you really are, always were, and always will be. By relinquishing ego thoughts, you realign with the source and so allow your authentic self to emerge.

What are your values? Your values are to do with anything that is important to you in life. Your beliefs about yourself and the world can affect the values you have in general. When you were younger, you may have taken on board the values of your parents, your teachers, and society. This was your way of adapting to your environment in order to survive, because you needed to belong and so feel safe. Your values can determine where you are heading in life. Values can also change with ever-expanding awareness and understanding about yourself. The closer you get to realizing who you are at your core, the truer your values become for you. When you are truly living your life in alignment with your values, you are fulfilling your purpose towards your mission in life. You are here for a reason, just like every other human on the planet; whether it is to remember once more who you really are or to gain some new experiences and feelings is for you to discover. You always have choice about how you perceive your life and the decisions you make. Your values guide you in the directions of your heart's desire. Follow your heart. Free will gives the choice of either connecting with your spirit or not. Free will determines your link with source and spirit, which reside within you. The finding of God is coming to one's self. This occurs when you know that you are already what you'd like to become and what you wish to accomplish is already there to be achieved. It emerges from within into your life, instead of you having to go looking for it. This is the same as thinking from the end, in pursuing goals. The spirit that is you, once remembered, expresses itself through you.

According to Einstein, "Your imagination is more important than knowledge." Your imagination is much more effective in linking up with the universal mind than is willpower. Strong willpower on its own is closer to ego. Your imagination allows you to create a picture in your mind, which you can then co-create into being in a physical sense. Your spirit of intent gives expression to whatever is desired. If you can trust and see yourself in your imagination, able to be something beyond your body, you begin to feel yourself as something beyond your body. With your imagination, you can visualize yourself as stronger than the task at hand. Your inner picture of purity and protection lets you do what before may have seemed impossible. Willing yourself to do the task is thinking from ego. Your imagination allows you to think from the end and behave as if it's already here. Imagination has no physical limits and is our connection with spirit. Spirit is a creative power that allows for evolvement and expansion. Being in an ever-expanding state allows for evolvement and self actualization. This means letting go of the way you used to think or be.

What is real is what you think is real. Everything outside is an illusion. Like attracts like. This is the law of attraction. You become as you think. Human beings' natural state is health and peace. Your ego prevents this natural state of balance when you identify your self with it. We all have the power to heal from within available to us, but we must be "connected" to the power of intention in order to receive and give this healing. You attract what you send out; "As above, so below, as within, so without," was inscribed by Hermes, on the Emerald Tablet, which dates back to about five thousand years ago in ancient Egypt. This is the oldest sacred text known to man. It suggests that everything is a microcosm of everything else in the universe. What is going on within you on a personal level is also a reflection of what is going on in society and the universe as a whole. This also means that the way you are on the inside is the way things are reflected on the outside. When you align with your true nature, you can create magnificent things on the outside, because you are already magnificent at your core. Your spiritual nature is your real nature, existing in infinity in the timeless now. *A Course in Miracles* states, "The sunbeam sparkles only in the sunlight, and the ripple dances as it rests upon the ocean. Yet in neither sun nor oceans is the power that rests in you. Would you remain within your tiny kingdom, a sorry King, a bitter ruler of all that he surveys, who looks on nothing yet who would still die to defend it? This little self is not your kingdom."(Schucman and Thetford, Ch. 18, VIII, 7).

Your Goals, Plans, and Expectations for the Coming Years

By living according to your true self, you become empowered. Through your own empowerment, you can be the change maker that empowers others to be all that they can be. This is what sets you and others free from suffering. The ripple effect that is created by your actions affects others and their actions also. You can continue to learn for the rest of your life about awareness and the power of the subconscious, as you will find it fascinating. Your curiosity for spiritual awareness has already begun in your search for insight. In studying and learning about your authentic self at your core, you come to realize that it is a journey to healing and becoming one with yourself and others. In reality, we are all one. I am truly grateful for the extraordinary external and internal experiences I've had thus far and look forward to more with curiosity, anticipation, and excitement. When the student is ready, the teacher appears. Having gratitude opens your heart to receiving from the universe. Trust and enjoy the direction of your life's journey.

A New Paradigm Shift

A paradigm shift occurs when you come to see things in a different light. There is a shift going on in the world at present in the consciousness of humanity. What is going on is an evolution of consciousness. We are moving from the age of information to the age of spirituality. Instead of focusing on the differences in the cultures of the world, the time has now come for humanity to recognize that we are all one in our true essence of who we are, both individually and collectively. Science and spirituality are being studied now in relation to each other and not in opposition to each other, as was the case in the past. To put it another way, each individual represents a spark in the light of consciousness. While the light exists in the spark, the spark on its own is a unique expression of this light. It has a connection with the light and is never separate from it. The spark and the light are both one and the same, yet at the same time, the spark is an individualized expression of this light. You, as an individual, have this spark of consciousness within your being at your heart centre. When you perceive yourself in this way, you realize you are part of a greater whole. Just like a drop in an ocean of consciousness, you form an essential part in connecting with the individualized parts of the whole. The drop is part of the ocean, and the ocean is in the drop. The part is in the whole, and the whole is in the part. This new perspective of how you view yourself now allows you to focus on your commonalities with your fellow beings. In so doing, you will have no need for competition or struggle for survival. Instead, collaboration and cooperation will be the norm for thriving. What you do unto others, you do unto yourself. By giving unconditionally, you receive. As greed, selfishness, and power-based systems fall away, this makes way for a new era in which prosperity and abundance are available to all based on equal opportunity and unconditional love. That way, instead of just trying to survive, everybody can evolve and thrive.

Your subconscious can be utilized by the conscious mind to access your innate knowing and wisdom in the "ocean of consciousness." You have access to the same power of the subconscious within yourself that all others have within themselves. The subconscious is that part of the mind that allows you to connect with the superconscious aspect of your higher self. Your superconscious mind has a direct link to the consciousness of the whole, higher intelligence, or God. Therefore, God resides within you at this deep level. The subconscious is where you can find solutions to your problems, and it can be accessed through guided visualizations or meditations. Your essential self or your individual essence is untainted as it is, and it can be tapped into via the subconscious mind, to bring it forth. Hypnosis can be used to reach the subconscious mind, bypassing the conscious mind and resistance itself. In this way, you can gain self-insight much quicker. It is you who heals yourself. All hypnosis is self-hypnosis. By lifting the veil in this way, you can become aware of your own self-empowerment, which gives rise to emotional release through letting go. Good internal communication between your conscious and subconscious mind builds alignment and balance within you in your connection with source. This involves listening at a deeper level, reflecting, and asking the right questions.

Orthodox medicine treats only the symptoms, not the cause. To get to the root cause of any problems you may have, you need to tap into your subconscious. When you get into rapport with your subconscious mind, you close the gap between the conscious and the subconscious mind. You learn to consciously make choices based on your internal feedback. In this way, you can be at cause in your life, instead of effect. With self-knowledge, you become aware of what self-limiting beliefs may have held you back before. You can change your beliefs to ones of empowerment. With self-empowerment, you have the belief that you have all the resources necessary to bring about self-healing. By trusting in the process, you learn to solve problems by tuning into your real self, with guidance from this book. You can then learn to live and be who you really are and not be under the illusion of who you thought you were any more. Your body, mind, and soul become balanced as a result. You learn to live your values and your life on purpose, and you are much happier in the process. In this way, you can evolve to new heights of awareness in moving towards and being your actualized self. The best way for you to move innermost towards your actualized self is by unblocking and letting go of blocked emotions. This frees you up to be congruent and true to your authentic self. In this way, your personal path of evolution moves in a direction of self-empowerment towards a life of purpose and inner happiness for you and others around you.

How can you overcome the problem of suffering in your life, instead, to advance towards your conscious evolution? The answer lies in expressing your authentic self. Conscious evolution is happening already on a mass scale. It's time to wake up and take back your own power! Expressing your authentic self empowers you to take control of your life. You are no longer a victim. Now you can be the hero in your life. You can let go of the old story of your life. Now you can make way for the new story, in which you are the lead actor and the hero. No longer are you the person in the background whom nobody can really see or hear. You are the director, producer, and actor in actively creating the life of your dreams.

When you express who you truly are, you are in alignment with balance, harmony, and peace with everything in this moment. Expressing your authentic self is your truth, and that's what sets you free. Imagine a world where everybody feels and is totally free. In reality, your real self is the essence of who you truly are; the spirit of who you are. Your authentic self is your own spirit of who you are. Your journey towards your self on the inside leads you to the source of all being and empowerment. In viewing others as spirits having a human experience in a body, you learn to appreciate that the real self is spirit. Thinking outside the ego mind means detaching while looking on as an observer in situations, without becoming offended, angry, or upset by other people. You learn instead to have compassion and empathy for those other people instead. You are responsible for your thoughts, not other people's. You cannot control what other people think or say. They, in turn, are responsible for their own thoughts and behaviour. You will find that the more you eliminate negative thoughts from your inner dialogue, the more your awareness increases and the less inner dialogue you have inside your head.

Exercise: Visualization

Now, sit comfortably and place your hands on your lap with palms facing upwards. Look at a spot above eye level. Keep looking at the spot while seeing all the way around to both sides of your eyes. Your look turns into a gaze. Your eyes may water a little. Now close your eyes. Take three deep breaths, each time filling your lungs deeply and letting go of any tension on exhaling. Envision yourself standing at the top of a mountain, looking down onto the sea, feeling a warm breeze on your face and really enjoying it. That's right. Your feet are rooted steady on the ground as you stand tall on the summit. You feel melodic and focused because you are at one with the beauty of this place and you feel in the moment. Realize that you are a loving being.

The light of the sun shines on you as you soak it up. Now you feel the heat of its rays in your body as the liquid golden light enters through your head, flowing all the way down through your heart to your feet. Every time you take a deep breath in, more light enters your heart, and as you breathe out, all tension leaves your body. When your heart is filled with light, imagine the light shining forth into your body and out into the world. As your body fills with the light, you see a cocoon of light around your body that is covered in a gold seal all the way around. There is only light within. In the present, your gift lies within. Your presence of mind is the gift by which you become a witness of your real self. Because you know that everything is as it should be, you are right where you are meant to be. Your journey to self-discovery is your inner journey towards your authentic self, so you can now express yourself to the world. You can shout from the mountaintop, "This is me! This is who I am!"

You know who you are now, and you deserve to be who you are now because you deserve to be all that you are, so you deserve to have all that you are. You create all the good things to come because of who you are. There is more stillness and peace. As you harmonize with your spirit, which is your real self, you listen to your self and other people in a way that allows you to hear more than just words because you listen with an inner knowing. Now you have more energy when you are at one with your self. Your innate wisdom that you were born with now makes it possible for you to remember who you really are. You are your authentic self; you always were, and you always will be. Now, with your eyes closed, contemplate your true essence in the stillness within, while focusing only on your breaths in and out. There is no thought in this space. It is the gap between thoughts. When you are ready, you may open your eyes slowly.

CHAPTER 2

WHERE ARE YOU NOW?

If you don't know who you are and where you are right now, then you don't know where you are going. If you don't know where you are going, then many roads will take you there. Without a true reference point to relate to in terms of who you are or where you are at this moment, your ability to move forward may be affected also. Knowing who you are and where you are gives you a solid foundation for moving forward with momentum, with direction, and with purpose towards a definite destiny. You can create your destiny, but you need to know what it is in order to move towards it. When you are stuck in your life, you may be confused about everything around you as you try to make sense of external things, and so you may have no real focus or drive. This can lead to procrastination or lack of motivation in getting a task done. You can avoid this sense of "stuckness," procrastination, or putting things off, when you develop awareness and self-understanding.

Self-awareness and self-understanding give you answers to all those things that held you back before. Knowing where you are on the inside is necessary before you drive forward with your plans. Otherwise you could end up going around in circles on the roundabout of life. Knowing where you are means you know how far you've come in terms of what you desire for your self. This means you also know what further steps or goals need to be achieved in order to get to where you want to be. Little steps need to be taken along the path of life to get to the big picture or vision of your dream. Looking at it this way makes it appear less daunting. Achieving each step along the way gives you a great sense of achievement and delight that you are moving towards what you want with your whole heart. This is in accordance with your life purpose and is the reason you are here. Everybody is here for a purpose, and unless action is taken in achieving goals, some dreams are never realized. Instead, life becomes one of regret for the missed opportunities, wasted time, procrastination, and a mediocre life. You can live the extraordinary life! Why settle for an average life that does not become you. Believe in your self and use the power within your authentic self, as well as your values, to give you direction. Don't go by what other people say; otherwise, you will be acting to fulfil their expectations and not your own.

You create your own self-fulfilling prophecy. So, in order to know where you are, you may need to re-evaluate your whole life and rise above it to see it from a different perspective, as though you are watching the film of your life. If you were watching this on a screen in the cinema, how would you feel about you, the actor, and what advice would you give to you, the actor? Where are you in your life, and where do you want to go? What is it you really want for your self? Whatever it is, you know you have a passion for it and love doing this. Whatever you have a passion for is linked with your purpose in life, and you can manifest abundance while doing it. Money is never the ultimate goal with your purpose, but it does seem to come into the picture as a side benefit when you are creating your dream with passion. Abundance is effortless when you follow your passion. When you love what you do, you will never have to work another day in your life.

Following your heart means bringing your heart's desire closer to you. You do not need to chase after it. In this way, your purpose finds you where you are. Acting on your purpose brings you closer to the dream of your heart's desire. When your self-concept is limited to traits, roles, and attitudes, your understanding of yourself is very much on the surface, like the visible portion of an iceberg above the ocean level. Beneath the depths of the ocean of consciousness lies that deeper part of you that is not visible to the naked eye. Your deeper self can be perceived when you tune into it by turning your attention inwards. Your attention to your authentic self means your energy goes in this direction – that is, inward. Your intention to focus on your authentic self means you bring it forth by allowing it to emerge into your being. This is your life, and you are responsible for what you create with the power of your intention.

Some people live their life according to what other people want, because of fear of non-approval, non-acceptance, judgement, and blame by others. By pleasing others in this way, you lose sight of where you are in the great plan of your life. You come first. It is important that you take care of yourself first. This is not selfish by any means. It is essential to be in control of your own life. When you have control from within, you take care of your own needs first. This does not mean that you don't care about others. It means that you are at your peak to be able to care for others. If you looked after others' needs first and not your own, you would get tired and drained pretty quickly. It is important to replenish you energy from time to time by whatever means are available. This could mean even taking time out for yourself to reflect on, pamper, nourish, and support your inner being. Replenishment of your inner being comes from clearing any tension or negative emotions; these things then become transformed and transmuted by the light of your authentic self. This is why it is important to align with your authentic self, because this allows you to become filled with a wholesome oneness of unity within your being. When you are congruent with your inner desire, you manifest that which you intend with grace and ease. Your inner balance and harmony mean you are living an effortless life. Your connection with your authentic self gives you access to your own infinite power, which comes from source or the universe.

Whose Life Is It Anyway?

Have you ever felt that your life is not your own? Whose life is it anyway? Are you in control of your life, and where you are going? Are your decisions influenced by outside conditions, such as other people's thoughts, assumptions, or opinions? If you ask yourself these questions, you get to look at your life and where you are at this moment of time in the world. Can you truly say that you fully own your own life and are free to make your own decisions? Yes, I know there are others around you who need you for this and for that. Are you being true to your authentic self, or is your life consumed by the needs of others all the time, leading you to feeling resentful? Are you doing what others ask of you, even if it means sacrificing your own needs? Sometimes we say yes to requests to avoid feeling guilty. Once you own your own life and take responsibility for your self before others, then you stand in your own power. This is not selfish; it is your birthright! To be who you are meant to be and not what others think you should be means taking responsibility for your self and having courage. It means being at the cause of your life and destiny and not having it carved out by other people. You have more inner power than you may think you have. It's the persistence you use to tap into it that counts. The first step is becoming aware and observing your self from inside your self. This includes your thoughts, emotions, and actions. In this way, you become the silent witness, or observer, of your own thoughts, emotions, and actions. At first, it may seem strange, but then, after a while, you begin to realize that you are more than your mind and your body, as well as who you think you are. What you believe you are, you are. When your mind starts expanding, in terms of what's possible, so do your reality and potential. A closed mind leads to a limited existence. The quality of your life comes from the quality of your thoughts and emotions in life. What you think, you become.

Thoughts are habits that can be changed. As Gandhi said, "Be the change that you want to see in others." You can't change other people; you can change only your self, your thoughts, and how you look at things. By blaming others and creating reasons or excuses for any shortfalls in your life, you are playing the victim role and being at the effect of others. By living with commitment and taking responsibility with action, you get results and are, therefore, at the cause of your life. Where do you spend your time? How can you use your time more effectively? Surround your self with a good support network of people who will lift you up and expect more from you than you do from your self. That way you can grow and evolve your being in this world, to the point at which you can lift your head up and see all the opportunities that are around. As you evolve your consciousness, your life takes on a whole new meaning. You will begin to see that you have a reason for being here and that there is a purpose for you to fulfil in this lifetime. By tuning into your authentic self, you are also tuning into your soul purpose. The more you connect with your real self, the more you notice changes in the way you express yourself and how you behave in the world. This includes the language you use also. Once you set the focus of your own compass, you will begin to see opportunities and will have a different perspective on everything. You will always find what you look for. What you focus on grows, and this includes your self. You deserve it! Think of your self for a change, even if it means stepping back from your own life to take a look at it. Go on, you can do it!

Watch Your Language

We speak without realizing what we're saying sometimes. On hearing your own spoken words, especially if they are habits, you can actually start believing them. As in science, your matters of fact can be revised in the light of your new experiences. Therefore, your concepts of the world can change also, and this is expressed in the symbolic form of language. Your concepts in total make up the reality of your knowledge. Your world view is what you say it is, according to you, because that is what you know from your experience. It is relative to what you understand in your web of concepts and is therefore communicated in the sentences of your language. Your concept of things does not necessarily give you their truth in reality, but only in terms of what that concept means to you.

The language you use gives you the ability to express they way you view the world. All meaning is context related, and your language reflects your understanding of reality. Things are meaningful for you in terms of the language you have learned in association with the way of the world. Your reality is what you say it is. With more experiences, you gain more understanding and more expressive language as a result. Your language as a whole can change in the light of a new, original experience. Your thought processes can evolve through learning, in terms of the language you use and what it means to you within your mental framework. You form your beliefs and use of language within the confines of your understanding. Your use of language describes your interpretation of the world through sentences as a whole. While your interpretation of the world shapes your beliefs, it is also shaped by them. Your beliefs shape your perception of reality. Your beliefs are subject to review when you have a new experience that changes how you look at things. Through learning and expanding on your use of language, you can redefine your concepts and beliefs of the world. You make sense of the world by the accepted truths within your language usage. Your concepts and experience in life cannot be separated, as you need both to make sense of the world. People have different ways of expressing the same thing, all of which are legitimate. People express themselves according to their own experiences and concepts. Sometimes people may disagree on the same thing only because they are using different sentences to describe it. Learning is achieved when you can negotiate, reinterpret, and understand different points of view when communicating with others. As you evolve, you can judge your truth as earnest and absolute as can be, subject to correction. This allows you to re-evaluate effectively with yourself what reality means for you. Reasoning and language work together in combination. You form your concepts with the language you use. This is how you learned language in the first place – from concepts of symbols or pictures. Your language is constructed from your perceptions of sensory input and conditioning, which come from ex- perience. You think in a language of sentences that make up your concepts.

Your beliefs and values shape your attitudes in life. As Henry Ford said, "If you think you can, or you think you can't, you're probably right!" When you have a positive mindset, your language represents this, while the reverse also applies. Once you become aware of your own use of words, you may see how you may actually be limiting yourself in life. When you say to yourself "I can't do this" before attempting a task or challenge, this leads to the same self-fulfilling prophecy. Because of this, a belief is formed that you were right in the first place, when you said "I can't do this." Also, when you focus on what you don't want in life, you may say "I don't want …", "I'm not good enough …", "I can't do …", "I don't have …", or "I don't deserve …" What you focus on grows. If you focus on the things you don't want in life, where does your energy go? Where is your time spent? What about the things that you do want? Are you thinking about them when you say "I can't"? Are you problem-focused or solution-focused? Which would you prefer?

Some people don't realize that they sometimes are going around in circles with their own language. It keeps them stuck where they are in their own lives, as a result. Maybe this is because the habit is familiar, known to the mind, and therefore considered safe. Also, when you say "I should …" or

"I must ...", these are pressure words that tend not to incite motivation. Instead you can say "I choose to ..." This puts you at cause instead of effect in your life. It means you have choice and not pressure. Similarly, when you tell yourself "I'll try to ...", you're really saying that you won't actually do it yet; in trying, you're not actually doing. When you say "I'll try ...", you are seeking approval for something you have already decided not to do. Instead, you can think of your self in the present tense as having already done it, by saying "I am ..." or "I have ..." Using words in this way is far more powerful in achieving your goals in life. Always remember to attach the emotion of having this goal also, at the same time.

Observe for generalizations or stereotypes that you may use. For example, "all", "everybody", "always", and "never". If you tell yourself everybody does that, this is a generalization that is not necessarily true. Also, be wary of limiting beliefs in your language use, and question yourself on it. For example, "can't", "not able", "impossible", and "don't deserve". Challenge your own assumptions. Be aware of when you make comparisons of one thing being better than another, and question yourself on it when appropriate. Champion, encourage, and support your positive attributes, learning, and achievements. Support yourself in the process of your journey towards your deserved goal. Be creative and flexible. Dance in the moment. Look on yourself as already creative, resourceful, and whole. Have the big picture in your mind. Allow yourself space to be. Use and follow your gut instinct or intuition. Have courage in taking risks for your own benefit.

As Einstein said, "We live within the boundaries of our thinking." Would you prefer to live in a safe and same life with no change, or a life in which you are continually evolving, growing, and learning with ferocious curiosity that gives you fulfilment? Your choice in using language makes the difference in how you represent the world to your self from the inside out. You have been conditioned to think from the outside in. That is why you think things happen to you on the outside. In this way, you may think that life is happening to you and that you have no active part in what happens. Words reflect thoughts, and thoughts reflect reality. Words are the expression of thought. You can speak in your language as if the world is a fearful place to be in, or you can speak as if it is a place of peace, joy, and harmony. By reflecting on your own words, you can gain understanding of how you perceive the world.

You perceive the world around you through your senses in terms of how this is re-presented back to you, the observer. You re-experience in your mind just as you see, hear, or feel the outside world through your senses. Your senses are visual, auditory, kinesthetic (touch), olfactory (smell), and gustatory (taste), and your inner talk is audio-digital. The visual system is how you create your visual pictures. The auditory system is how you rehear a mixture of words and sounds, even in imagination. The olfactory system deals with smells, and the gustatory system, tastes. The kinesthetic system comprises your internal and external feelings of touch and bodily awareness. Emotions are also part of this system. As people are unique individuals, they usually have a preferred representational system that dominates what they perceive through their preferred sense. This preferred system is subconscious. In becoming aware of your word usage, you can ascertain the mental origins of the words or phrases in terms of sensory-based mental origins. Most people's preferred representational system is the visual system. Whatever is preferred shows up in the language you predominately use. If you have a visual preference, you may say "I see what you mean." If you have an auditory preference, you may say "I hear what you mean." If you have a kinaesthetic preference, you may say "I feel the same way." Once you know what your preferred system is, you can use this when creatively visualizing your goal, by emphasizing that system more.

What most people don't realize is that they have a choice in how they perceive the world around them and the position they hold in it. Nothing is set in stone, even if others try to convince you of this. There is always room for movement towards what you want in life in order to be in the flow of life, being carried to your destiny-ation. Isn't it better than resisting the current and staying in the same spot as a result? Thinking outside the box means thinking outside of a problem from all angles as a challenge to be overcome, and therefore it gives you strength of character. There are no mistakes in life; there is only feedback. There is no point in having regret, shame, or guilt over past feedback, as this does not serve you in any way. Feedback is there to be learned from so that you can learn to become a better person for it. That's what life is about. A person who learns and grows is living in alignment with nature. Nothing is permanent or ever remains the same in nature, and it's the same in life. In trying to cling to something familiar without letting go, you hold yourself back – from your own freedom, ultimately. Your position is constantly changing. If you ever felt you were stuck in a rut, it's because you were not moving in life. Life is meant to bring constant movement. Life brings growth and change with constant evolvement. When there is resistance to change through fear, this leads to the stuck-in-a-rut state. Know that you can be, do, have, and create whatever it is you want in your life. Know that you have everything you need already. Believe it! Live the life of your dreams starting right now, one word at a time! Watch your language! Say "I can do this!"

Clarify Your Goal

Everybody has a purpose in life, whether he or she knows it or not. What is your goal for your life, and where are you in relation to your goal? Look at your goal in the context of your whole life. You need to know where you are before you know where you're going. This is because you need to know where you are coming from, in order to move forward in your life. When you know where you are, you can focus on this goal and clarify what exactly it is you want in relation to this goal. Imagine what it will be like when you achieve this goal, in terms of what is seen, heard, or felt. The more the picture is painted, the more real the goal appears to be. Setting a goal for yourself is where it all begins. The goal in itself involves a journey towards what you want, as well as what you are to learn along the way. This journey to your purpose involves "quest-ioning" yourself on an ongoing basis about what your goal specifically is in the long term and where you are in relation to it. The quest of questioning yourself takes you on a journey from where you are now to where you want to go.

Things may not be as they seem to you. You can ask yourself powerful questions like "What do I want?" to get yourself moving. It is important to do this, because when you think you have all the answers, do you learn anything new? Without asking yourself questions about your life, what changes? Once you start the process, you unravel your progressive insights and personal development towards your dream. Your circumstances may change, so wherever you are, hold the vision for your goal, as your viewpoint may change. As you get to see your goal from different angles, see it as it is or as something better. Keep an open mind. Don't restrict your thinking to only one way of doing things or only one result. Identify your intermediate steps, or short-term goals, for achieving your goal. At the same time, always hold the vision for your dream. By asking yourself where you are now, you become aware of how far or near you are in relation to your goal. Know that you may have more resources than are apparent at the present. You clarify your present reality and perceptions through questioning yourself on any concerns, who else is affected by them, how much support you have, who is in control, what has been done already, and what stopped you from doing more. You can also clarify any potential obstacles so that you become aware of what needs to be overcome, externally as well as internally, in achieving your goal.

As you become aware of options that you wouldn't have considered before, you develop fresh perspectives and gain more choice in actions and decisions to be taken. More choice gives you more freedom for moving towards what you want. It's about not limiting the search for information to the normal sources. Fresh perspectives broaden the horizon and increase options available to you, providing a totally fresh point of view. It's all about thinking outside the box. When you see beyond the previously self-imposed limits, this gives you motivation and enthusiasm to pursue your goal. You can look at any potential obstacles, as well as how these can be overcome. You can clarify options by asking what will be achieved, how they will be achieved, in what way they will be achieved, to what degree they will be achieved, how often they will be achieved, when they will be achieved, by what date they will be achieved, and how often things need to be done. It's the questioning from different angles of how the goal is to be achieved that allows you to see the fresh perspectives for yourself. You can also clarify your own resources: is the goal realistic, clear, or specific?

The times and measurability of smaller goals can be looked at also. That something needs to change implies that there can be change. By asking what the main hindrances are, you can bring any potential blocks to movement towards your goal to your awareness so that you can deal with them. This may also bring you some awareness into your feelings about certain things and how this may be blocking you from moving forward. Observe where you are now in relation to your goal, after expanding on available options. It is also good to clarify your will to reach your goal. Sometimes you may receive a secondary gain in not achieving a goal. You could ask yourself "What will I gain by not achieving this goal?" in trying to find your secondary gains. Other questions you could ask yourself include the following:

- What will I not gain by not achieving this goal?
- What will I gain by achieving this goal?
- What will I not gain by achieving this goal?

Asking questions in this manner allows you to see all angles of a situation. You get to see the implications of actions from all perspectives in this way. The answers will also bring insight into your own self-limiting beliefs that hold you back from moving forward. You may also get some insight into your motivation to take action. You may realize that you feel you don't deserve to succeed or you are afraid of succeeding because it means change. Secondary gain means it may be more comfortable and safe to stay in the same situation than to make the effort required to achieve your goal. Secondary gains are the reasons and excuses that stop you moving forward because of fear of change and what it may bring. When you let go of the fear, you become fearless and there is nothing to stop you. Clarifying your goal means you are also clarifying where you are in relation to it. Getting a clear picture of your goal also gives you an idea of what steps to take next.

Clarify Action Steps

Now that you have explored your options for your goal, next you can clarify the action steps to be taken in a specific, timed fashion to move you towards your goal. This is where your action plan comes in. With a complete action plan, you know what intermediate goals or steps you need to achieved. Also, you know precisely where and when each is achievable in a flow of succession from one step to another. It is important for you to assess, clarify, and become aware of any subconscious beliefs you may have that prevent you from reaching your goal. Is the goal congruent with your capabilities and purpose in life? Become aware of where you need to make changes in any current behaviours, or whether new skills are needed in order for you to be successful. When devising your action plan, you can ask yourself what will be done, by whom, how it will be done, and what resources are to be used. Sometimes you may need to review your plan. What worked previously can be incorporated into the plan, as can knowledge gained from what didn't work previously and why it didn't work. Become aware of what may have held you back in the past and how you can overcome this. This prevents the same thing from happening again. How do you measure your success? Who needs to know about this action plan and what support is available or needed? It is also good to clarify the goal's ecology. Ecology refers to safety for you, other people around you, and the planet as a whole. You can check the goal's ecology by asking yourself four questions, as follows:

- What will happen if my goal is achieved?
- What will happen if my goal is not achieved?
- What won't happen if my goal is not achieved?
- What won't happen if my goal is achieved?

This kind of questioning clarifies all angles of a situation and gives you more answers than you may have anticipated. The answers you get can confirm if you are on track or not. They also give you an idea of where you are in relation to your goal or what you want.

Expectations predict outcome. Once you know what to expect in terms of the outcome, then you can be fully congruent with being at cause in your life. This comes from being in alignment with your values, beliefs, and emotions instead of being at effect of what happens to you. When you are moving towards your goal, this sets you on the path to your goal. This is in accordance with your heart's desire or calling in life, because that is what you truly want. So let's say you know where you are right now. Great! Now you can monitor your progress towards what you want. You can also understand what blocked you in the past and why you weren't moving forward in life before. Self-understanding in this way helps you to take action in your life, instead of procrastinating any longer as to what you "should" be doing.

Self-awareness also fosters continued learning during self-reflection, and this empowers you for continued self-development. Learning and self-discovery create conditions for momentum to take place in how you get things done. This momentum moves you forward in taking actions, while picking up speed along the way. You deepen your learning that takes place as you journey towards your goal. As you increase your awareness from learning on the inside, your external world also changes. Your external world is a reflection of what is going on internally. Moving your action forward while deepening your learning means you are moving from where you are to where you want to be. Without action, there is no learning. Without learning, there is no action.

Through curiosity, intuition, self-management, and active listening (internal and external), you can learn to think outside the box. From this space, you can view things from a different perspective. In this way, you expand your options and your view of your world. Having courage to take risks in a safe environment is possible while trusting the process of designing your own future in the present. You can take your whole life into account when tapping into your motivation, curiosity, creativity, resources, and goal in life. This is what moves you towards your soul purpose.

The subconscious looks at the big picture of things and does not deal with specifics. By holding the vision of your overall picture in mind, you are tapping into the power of your subconscious mind, which processes everything at once. At the same time, your conscious mind deals with the specific actions to be taken in a sequential manner. You are already creative, resourceful, and whole. The answer lies within already, in your authentic self. The solution is already inside. Your action plan can include tasks that keep you motivated and focused on the task to be done. Structures are the cues that you create to remind yourself of a task to be completed, like messages on Post-it notes. Your expanding self-awareness lets you know when you reach the limits of your own self-boundaries. With this awareness, you can now consciously push past these boundaries that were limits for you previously.

If you are not being true to yourself, you may have hesitation or a forced manner of speaking that doesn't ring true with what you are really trying to say. This vibe can be picked up by other people subconsciously. Your expression of your true self is subconsciously picked up by other people as just that. Self-awareness also gives you insight as to whether you are moving away from or towards what you want. With self-awareness you develop the feeling of either balance or resistance, according to where you are now and whether you are on track with your goal. As a co-creator with the universe, you take courage in speaking your truth. It can be very beneficial for others to hear your truth, even though they may not like it. Sometimes the truth can hurt; but it hurts only momentarily, because it wakes you up to the illusion that you have been living under. When you speak from a source of integrity, your intention is what counts. Your words of truth carry enough power to bring about transformation in other people and in the world. When your intention is in the right place, you speak from your heart. Expressing your authentic self means speaking from your heart, from the very core of who you really are.

By comparing your current situation with the big picture of your vision, your learning comes from the context and not the situation. This way, you can see where you are in relation to your ultimate goal in your life. Your current situation does not determine where you go; your potential does. Your perception of your situation is the meaning you give to it from where you are in your life right now. Acknowledge the values you honour in taking an action. Become aware of your perception of the world that has subjective or personal meaning for you. Become objective once in a while also, as if viewing yourself and your current position from the outside. Hear the words, predicates, and phrases you use according to visual, auditory, kinaesthetic, and audio-digital internal representations. From this, you get insight into your own model of the world.

Your model, or world view, is different to other people's. Respect other people's models of the world. How they view their world comes from who they are and where they are on the journey in their life. It is not for you to judge other's beliefs and points of view. Your journey to self-discovery leads to your own answers via the challenge of thinking at deeper levels for yourself. Your answers do not come from other people. Questioning where you are can clarify your direction and expectation in relation to your goal in life. Your focus and commitment determine your movement forward in achieving the steps towards your goal. By empowering yourself to find your own answers through a process of self-discovery, you gain insight and choice. In gaining self-awareness, you become active in making your own decisions. Speaking your truth enables you to become aware of where you were holding yourself back in the past.

Your subconscious mind hears every word you utter. Monitor what you say for a while to become familiar with your language. It can be very revealing. The more you are being true to your self, the more this will be reflected in your language. In self-expression, you are overcoming your previous habit of denying or procrastinating what you need to do next. In this way, you keep yourself on track towards your plans and goal in finding your purpose in life. However, it's not enough to just be on track. Movement is required by taking action to avoid the train of thought that keeps you stuck. In this way, you overcome your inner critic in the process. Any obstacles on the track can derail you if they are not worked on and overcome before passing them.

In keeping yourself accountable, you know you are responsible for maintaining movement and momentum towards your goal. You are responsible for yourself regarding the actions you take and the actions you don't take. Through self-awareness you can move towards your destiny at full steam. Self-awareness brings you closer to your own self-empowerment, courage, and confidence. By bringing out the best in you, you foster and maintain commitment towards action. Through self-discovery, awareness, and choice, you learn to close the gap between where you are and where the goal is.

By achieving results, improving performance, and learning along the way, you have learned to be at the cause side of life and not the effect side, where "everything" happens to you. Being at cause involves choice of thought, action, emotion, and way of being in life. You come to realize you are on an inner journey of self-discovery that is reflected in the outer journey. The inner journey of self-discovery can bring about awareness at deeper levels than you've ever experienced before. This can create a shift in your thinking. In the outer journey, you take action towards your goal also. When inner shifts occur, the outer journey immediately shifts also. How you perceive the world affects what is seen in the world, as well as how it is related to and processed in turn. The more awareness you have, the more you realize that concepts of reality can change. There is no fixed reality; there is only your subjective impression of what is reflected back to you. What you see at any fixed time is in direct correlation to how you view the world. The more awareness you develop, the more choice you have in your life and the more options you can see. You can always choose how you feel, no matter the circumstances. There are possibilities for every situation. There is a solution for every problem.

By finding the bigger why in your life, you can propel yourself past your present experience and habits. When you know what you want, you also need to know for what purpose you want it. What would it give you, and how could you benefit others by obtaining it? By accessing your deeper values of what is important to you in life, you gain a new sense of purpose that will automatically propel you forward towards your heart's desire. When your values are in alignment with universal intent, your purpose flows to you effortlessly. The universe knows where to find you when your values resonate with its own. Believe in your purpose and it will flow to you without effort. Stay focused on your dream, which is already a reality in your mind. It exists already in potentiality.

Commit to an action plan when you know where you're coming from. See where you are now and plan your action steps one step at a time. The journey of a thousand miles begins with a single footstep. Any one of your action steps could be the giant leap that skyrockets you to instant success. By keeping on the path, you make steady progress towards your ultimate vision and purpose. Knowing where you're at means you can decide which step to take next. When you know where you are in relation to your big picture, it is easier for you to make decisions along the way. Determination and drive are two values that can be useful for persisting in your journey. Know what your true values are, and start living your life from them. When you are in alignment with your values and living from them, your journey becomes smoother and easier. While obstacles may still arise from time to time, you find that living from your values allows you to overcome them much quicker than before. You are responsible for the life you create. You experience what you are, and this also includes what you intend for yourself. When you know where you're going and how you fit into the picture, your life becomes richer as you see the progress you make once you start moving forward.

You can measure your success and achievements when you know where you are. You also then know whether you are moving closer to or away from your ultimate goal and purpose. In this way, you can correct your direction once more to what you want. So, in the process, you close the gap between where you are now and where you want to be. Avoid distractions or self-limiting beliefs getting in your way. In this way, you make steady progress towards your goal, one step at a time. You create everything that comes into your life through experience. Therefore, by saying to yourself that you are responsible for your own life, this prevents you from blaming and judging other people or situations. Believe that you can do it!

If you make excuses or give reasons for your failures, then you are arguing for your lack of success. Stay on track. You are not a victim of circumstances. You do not need to be rescued, in reality. It is you that creates the breakthrough in your own life. You have the power within to change your experience of life in any instant by changing your perception of it. Your perception affects the way you act in the world. What you see around you is in the form of appearances only. You create your reality from within, which brings into being your reality without. When you know you are responsible for everything you create, this makes only you accountable for all the results in your life. This takes your focus off what others are saying or doing when carrying out your goal, because you are self-determined and uninfluenced by them. Your control comes from within, because you know where you are. When a person is controlled by outside events, people, or situations, that person's control lies outside of him or her. Lack of inner control can lead to confusion about what direction to take and what decisions to make. In this way, you lose sight of where you stand in relation to your goal. If you allow other people's opinions to influence you, then you may find yourself going down a path you don't want to take. This may have been a pattern for you in the past. You can change your story right now by making a decision to stick with what feels right for you.

You can become fulfilled in life by following your heart and what feels right for you. Taking responsibility for your life in this way means you no longer blame others for what happens to you. Having an inner locus of control brings clarity instantly because you know where you are inside and, hence, outside of yourself. Your plans are not diverted when you control your own reality. You know that whatever happens, it is because of the decisions you make now in your life. Your life becomes on purpose when you tune into your soul purpose, mission, and vision for your life. Stay committed to the process by holding the vision in your mind from time to time. Your commitment keeps you on your path to your heart's desire. Each decision creates its own potentiality of many other roads to choose from. Take a step in the right direction each day from where you are now. Your life is unfolding continuously, and the good thing is that you get to choose what direction you take. This is much easier when you know where you are than it is when you are lost.

Being honest with yourself means allowing yourself to speak your truth. Honesty comes with courage and having trust in yourself. If you can't be honest with yourself, how can you be honest with other people? When you are up against the boundaries of thinking that keep you in the box, you may need to challenge yourself. It's the only way to release yourself from the chains of illusion. Sometimes you may think you don't know what to do next when your perceived limit is reached. By challenging this perception, you can help yourself to stretch out of the comfort zone. In this way, you are expanding your previous limits. You can stretch yourself by asking these powerful questions:

- What challenge do I face?
- What can I learn from this?
- How can I overcome it?
- What lessons can I take from this?
- What do I need to do to get past this?
- What do I need to let go of?
- What do I need to do differently to avoid self-limiting habits?
- What habits or beliefs are holding me back from my ultimate goal in life?

- What is my dream life like? Where am I? Who is with me? What do I feel? What am I surrounded by?
- How can I and others benefit from my success in achieving what I want?
- How can I break past my previous limitations that held me back?
- Which resources and skills do I already have? Which do I need to get?
- What are my self-imposed limitations that hold me back from my dream?
- What are my self-limiting beliefs and habits costing me?
- What are my habits of success?
- Could I make the change?
- Would I make the change?
- When do I start? Am I ready now? Can I make that decision now?
- What is the next step?

Questioning yourself like this means venturing into unfamiliar territory outside your mind map – the map of reality in the mind. The map is not the territory. By looking outside the map, you learn to see things as they really are. Take some time to reflect on these questions and write down the answers. Your answers to these questions need to be followed in turn by empowered action.

By taking courageous action, you stretch beyond your comfort zone, which expands in the process also. In the process of expanding your boundaries, you evolve and grow. The next stretch is another step or challenge further. Allow yourself to celebrate success. When you are neutral, genuine, objective, and impartial with others, you do not take anything personally. There is no judgement, assumption, opinion or advice given towards others when you are being neutral. This doesn't mean you don't care. What is right for you is not necessarily right for others. The difference is that when you express what is right for you by speaking your truth, this can help others when they identify with you. Others are responsible for their own self-awareness and self-discovery, just as you are for yours. They may not see things the same way you do, no matter how hard you try to tell them. Whatever surfaces for you is always relevant, as this leads to further self-discovery and, therefore, self-empowerment. Learning in itself can be fun and in itself is a good motivator. This also means that you don't have to take yourself too seriously. Your understanding of the language you use, the way you behave, and how you view the world can determine your flexibility and creativity in your progress towards your goal. Become aware of why you do what you do, so that you know where you are in relation to your goals in life. By knowing your previous limited habit patterns of thoughts, beliefs, and actions, you can begin to change these consciously from the inside out to suit your needs.

Release the fear that has held you back previously, and become fearless in your living. Become aligned with the vision you hold for your life. This comes from doing whatever it takes for your highest good and the good of all. Also become more aware of your time management, which some refer to as self-management. You can now set an action plan for getting things done in a systematic fashion. This starts with writing down your short-term and long-term goals while dreaming big, without limits. It is in breaking through your old negative emotions and habit patterns that you can let go. By letting go of what you don't need, you can take off in a new direction in your life. You set the course of your life by aligning your values with what you want. What you want is the vision you hold for your life.

When you want to know where you are, just see the bigger vision and make headway towards it. This may involve making alterations, adjustments, and changes as you keep on track to the life of your dreams. Rise above any situations or people that may block your path. Everybody is on his or her own path in the journey of life. Avoid resisting, because then you push against what is. Allowing and accepting all that is speeds your path towards your destiny. Even though your path may cross with others', you do not need to follow them. Become your own leader. Become your own guide by connecting with the core of who you really are. When you are connected with your authentic self, you know your place in this world. The world needs you to be present in your self, because it is from your source that you give the gift of who you are to all. In your journey of self-discovery, you gain insight into your potential that always was, is, and always will be. It is also by knowing your authentic self that you know where you are in your life.

Your position in your life determines what you want. Are you in alignment with your goals? What do you need to understand in order to know where you stand? When you detach from judgements of situations or people, you free yourself up to discern instead the right path to follow. Discernment comes from your ability to tune into your gut feeling or intuition. Your intuition is your guide that comes from the core of your being. As it guides your forward towards your heart's desire, you avoid distractions that would otherwise have held you back. Judgements are in your head. Discernment comes from your knowing in your heart and soul of what is the right step to take next. As you navigate to find your place in the great plan of your life, knowing what the next move is in the game of life becomes easier. In this way, your life becomes easy and effortless as you are shown the way by your higher being through synchronicity, opportunity, and being in the right place at the right time. When you think, feel, and act in accordance with your higher purpose in life, you are right where you are meant to be. You will be shown the way. Trust and believe that this is so. Fear and doubt put blinkers on your eyes so that you can't see the vision that lies ahead. When you detach from fear and doubt and instead travel with hope, faith, love, and compassion, your vision of what you want to create becomes your destination that is always visible to your insight. Your vision of your heart's desire is what drives you forward towards it, or so it appears. When you are in line with what you want, or aligned with it, you are actually attracting your desire into your experience of reality, where you already are. Sometimes, you may need to shift the direction of your life path after you discern the next best step to take. As you do, your life becomes better and better as it expands with more potential and possibilities. As you move forward in the direction of your dream, you know that you already have what you want and you are grateful. Gratitude opens your heart to receive more of what you are grateful for.

Trust that no matter where you are, you have the power to decide where you are going in any given moment. You control your destination. No matter what appearances are like in your experience of the world, this does not necessarily represent the reality of your situation. All situations, events, and relationships with other people are neutral in themselves. It is you who gives meaning to them from the context of your perceptions of where you are in your life. What you see in others is a reflection of what is inside you.

When you can look on other people as spiritual beings who are here on earth to learn lessons just like you, then it is much easier to look on them with compassion instead of blaming them. By understanding where you are, you learn ultimately what you need in order to realize your wholeness.

Becoming whole, or at one with yourself, ultimately allows you to become more congruent with your purpose in life. When you know yourself in this way, only then can you discern what others need in order to be complete and at one with their path in life also. You are responsible for your own life and the path you follow. Others are responsible for theirs. Life is full of choices, not shoulds or have tos. Everything you do in life is a choice that creates your reality. Also, those steps that you do not take create your reality also. Knowing that you are fully responsible for your life means no longer looking at yourself as a victim waiting to be rescued. You can be the hero in the story of your life. Know where you want to be in the now. Don't worry about the future. The future will follow automatically from where you place yourself right now.

Tapping into the infinite potential for your life puts you behind the steering wheel and accelerator of the vehicle that drives you forward to the life of your dreams with speed and intensity. You are the driver for your life, and you get to decide where you and your life go in this very moment. Your life flows through you and not to you. You move forward from your inner being in reality. Tune into your power within. Start up your internal love engine by turning the key of your heart or the heart of your key to your soul. Your soul is the essence that drives you onwards in carrying out your mission here on earth. Your mission is to serve others by carrying out your life purpose. Your life purpose is your means of creating and manifesting your vision right now. It exists already in potentiality. Moving towards your life vision is what actualizes your destiny-ation. As you move closer to your destiny, it becomes clearer and moves into focus on your horizon. You can see it, so you know it is real. You know where it is. Now you can move towards it with excitement and passion. The more you move in that direction, the more it manifests into your reality. You know it is possible, and this belief makes it so. You have conviction, which gives you power and strength as you move forward with determination. You are inspired by the vision ahead. You can feel, hear, see, smell, and almost touch it. It is within your reach as you move evermore forward.

You realize now that procrastination is a thing of the past. It had kept you from realizing that your vision was there all along. Your new friend, guided action takes you where you want to go, from where you know you are now. Trust your inner guidance and act on it now. You will be rewarded in ways beyond what you can imagine to be possible. The life of your dreams becomes reality for you when you act with courage from your inner guidance system. This inner guidance system is the soul compass of your life. It will always be there to guide you in the right direction. To access it, close your eyes, look down towards your heart, and become quiet and still. Contemplate and reflect in a meditative state, even while listening to music, on your ultimate goal in life. As you go deeper and deeper, you receive guidance in the form of a feeling, a hunch, an insight, or a gut feeling about what direction to take next. As you practise this more, your intuition becomes stronger. Your direction towards your heart's desire becomes focused more and more with laser-sharp precision as you bring it forth into physical being.

This is why knowing where you are carries such power in your life. Where you come from does not determine where you are going. Your past does not determine your future. The decisions you make now and your state in this moment actually create your reality right now in bringing it forward towards you. Each moment that has passed is no longer now. What has passed is past and no longer is. With each moment in the now, you create your reality evermore. When your focus is on your vision and you can see it in your mind's eye, you create it in every moment of now. It will not happen by anticipating it in the future, because then it will never be present, now will it? Your true power lies in the now. Your every moment of now is when you get to create and move towards that which it is you want. As you do so, the future you want moves towards you and comes into focus in your reality. Now is all that is in reality. Where are you in the now? Where do you want to be now?

Decide now. Commit now. Act now. All else will follow. You can be at peace now in knowing this, and so be it. There is no time in actuality; there is only your experience of what is now. When you release your past now, you are letting go of your old story. Where you end up now in the new story of your life comes from what you choose right now in each passing moment that is now. There is only now. This is where you are. What do you choose right now? Where do you want to go from here right now? You always have choice in deciding where you are now. Your decision in turn affects your perception of where you are – or should I say, where you think you are. You can be where you want to be, depending on the decision you make. In the unlimited possibilities that stem from now, you have the power to choose where you are and where you are going. Where are you? Where are you going? You get to choose right now. What is your story right now, and where are you in it? What is your destination that moves you towards your heart's desire? Only you can decide this right now. Every move you make with conscious awareness in this way frees you from the old patterns that kept you stuck before. Now you can move with renewed energy towards what you want, from knowing where you are in every moment of now. Now you can move forward towards your dream in every moment of now. When you move forward from your authentic self, your life takes on a whole new meaning. Now you can know your place in the world. Go in peace, with grace and ease. You are not alone.

Exercise

Get a pen and paper for yourself and start thinking about what you want to achieve in terms of goals. When setting goals, they should be written concisely in the present tense. Which areas of your life need more attention? What do you need to change in your life? Your goals can refer to the different aspects of your life, such as the following:

- health
- wealth
- friends and family
- romantic partner
- fun and recreation
- career
- physical environment
- personal growth

When writing goals, you can phrase them starting with

- I allow my self to have …,
- I have …, or
- I am …

You can also add a future date to the goal in the present tense in this way:

> It is 14 March 2016, and I have successfully published my
> book; this or something better.

It is always advisable to add "this or something better" at the end of the overall goal. In that way, you are not fixed on one outcome, as there are many possibilities in the universe. Then you can detach from the goal once you have sent it off to the universe. In this way, you are not attached to one single outcome, and it also allows the universe to provide you with a better outcome than you could have imagined for yourself. If you remain attached to the goal, you remain attached to the state of wanting and lack. Trust and allow. Never worry about the how, because the universe takes care of that. Once you set an intention and put it in writing, this sends energy out into the universe, as all thoughts are energy. When you combine the emotion of having the goal, this adds more power, or juice, to get the wheels in motion. Trust that it is done and it is so now, once you have written it down. Then let it go. Also, at the same time when you are writing it, create an image in your mind's eye of what the end result will look like. This could be a film reel or a still photo of the evidence of having achieved the goal. First, see it as though looking through your own eyes, and then see yourself in the film or the picture. Say to yourself, "This or something better." See what you see, hear what you hear, and feel what you feel when you have the feeling of knowing you have achieved your goal. Make it compelling! Imagine a dial and turn it up. Make the colours bright, hear all the sounds, and turn up your feelings intensely while creatively visualizing your goal. You can look at your goal daily or read an affirmation of it being present "as if now" in your life. This reinforces your intention regularly, while allowing you to just forget about it consciously afterwards. Get on with your daily life and just trust that all is in order. You are right where you are meant to be in this very moment.

CHAPTER 3

WHAT DO YOU WANT?

Do you know what you really want in and from your life? Without knowing what you want, you will not know which direction to take or which steps to take. Knowing what you want allows you to focus on it. Would you rather wander aimlessly in life to see if things work out, or would you rather marvel at the wonderful path you have taken towards your dream? Without a vision to focus on, you may not know if you are achieving what it takes to move closer to your dream. With a destination in mind, you can steer the course of your life towards it as you follow your heart. There may be challenges along the way, and you can view these as opportunities to accomplish whatever you need to overcome in moving towards your goal.

As you journey to self-discovery on the inside, you also allow yourself to move towards your dream on the outside. When you go inwards and learn who you really are at your core, everything on the outside changes. This will involve you stretching your self at times, as you expand the boundaries of your awareness. This also means that you are courageous when you need to be. It is fear that stops people from moving forward in their life. Fear of what? Fear of the unknown? What is familiar is considered safe, according to our survival in evolution. It may seem comfortable and safe to stay in your familiar space. Familiarity and comfort mean you are not moving outside your comfort zone. Moving into the unknown can be scary and exciting at the same time.

By clarifying what you want in terms of your goals, you can also find out what your values are. Values provide energy and drive to move towards your goal. Know what your present reality is in terms of your beliefs, limiting beliefs, outlook, perspectives, and perception. Reflect on your options and resources. Clarify your commitment to take action and to do whatever it takes in achieving your goal, at the same time. What are the consequences of your goal? How long do you think it is going to take? When do you expect to achieve the outcome? How do you know you have what you want? Set out what intermediate steps are to be taken between now and the goal outcome. It is more powerful when you write this all down in a journal, which you can write in from time to time. Writing your thoughts and feelings on paper helps you to let go of them easier, as well as to become aware of your self-limiting beliefs. Thoughts and feelings in themselves can be habits. These habits can change once you shine the light of your awareness on them.

The reality you experience right now mirrors your level of consciousness on the inside. When you move deeper and deeper towards your authentic self, your experience of reality changes on the outside. You determine what you create in your life by your consciousness, or state of mind. Your mindset is how your mind is set, or how you set your mind. You can adjust and change this setting at any time through conscious awareness and self-knowledge. By moving deeper into who you are and where you are over time, you come to know what you truly want according to your heart's desire. What you want is no longer influenced by what others want for you. This is because your control comes from the inside, from that very part of you that is your authentic self. You know this to be so when your mind is still enough to hear the inner voice of what is true for you. By getting to know your self deeper and deeper, you get to feel what is true for you. Your feelings, and not your thoughts, become your intuitive guide for which path you must take and what you truly want. Feeling comes from the heart of who you are, while your thoughts come from your head.

As you learn about your authentic self more and more, you grow and create a better and better life for yourself. You also learn that by moving out of your head and into your heart, you will be guided to what you really want and not what you think you want. As your awareness expands with growth, you evolve into a higher level of being, both on the inside and the outside. In this way, you continuously change and grow through a process of transformation. What you want for yourself also evolves as you continue to grow. Therefore, while you gain self-knowledge and self-awareness on your journey of self-discovery, you are constantly shaping the reality you live in. At the same time, you are gaining self-mastery. You create according to your journey to your authentic self. The deeper you go, the more "in-sights" you get into a new way of being and feeling in the world. What you want is related to your concept of who you are and where you are right now.

As you move towards your authentic self, what you want becomes more colourful, compelling, expanded, and possible. Whatever you wanted originally might not change, but as you move towards the core of your being, it will expand, become bigger, touch more lives, and have more impact for the good of all. Your potential for creating what you want is very much linked with your self-knowledge, your stage of personal development and self-understanding. We are all on a journey of learning and growth. When you learn that you can create a better reality, you grow as a result. You learn what works and what doesn't. These lessons in life increase your level of consciousness. When you are at one with what you want, it is yours already. It exists outside of time in your imagination and so must come into being when you hold your belief in it. Your subconscious always acts on your beliefs as they show up in your behaviour.

The process of creation in your life is a reflection of your inner consciousness. You always get what you expect. Your thoughts have the power to create. They are more powerful than you may realize. The world around you is a mirror reflecting back to you what you project onto it. In your journey towards self-knowledge and self-realization, the ways in which things appear to you on the outside can change over time as you change on the inside. As you move towards your authentic self more and more, your creation of reality on the outside also moves to a deeper level. As you move deeper into your self, you gain more knowledge and realization about how things in themselves really are, versus how they appear to be. This journey towards your true self also lets you know what you truly want, if you didn't know it before. It comes to you at any time along the journey, from out of the blue, in a flash of inspiration (in spirit).

What you truly want is linked to helping others, for it is in helping others that you help yourself. What you want is also linked to how you can be in service to others. What you want is linked with your soul purpose and what you came here on earth to do. It is what gives you joy and makes you feel alive and excited. What you want means you can do what you know. You can become the person that can just *be*. When you have what you want, it becomes integrated into your very being, because it is a part of who you are. It was always there, but it only emerged when, like a seed, it was nourished and supported in the right environment to allow it to grow and show itself above the soil. It always has potential to come into being. What you want just needs focus, attention, belief, faith, and a deep knowing that its creation is possible in a material sense. You can manifest that which you desire by stilling the mind in the absence of thinking. Your thoughts can get in your own way sometimes. In order to get out of your own way, you can maintain this inner silence as much as possible in keeping your connection to your authentic self at the source of your being. Also, by surrounding yourself with people who have what you want, in terms of what you want to do, you can influence the changes you need in order to create what you want in your life. Being surrounded by these happy, successful, abundant people increases your ability to create what you want dramatically in achieving the life of your dreams, when you are following your heart's desire.

If your willpower and imagination are in conflict, imagination always wins. Your imagination, or what you see in your mind's eye, is everything! According to Einstein, all your problems are of the imagination and all your solutions are of the imagination. It's all about how you look at it in how you play the game of life. Excuse yourself from excusing yourself with reasons for your perceived limitations. Instead, know that when you have belief in yourself, you expand and play big towards living your extraordinary life! In the process, you have effortless access to being in the flow of the universe. Incongruence within yourself leads to a state of stuckness, conflict, or limbo.

When you try not to do something, it inevitably becomes a self-fulfilling prophecy in reverse, as in Coue's law of reversed effect. You cannot try not to think of something without inevitably thinking about it. The imagination responds to the images presented to it. For example, if you hear a dripping tap and try not to think about it, this leads to a self-fulfilling prophecy in reverse. Whatever you focus on (even if it is something you don't want to think about) is where your attention goes. The possible frustration associated with trying to go asleep and being distracted by the dripping tap adds emotion also, which increases the likelihood of indirect suggestibility to yourself that the tap's dripping prevents you from sleeping. The best thing to do is either turn off the tap or focus on something else that may help you to sleep, such as your own breathing. As Chris Howard says, "You can't think about something you don't want to think about without thinking about it."

When you integrate all aspects of your being in mind, body, and soul, you become complete and whole in your thinking. In fact, you are already complete and whole. When you align with being whole in your being, your thoughts flow more from the heart or source of your being. This includes knowing what you want. The world is always a reflection of your consciousness. The world reflects back to you how you are on the inside. How you are on the inside affects your results on every level. Who you are determines what you look for in life. When you expand on who you are in your consciousness, what you want for yourself also expands. Your values and beliefs affect how you deal with decisions and challenges that arise. Who you are affects what you allow to filter into your life. People cannot behave towards you in any way other than the way you perceive them to be. You create everything that comes into effect. You are at cause for everything that happens or doesn't happen in your life. Everything is your responsibility now. With awareness comes responsibility. While before, you may have blamed yourself for problems, they are not your fault. This line of thinking comes from your conditioning of how you view problems and why they happen. When you look at all problems as challenges to be overcome, that provides an opportunity to learn, and you can say to yourself, "Bring it on!"

Your focus on what you want determines your results in life. When you want something, focus on just that and not on what you don't want. If you keep thinking about what you don't want, then that's what you get. This means letting go of your emotional baggage. That means letting go of your judgements and blame. Only then can you be light and free to move forward, unburdened, with ease and grace. As you pick up speed, you close the gap between where you are now and what you want. As a result, you increase your quality of experience in life, because you can transcend what may have bothered you before. This used to consume your energy in the process. Don't waste your energy on stuff that doesn't matter ultimately, in the grand picture of your life. Know that there's something to learn on the inside, and that is the truth of who you are essentially. Start with the basics in learning who you are at your core. First of all, you could ask yourself questions that bring about awareness as to why you may be stuck in life. The answers will give you insight into areas you may not have looked at before. You could ask yourself the following questions:

- If I am not living according to my full potential, how do I block myself with my self-limiting beliefs?
- Are my relationships influenced by other people's judgements, opinions, or assumptions?
- Did I put everybody else first before now, in sacrificing myself and my needs for others?
- Am I drained of energy because I spread myself too thin, leaving little for myself?
- Am I making excuses of not having enough money, time, or resources when I know I can do it?
- Do I withdraw when low in energy and in doing so close myself off to opportunities?
- Am I conditioned to think of others and forget myself?
- Do I believe I deserve wealth and abundance?
- Do I think that I don't need money to be happy?
- Do I separate the idea of money and wealth from happiness in my life?
- Does my stereotype of rich people and poor people differ in that I view only poor people as happy?

Remember, your thoughts are powerful. Asking yourself these kinds of questions impacts your awareness of where you are most stuck in your life. With awareness, you can make changes in your life. All change is instant and takes place in your subconscious mind. Change itself comes from having learned something about yourself, just like when you have an "Aha!" moment. This is where the light bulb goes on over your head and you just know something to be the case. It is the same with self-awareness. The more self-aware you become, the more you know what you truly want, according to your heart's desire. You can make the necessary changes in yourself after taking a look inside in this way.

When you know what you want, you give yourself a chance to fulfil your dream. Your knowing gives you the energy and dynamism to achieve whatever it is you want in life. You become resistant to negativity because there is no holding you back. Your determination propels you forward. When you learn more about yourself, you can interact with others according to your true self. This is what sets you free from your old ways of being or doing. Now you can be free to have and share joy with others. You communicate better from a place of knowing more about yourself. In this way, you are less affected by others' opinions or assumptions. Your connection with your self-knowing means you know you can live where you want to live and be where you want to be. With ease of mind, you can focus on what you can and want to do, while being open to possibilities. Your internal strength gives you vitality to do the things you want to accomplish. You know you can shed the old and enter the new way right now, in your journey to creating what you want. By getting to know who you are, where you are, and what you want, you can take off towards your vision much quicker. Sometimes there seems to be a lot of choice as to which direction to go next, and this may seem daunting or even confusing at times. When you know your self deeply, your choice is always easier. Knowing your authentic self is the shortcut to knowing and getting what you want. This is because you can tap into your power within, from where your life emanates. You can feel the momentum building in your life, and you know you do not have to put up with what does not serve you any longer.

Your values hold what is important to you about any aspect of life. Your values in life determine where your attention goes, and this in turn determines your results. Increased self-awareness leads to better action for yourself. What values would somebody need to have to achieve what you want? Think about it. I wrote my own list of life values years ago. Here they are as an example in their order of importance to me then:

- love
- empowerment
- control
- resourcefulness
- strength
- altruism
- decisiveness
- discernment
- peace/serenity/calm
- trust/faith
- determination
- enthusiasm
- adventure
- zest
- fun
- belonging
- interdependence
- curiosity

I know now that this list of values has changed since then, as my vision of what I want expands and grows continually. Everybody's values are different, and one person's values can change from time to time. I know that my values of interdependence and curiosity have definitely gone up the ladder since then. I also know that the whole arrangement would look different if I wrote it down right now. When you live your life in alignment with your values, you are in congruence with your self. The key to living a full life is doing what you love. When you know what you want, you can live your life on purpose with a sense of mission to bring about positive change in other people's lives. These positive changes you envision for others come from listening to your heart while leaving logic aside. The universe, in turn, rewards you greatly for being in service to others while following your heart. Celebrate by living your life on purpose when you know what you want.

Develop an attitude of gratitude also, as this shifts your attention to what you have in the moment. When you are in the moment, you are tapping into your power. Having gratitude becomes a habit over time. You can be grateful for your health, as this allows you to do and be everything that you are in reality. You can thank your family for the lessons you've learned and for all the good times you have had with them. You can be grateful for your insight, through which you learn about yourself, others, life, and the universe. You can appreciate the relationships, connections, and friendships that have led you to now. All of this has given you the opportunity and potential to be who you can be. You can express gratitude for all the people who have turned up to help you change the course of your own life by encouraging you to go beyond your beliefs. You can also think of all your possessions and facilities, even water, that have helped make your journey easy along the way. You evolve from the here and now towards your dream, which is your vision of what you want. Knowing where you are right now gives you the foundation from where you can move forward in your life. Knowing where you are gives you a reference point that shows what direction you're coming from and what direction you're going towards. When you know where you're coming from, you're going towards what you want.

When you know what you want, you need to set a strong intention to bring it into being. This requires concentration through focus of mind. If you are distracted, this can lead to procrastination and lack of concentration on what you want. As you increase your concentration and focus daily on what you want, you are in the moment, thinking only of what is relevant and avoiding distractions. By growing the seed of your intent, you can reap the rewards. When you have concentrated focus on what you want, according to your life purpose and vision, you are in the zone, in the now, where there is no thought. When you are in the zone, your superconscious, conscious, and subconscious mind are in alignment, acting as one in harmony and balance. In the zone, you are in the flow, where everything seems to go easily and effortlessly without thought. So, in order to create anything you want in your life, get into the zone as much as possible. If your reality is not reflecting what you want, it seems you have not accessed this state of flow in the zone enough times. This is how to get the law of attraction to work for you. Through concentrated focus in the zone, while remaining connected to your authentic self, your ability to create and see life in a different light is possible.

When you know where you are, you know where you're moving from. When you know where you are, this means you know where you come from and how you arrived where you are right now. Knowing where you come from means you understand what had to happen for you to be here right now, as you are and where you are. Knowing this can in itself act as a foundational platform for you to move on to higher planes of existence while you achieve what you want. As you navigate through life, do you know where you're going? What direction do you want to take, and what is your destination? Are you moving towards your heart's desire for what you want in your life, or are you moving away from it? If you were to rise above your life and take a look at where you are and where you are going, what does it look like? Do you like what you see? Does your mind map match the plan to reach your destination? Remember, the map is not the territory. In order to achieve a goal, you need to have a plan. This plan can show you which way to move in the outside world, but it does not really show you the inner resources needed to get you there. The foundation from which your attitudes and behaviours flow is the driving force that sets the compass for what you want. This comes from how you view the world from your own point of view, so to speak. So, when you know who you are and where you are, your mind map is more likely to represent the territory for your journey to what you want. When times seem difficult or challenges get in your way, then it's a matter of adjusting the inner map to get through and over whatever arises.

Doing the same thing over and over again and expecting to get different results doesn't work. Trying harder doing the same thing doesn't work either. It's like repeatedly banging your head against the same wall. It is by learning to change your inner map to match what you want that you make your desires and goals come about. If you ask a person what he or she wants most, that person might answer you by saying he or she wants to be rich and have a boat or a big house. While it is good to have nice things, being wealthy is not just about having material possessions. True wealth allows you to live your life with zest, comfort, joy, and aliveness. It does not mean living a luxurious lifestyle that has no meaning. While there is nothing wrong with having luxury, true wealth means you have all that you need to carry out your life's work. This may not seem like work to you, because you have a passion for what you do and you love doing it when you carry out your soul's purpose. There's a saying that goes, "When you love what you do, you'll never have to work another day in your life again." You can have luxury even while carrying out your purpose in life. Some people have beliefs that wealthy people are not honest or that rich people are not righteous. This is not the case. The universe is abundant, and that means that there is enough for everybody on the planet. Abundance is not about satisfying the ego needs of material gain. It is, in fact, about having everything you need in terms of tools, resources, and environment to do your life's work. At the same time, abundance has no limits, and this is how the universe operates. When you genuinely set out to be in service to others in following your purpose, you will be right where you are meant to be at the right time, when you follow your inner guidance. When you hold this focus in the background of everything you do, it will ultimately lead you closer and closer to what you want.

Be Committed to What You Want

Be committed to your intention or goal, once you know what it is. By knowing where you are in your realistic commitment to your goal, you know what obstacles can arise along the way. You can then face them while knowing what reward lies beyond. You can also make room for whatever needs to be done in achieving your goal. Having commitment gives you control, especially when you state your commitment out loud to yourself. Commitment is not just intellectual; it is also emotional. Your subconscious hears your commitment as you say it out loud. Action and perseverance are more likely to occur when you are emotionally engaged in your quest for the goal of living a truly happy, fulfilled life, according to what's important for you. By eliciting your values of what's important to you in life, you can use the values compass for what you want on your journey towards your ultimate vision (or goal). The action steps or small goals along the way are the signposts on the path or mission towards the outcome. You can gain strength as you pursue your goals with momentum, determination, and an enthusiasm which was not apparent before, because now you have a focus.

With focus, you can take risks and challenge yourself. In getting to know where you are, you can have empathy and compassion for your perceived problems and suffering, while knowing at the same time that you can make the change that is needed. By accepting yourself, you are free to express your truth. The only limits are the ones you set for yourself. In having trust and empathy for yourself, you instil self-belief. This self-belief allows you to move forward in life, without distraction or hindrance from other people. Freedom and direction come from the trust and empathy you give yourself. Humour also allows you to look at something from a different angle, and this can also help give you the results you want in achieving your goal.

Within your authentic self lies courage, and courage is what gets you to where your goal is. That which already is can be reached by drawing to it the same that it already is. In moving towards your core, your source, the key to unlocking the door is to use what is already behind the door in terms of what you already are. You can tap into the qualities of your real self through courage, persistence, and determination. As you get closer to your authentic self, you will get a more definite idea of what you want. What you want includes what you want for your self and others. Your main goal will contain that thing that gives you a feeling of passion and drives you as you are doing what you love. You know you have purpose when you are moving to fulfil your purpose. This is your reason for being on this earth. This is what you are here to do. Your goal involves helping other people by serving them in some way as you live out your dream. Once you know what your goal is for the big picture of your life, you can set your intention. When you set goals for yourself, your desire represents the big picture goal. The steps needed to get there are the small goals along the way. When you move towards your ultimate goal through steps, or small goals, you find that success builds upon success. With each success, your confidence and belief in yourself increase. This creates further momentum in the right direction, moving you from goalpost to goalpost.

Focus on what you have and not on what you don't have. You can build on what you have. You create lack by focusing on what you don't have. You know that what you have and are in this moment was created from a possibility before it became manifest in physical form. You have the power in this moment to manifest what you want also. When you believe and know this to be true, you can manifest any possibility you set your mind to. You can bring a different possibility into being. In doing so, you realize that what you create in your life is your responsibility alone. There is no point in waiting for others to give you what you want. While other people can help, it is your intention that creates the end result, ultimately, through being open to a synchronicity of events. An intention is more likely to become manifest when you stay focused on it in a relaxed manner, no matter what happens in your daily life. Staying fixated on your intention behind the scenes of life sends a message to your subconscious that incorporates what you want into your programming. In this way, what you want and who you are at your core become one. When you are one with what you want, it is yours already.

Setting an Intention

When there is no conflict between what you want and your inner self, it is already in your very being in potentiality. This is because you know it is possible. Your authentic self is your inner knowing and your deepest consciousness, where all is one with the universe. Your authentic self gives you the connection to the source of all being. It is the key that unlocks the door to the universe and the quantum soup of possibilities, which some also call the quantum field. When you are one with what you want, it is reflected in your beliefs, which are acted out in your behaviour. Your actions then reflect your beliefs as you steer towards that which you want, without distraction from anything that lies outside your beliefs.

Changing your present picture may not happen immediately, as it may have taken some time to bring it together according to your old beliefs. For any aspect of your present picture that you do not want, you must focus on what you want to replace it with instead. This means focusing on your intentions and beliefs that will bring you what you want. Ignore that which you do not want, and it will fade away. Use the path of least effort. Do not resist what you do not want, for then you energize it, which keeps you stuck to it. By simply not paying any attention to it, you cause it to lose its energy and fade right out of your life. Pay attention to what you want, because that is where you want your energy to go. This is where your free-will and choice come in. You design your destiny by the intentions you set. You design your future from your power in the now. If you are more visual than hearing or feeling in perceiving the world, then use visualization. If you are more auditory, then use repeated affirmations, in your head or spoken aloud, on a daily basis. By using your senses to get what you want in this way, you are concentrating your whole being on your desire. Use all your energy and focus when setting an intention. Then detach from it and go and do something else.

When you know it is so, you do not need to check up on the universe and its abundant supply. If you doubt, or if you focus on lack, you disconnect yourself from the flow to and from what you want. When you are connected to what you want, you don't need to hang on to it or look to see if it's there. Your connection guides you in the flow. You just know and feel it within your very being. What you want will manifest when the time is right. All is in divine order. When your intentions are clear and simple, in a nutshell statement in the present, there is no room for doubt or error. Remember that the existence of unlimited possibilities means you need to be precise when setting an intention. When you want something, that means you want that possibility or something better. The universe will always give you what you ask for or something better, when you believe in it. In clarifying your intention with laser-like focus, you are clarifying exactly what you want, while allowing for something better also. That's when you get what you want. Once the intention is set, just let go of it and the universe will take care of the how.

Setting intentions in the form of goals is powerful, especially when you write them down. You can also write down small goals that are action steps to your main goal. Write down ten goals and focus on the most important one at first. Put this goal on your mirror and say it to your self every day. Through repetition, on a regular basis that is consistent, eventually this goal will go into the subconscious. However, this form of reprogramming takes time. A quicker method would be to use your positive affirmations or intention during hypnosis, when your conscious mind is at rest. When your mind is in a deeply relaxed state, it is more open to accepting suggestions. As a result, these suggestions become integrated into your automatic behaviour. Once this happens, your subconscious, which has a connection to source and the universe, manifests whatever you need at a given time, in moving you towards your goal. The path may not be easy at times. Follow your gut intuition, which is linked to your subconscious, as this will give you some direction before making important decisions in your life. The world that surrounds you is created by what you think, feel, and believe. You cannot see, hear, feel, taste, or touch beyond your expectations of such. Einstein said that we are confined within the boundaries of our thinking. What you expect, you get. When you intend something, you take a more active role in what you surround yourself with, rather than merely just perceiving your surroundings. You may not notice it at first as the outside world mirrors your thoughts, feelings and beliefs. As you change your thoughts, your outside world will change in your perception of it. This will bring new things, places, and people into your life. This you have created by changing on the inside to become more like your authentic self.

The source is where all creation emanates from before it is manifested into this world. The field of intention is present in the source and is a field of infinite potential and energy. It is universal and exists everywhere, always was, is, and will be. In setting your intention (goal), you are tapping into this field of possibilities. Through believing and expecting it, you bring it forward to you effortlessly. Also, feeling the feelings of having it now, when setting your intention, makes the intention more powerful. It is as if you feel as though you have it already. Once you set an intention, you can then let it go. It is important to do this, because if you remain attached to it, you remain in a state of wanting. If you are in a state of wanting, you are saying you don't have it now. In letting wanting go, you allow what you want to come to you. This is the law of detachment. You can only receive that which you are not trying to get all the time, for if you were constantly trying, that is the state you would remain in. By detaching from what you want, you allow yourself to receive it. This means you have surrendered and trust in the process, when you know you have it in the now.

As you grow and evolve, you move closer to what you want. All learning leads to growth on some level. You can learn through either joy or pain and suffering. Either way, you will learn what you need to learn. The path of joy is effortless, easy, and direct, and on that path learning makes you feel light and moves you quickly towards what you want. The path of pain and suffering has its lessons of learning also, but this takes a bit longer, as the path meanders, twists, and turns. When you see the world through eyes of joy, it is a friendly place where cooperation, sharing, and collaboration are seen as means of getting things done. Joy is expressed in embracing the flow and change in life, where the world is seen as safe and open. In a state of joy, opportunities abound, as does the potential for making new friends. Joy seeks to spread love and happiness. Learning the painful way is heavy and resentful. The painful path is one of competition and greed that comes from ego. This pain is expressed in resistance to change, as well as rigidity in changing itself. The painful path sees the world as threatening and focuses most on safety and security. With awareness, you can choose the path of learning with joy and put an end to your suffering. Buddha said, "With enlightenment, comes the end of suffering." When you know what you want and can move towards it with joy, you become a magnet for attracting your heart's desire.

Harmonize with Your Authentic Self

Live in the moment. Don't dwell on the past. To bring about knowledge, understand from the past why you are the way you are. With self-insight, you come to realize where you are in your life, in relation to what you want. With self-knowledge, your awareness increases regarding how to replace negative thoughts with positive ones. This is achieved by harmonizing your thoughts with your authentic self and what feels right for you. Only then can you know what you truly want for you. Be the change that you want to bring about. Give to others what you yourself want to receive. Be patient with yourself and others. Change is a process and therefore is not instantaneous. It requires reflection and contemplation to bring about awareness. All learning and change takes time. By harmonizing who you really are with your being and your thoughts, you resonate with the same energy in the quantum field of infinite possibilities, where anything is possible.

Synchronicity becomes more frequent as you learn to tap into the power of the subconscious within. Your innate wisdom enables you to focus and be patient, as you bring your thoughts, feelings, and beliefs into harmony with your authentic self. Once you know what you want and you get to do it, you love what you do and do what you love. This in itself leads you onwards towards self-mastery. Self-mastery involves self-discipline and commitment to do whatever it takes to get where you want to get to. Paradoxically, surrendering to your authentic self is part of this process also.

You always have a choice, and your free will is yours to use with or against your authentic self. Your intention or goal setting concentrates on what you focus your attention on. Your thoughts and feelings influence the way you use your free will. By using free will to focus on your authentic self, you can concentrate your creative energy upon a precise moment in time and wait in patience for its unfolding. On the other hand, free will dominated by ego moves you away from your authentic self to the lower energy field of feeling down and out. Free will gives you the choice of either connecting with spirit or not. Free will and the power of your subconscious can coexist in allowing yourself to be guided by spirit towards your authentic self. Your choice determines your link with your own authentic self in this way. You can avoid being average by using your free will to be aligned with your authentic self. By recognizing when you're out of harmony with you real self, your awareness allows you to reconnect and realign with your purpose. Whatever your task at hand is that you wish to accomplish, it exists already in spirit. Your intention brings it forward into the physical world. Your intention can be set as a goal or even as a prayer. "Ask and you shall receive." "Seek and you shall find." You will always find what you are looking for. When you ask for help in the form of prayer and have faith, it is always answered in some form or another. Asking for help is better than not asking to receive guidance about what steps to take next. You will always reap what you have sown.

If material possessions are the focus of your life, you may want to get the biggest, largest, and most expensive thing you can imagine. By placing your focus on material gain, you leave less room for connecting with your true power that comes from your authentic self. Your authentic self is what provides you with access to the power within, through the source of all that is. When you chase the illusion of happiness and fulfilment on the outside, you lose connection with your real self. While it is good to have nice things, it does not serve you to have material items as the end of your means to achieving what you want. Your abundance in life comes from the truth of who you really are. Abundance and prosperity come from your deeper meaning and connection to your authentic self. While it can be good to have luxury in your life, even in the form of material things, your connection with source means that you are not caught up with them. In this way, you are not identified with material gain.

Abundance covers your health, your wealth, your relationships with other people, and your way of life. Abundance allows you to serve others to the best of your ability. The more abundance you have, the more people you can serve, and that leads to more abundance in turn. The more you connect with your authentic self, the more you let go of former dense emotions that previously clouded your mind. Now your connection with source means you allow in the light of your higher being, which becomes your inner radiance. From within, you now radiate forth your true light as you move towards what you want with passion and purpose. This is because you are on purpose in your life when you have found your purpose. To discover your purpose, you need to move past the illusion of your life as you see it. In order to move past the conditioning of your life, you must learn to become aware of your conditioning and programming that shaped your perception of life. Know that your beliefs are not necessarily true. Your beliefs can be changed by you more directly than before to get what you want. You can save yourself a lot of time and lessons by changing your beliefs. First you need to learn which ones serve you and which ones don't. In the process, you can start letting go of those self-limiting beliefs as they become illuminated by the light of your inner knowing.

Your authentic self cannot be reached with negativity, such as doubt, limitations, or lack of self-belief. As Aldous Huxley said, "The spiritual journey ... consists in the dissipation of one's own ignorance concerning one's self and life, and the gradual growth of that understanding which begins the spiritual awakening." The finding of God is coming to one's self. Know that you are already what you'd like to become. What you wish to accomplish is already there to be achieved. This is the vision of your heart's desire, which already exists in potentiality. Think from the end in pursuing your goals. Your authentic self has an inner awareness, or silent knowing, that doesn't involve trying to reason or think your way through life. Rational thinking needs to be set aside, and doubt eliminated from the mind. Through practise with meditation and deep relaxation, the monkey mind can be emptied of all thought and just *be* in a state of no thought. From this state, your mind can move deeper and deeper towards self-actualization. This is why it is so important to quiet your mind. Your mind is quiet when it is empty of thoughts. An empty mind has more focus, clarity and precision in what it is aiming for. It remains undisrupted in its intention for achieving its goal. It continues to create whatever you give attention to for your purpose. For this reason, your creating ability is limited if you contemplate a lack of things, as this goes against aligning with your authentic self. Instead, contemplate everything as it should be for what you want, and trust that conditions for the end results surround you now. This mindset manifests conditions that bring the end into focus. Contemplate the intention you've set as working for you and not against you.

What you want is for your higher good and the good of all. It flows from the integrity of your being. Your integrity with yourself is what brings you into alignment with what you want. That integral part of you, your authentic self, is what links where you are now to who you really are. What you want comes from source by means of your authentic self. Your authentic self is the doorway to your heart's desire. When you connect with your inner being, you are on your way to what you want. As your authentic self becomes more prominent in your life, so does your personal power. Your ability to rely on yourself saves you a lot of time and unnecessary struggle. Your connection with your inner source gives you all the encouragement, support, and comfort that you will ever need. It is also nice at the same time to surround yourself with people of the same mindset as yourself. That way your external surroundings will reflect your inner state of being as you proceed towards what you want.

Your outside world is a reflection of your inner world. As you become more in alignment with who you really are and where you are, what you want becomes more authentic for you. As you move closer to the core of your own truth, you are also moving closer to the source of what sets you free. What you want in life is what gives you freedom to express your truth to the world. Your connection with your authentic self means you no longer hinder yourself from your self. You are free to move forward when you are living your truth. Your truth becomes what you want. Your connection with your authentic self means you become what you want in the process. This may seem a bit confusing right now, but read on and all will be revealed. Be patient with the process as you take on board the truth of your being. You have much more power than you know. Believe in your own power and pursue your dream with passion.

The more you get to know your real self, the more you get to know what you want. The two go together, because you can only want that which comes from who you are. When you know what you want, that's a step in the right direction. You have more steps to take, but you must take them one step at a time. Going for what you want means you are also learning to forget what you don't want. You are learning in the process that your focus determines what you get. When you want something in this way, you just focus your attention on it. The more attention you focus on what you want, the more you aim your energy in the right direction for your way forward.

As you walk on this path, you realize you are on your soul's journey to your authentic self. The further you go within, the nearer you come to your authentic self. As your authenticity emerges into your being, it merges with who and where you are. From this, you can access all that you need much easier from source. As you move along your life path, you begin to realize that everything is not as it seems. Appearances are just that, and you are not taken in by them any more. With your inner empowerment and awareness, you can go directly for what you want in itself rather than for what it appears to be. No longer are you swayed by the illusions of life. For this reason, you can remain steady on your path with balance and control. Your balance and control lie within, grounded in your being with who you really are. You are in tune with your own power when you know for certain that you can have what you want. This is not ego's knowing, but a knowing that you can feel in your own body. This knowing is what is right and good for you, other people, and the planet. What you want is for the highest good of all.

Exercise

Focus on your goal by writing your intention down. You can begin the writing with one of the following:

- I am ...
- I am attracting ...
- I am intending ...
- I am creating ...
- I am allowing ...

Then just add whatever it is you want to achieve in moving towards your vision and purpose. It is important that when you say your intention out loud, you also feel it to be so. In this way, your subconscious is in agreement with what you want to create. After writing your goal down, you can "future pace" by closing your eyes and imagining having achieved that goal on a certain date in the now of the future. In future pacing, you can see what you see, hear what you hear, and really feel the feeling that you have already achieved the goal. Turn up your feelings of happiness, achievement, and success in achieving your goal, as this makes it more compelling. Celebrate your success as if you have it now. Make your goal bright, colourful, and loud. If appropriate, hear the voices of people applauding you and their hands clapping right now in the moment. You are standing in your own power. How are you standing? You are in your moment of achievement. How are you feeling? You know now what you needed to do to get to this moment. You can ask your future self what this is and what the next step is. Write down the answer and take action on it this same day.

As Nike says, "Just do it." If you procrastinate, you may put it off. As long as you want a specific goal, remain focused on it and persevere until it is accomplished before moving on to the next goal. During visualization, you can form an image of what you want to create in your mind. Visualization of your end goal draws to you its physical form as you use emotional energy and power when you imagine it at first. By changing the image you see in your mind's eye, you can change the picture of your life at any time. The picture you paint for your life can be changed in any given moment, when your belief is aligned with it. Your present picture is just one life picture which you have created from the infinite possibilities that exist in potentiality. What you really want may be dormant, awaiting your activation through your power of choice. The skills and talents you need are already available to you, once you know how to access them. When you realize this, you know that what you have and what you do in your present life right now has been created by you. You realize now also that you can manifest what you want when you set an intention with conviction and emotion while seeing it in your mind's eye. Seeing is believing, just as believing is seeing! What you believe is what you see, and what you see is what you believe. Believe in what you want. Believe it is yours now. So be it, and so it is.

CHAPTER 4

THE ILLUSION: CONDITIONING AND PROGRAMMING

Can you imagine that your mind is like a computer? Imagine that your brain is the hardware and that your conditioning (or programming) comes from your parents, society, the media, and advertising. Your conditioning is the "software" that gives rise to your "programming", or ways of thinking and behaving. The way you have been conditioned is stored in your subconscious, and it is your subconscious that directs 95 per cent of your behaviour. Have you been conditioned to think that you are a limited being or a self-empowered being? What is the true nature of your being? Your software may block your access into the true database of who you really are.

Conditioning is the way you have become programmed by your environment. Your conditioning affects your concept of your self. When you become aware of the illusions that your conditioning brought about, you also become aware of your self-limiting beliefs. Do you know who you really are at your core, and are you living your life in alignment with that? The good news is that your programming can be changed. It is not static. It can be changed through awareness and self-understanding. This involves a process of self-discovery through which many lessons are learned about the true nature of your being. It is like peeling off the layers of an onion in order to get to the core. The closer you get to your core, the easier you can tap into your authentic self. This means taking a journey inwards with consistent movement while shedding off the layers along the way. In this way, you become more integrated with your self. You are already whole and complete, but your conditioning has lead you to think otherwise. You are enough already. You do not need to strive to be anything else. Just be your self, because in reality you are one with your self already.

The journey inwards becomes easier with acceptance of just how powerful you really are. This means letting go of your limitations and self-defeating beliefs. They do not serve you in any way; instead, they hold you back from the life you are meant to live. Self-limiting beliefs are part of the software that was programmed into your mind over time. This happened without your conscious awareness, because you just accepted this as the way of the world when you were younger. Your conditioning was not your fault, and there is no blame there. What you learned as you were being conditioned was to survive and adapt to your surroundings and the people around you. When you take on board others' views as your own, this pattern can continue on into adulthood, thus limiting your own awareness of self. Lack of self-awareness can lead to a "trance of disempowerment" which is mistaken for your reality. So, in the past, what you took for reality was really your disempowered state of conditioning.

When you wake up to your authentic self once more, you realize the truth of what is. With this awakening to your true self, it becomes your responsibility to live according to your own truth. You are not a victim. Your power comes from within and not from the outside. You control the power in your life from within. When you are at cause in your life, you control who you are, where you are, and what you want in life. If you think you are a victim, then you are at effect of what happens on the outside. All that is, is within. The outside is merely a reflection, like a mirror, of what is happening on the inside. Nothing is really happening outside of you. At your core, you are consciousness, where you are connected with the consciousness of all that is in the universal realm. What you intend with your mind controls the results in your life. Everything in your life is created by your intention. Nothing happens to you from the outside. Life happens through you and not to you. By realizing this truth, you come to know that you are co-creator with the universe for everything that happens in your life. When you have set an intention for your heart's desire, whatever way it comes about, this is always linked with your initial intention that brought it into being.

Even though unpleasant things may happen to you, this is for the purpose of moving you towards what you want. Those unpleasant things are subconsciously created by you on the inside not to harm you but to move you in the right direction towards manifesting your intention. When you learn the lesson, you do not need the experience any more. Your subconscious is always there to protect and guide you. It is your link with source that can tap into the infinite field of possibilities in the universe. The power of your intention causes the universe to arrange and rearrange itself to move you closer to where you want to be. It is you who controls this through your intention. You are in control of what happens to you. The illusion you have been living under is that everything happens to you and not from you. You have full power and control in your own life. Let go of the illusion that control comes from the outside. By aligning with your authentic self, you come to realize that you create and control all that is in your life. When you focus on what you can do to create what you want, you take back your power. When you give your power away to others, you become a victim. Your intention for your heart's desire is what drives the universal energy to create what you want. Everything that follows is linked with your initial intention.

Are you at cause or effect in your life? Do you have control over what happens in your life, or are you influenced by others' opinions and assumptions? When you realize that you are creator of your reality, whatever it is, you realize that you can also change it to whatever direction you want it to go. For this you need your locus of control to be on the inside. An inner locus of control means you are at cause. If your locus of control is on the outside, you are at effect in your life. An outer locus of control means that your life is influenced by outside events and the people around you, not by you directly. This occurs when you have given over your power to other people and so have lost control of your own life. With self-realization, you realize that you had control all along and that you just gave it away without realizing it. In realizing your control once more, you know that it all starts with you.

Everything that flows comes from you on the inside. You attract to you from the inside like a magnet, according to which signals you send out. No longer do you wait and hope for things to happen. Instead of following others, you become your own leader and others follow you automatically. Instead of letting situations control you, you take control of situations and direct them as you desire them to go. At cause, you become the initiator of events and experiences. By tapping into your inner power, you become empowered. Your inner knowing means you can make decisions and follow them. By focusing on what brings you success, you do those things that make this possible. Success builds upon success, and with success, your confidence builds. The more you use your internal power, the easier it becomes. Like a muscle exercised over time, it becomes stronger with use.

While there may be risk at times of not succeeding, persist in your being at cause with courage and confidence. The more you learn to handle challenges, the more you will experience on a greater scale. If you play it safe out of fear of losing, then you have already lost out on what could be. By mastering your fear of change, fear of success, fear of growing, or fear of rejection, your overcome your resistance to what can be possible. This means taking risks sometimes. Life would be boring if everything were already laid out for us. Taking risks means you can plan the journey and get the most out of it along the way. It also means you get to learn those vital lessons that move you deeper towards your authentic self. Risk is relative to how competent you are in dealing with it. You achieve greater power and freedom in life by thinking big rather than thinking and living small.

As you think, so you are. What this means is that your life is a reflection of your thinking. If you think big, you aim for bigger things in living an extraordinary life. If you think small, you remain in your familiar comfort zone, where life is average and mediocre. You create in your life as you think on the inside. The way you talk and behave is what you express on the outside. When the inner and outer are aligned, you create your reality according to your mindset. Being fully aligned means that your thoughts, feelings, speech, and actions are all on the same wavelength. If you say something without feeling it, you are not fully congruent in your being. Full congruence with yourself means you have no conflict within yourself.

Becoming aware of how you communicate with yourself and others in your thoughts, feelings, speech, and actions can be very enlightening. How you communicate in general can mean the difference between being abundant or experiencing lack in your life. By listening to your inner and outer voice, you become aware of how in balance you are with yourself. By tuning into your authentic self at your core, you are tuning into your own complete balance as one whole. Ultimately, you are tuning into your own truth. By reconnecting with your true self, you are aligning yourself with your authentic flow in following your life's passion and purpose.

If you think you have lack of control in any area of your life, then that is an illusion. You create everything in your life, because your control lies on the inside. At your core, that part of you – your authentic self – is at the source of your very being. At your source, you have connection on an energetic level to all that is in the universe. What you bring into your life comes through your connection with source. You get to decide what that is according to your beliefs and expectations, as well as your conscious decisions and intentions.

All power is within; therefore, you are not a victim. If you believe that everything happens outside of yourself, then this is another illusion you have been living under. Living under this illusion makes you think you are a victim. In reality, everything is happening within you. You are consciousness at your core, where you have a link with your higher consciousness or divine self. This is your connection with universal intelligence. Your mind power creates and controls from within. Your desire acts as the underlying fiery, forceful energy that is directed by your willpower in a strong, determined, controlled projection of energy. Your burning desire is backed up by your willpower, which says only "yes" and "can". Let go of the belief that you are not in control, for then you are letting go of the illusion that you are a victim.

You are the creator of your reality. When you focus on your power to create, as in what you want and what you can do to achieve that, then you take back your own power. Everything you create can be linked back to your original intention from the knowledge, awareness, and energy you gain in order to achieve it. In order to gain and achieve what you want in life, be ready to receive it. Expect and receive what you want. You are more likely to create what you want if it is connected with your life's work. What I mean by your life's work is not your job, but the reason you are here. What is it that you are here to fulfil in alignment with your authentic self? When you are living your life with authenticity, what will you be doing? When you do what you have a passion for, you are doing your life's work. When you are doing what you love, what is it that you are doing?

Personality

What about your personality? You are not your personality, even though you may think you are. Your personality is shaped and moulded by all your experiences since birth. Some theorists say that personality is partially inherited from your parents. That is debatable. Karl Jung's theories of the human personality enquire deeply into the nature of mankind and the way a person functions. He examined the ways in which we view ourselves and the world about us, as well as the ways we can function in the world. Jung's psychological types embrace the well-known introvert characteristics and extrovert characteristics that are governed by our attitudes and our orientation to the world in which we live. A healthy, balanced attitude would be an equal mix of both outgoing and introspective characteristics, according to Jung. In his view, one is usually more highly developed than the other.

The extrovert is usually responsive, with a ready acceptance of external happenings, a desire to influence and be influenced by events, and a need to join in. He or she enjoys bustle and noise, gives constant attention to the surrounding world, and cultivates friends and acquaintances. Extroverts give great importance to the person they represent, and they are not afraid to make a show of themselves.

Introverts, on the other hand, are by nature usually interested in their own needs and may appear withdrawn and self-reflective. They need their own space to generate energy, while holding back from new experiences with a seeming lack of confidence that may appear unsociable.

Jung also refers to the way people can perceive and acquire information and how this can lead to the development of habitual reactions. According to him, these habitual reactions depend on a person being more prone to either sensation, intuition, thought, or feeling. According to Jung, the way in which you function will be affected largely by your attitudes toward life, in terms of your character type. Jung identified four functions we use to orientate ourselves in the world (and also our inner world). These are (1) sensation, which is perception through the senses; (2) thinking, which gives meaning and understanding; (3) feeling, which weighs and values; and (4) intuition, which tells us of future possibilities, while also giving us information of the atmosphere which surrounds all experience.

According to Milton Erickson, you are an integral part of your environment. He laid stress on the importance of your interaction in the social world. Erickson believed that healthy psychological development occurs when the conflicts of each developmental stage can be resolved in readiness for the next one. In this way, your personality builds up like building blocks, to a position of strength. A lack of resolution at one stage may mean that the unsettled score will remain within your mind to impede later development. A positive outcome and transition from one stage to another would mean that you are able to adapt smoothly and integrate successfully with your environment. A problematic passage from one stage of development to another, however, could mean that you are unable to adapt to your social and cultural environment. Your personality, of course, will contain a mixture of adaptive and maladaptive developmental processes. According to Erickson, all successes and failures are accepted as an integration of your life. Without this integration, regret and despair about the past can occur that causes a block in your life, preventing you from progressing along the evolutionary path to greatness.

Healthy resolution of conflicts means that you can adjust to the changing demands of roles during the period of adolescence, while still retaining a strong sense of your own lasting personal identity. If the increasing demands of adolescence were to place too great a stress on you, identity diffusion would result, causing you to become confused about who you are. This is because of all the different roles which you seem to be acting out. When you have achieved a true and sound identity, you will find that your inner strength is a great asset in addressing any conflicts or challenges in your life. When you learn to identify with your authentic self at your core, you realize that this is the truth of who you really are. When you know this, you bring the truth of who you are forth into the world, through expression with freedom.

Motivation

Your interaction with your environment provides the key to your motivation. Your personal interpretation and evaluation of your environment is linked to your conscious thoughts and images. When you view situations objectively and can make an objective evaluation of a challenge that arises, you tend to be more motivated. How we perceive things determines how we act towards them. For this reason, distorted perceptions can produce an unnecessarily disturbing interpretation of what is going on around you. These distorted perceptions can affect your behaviour in ways that are maladaptive and damaging. When you can identify and change these distorted thoughts, you can begin to deal with life more positively. Your motivations stem from the way you expect you will react in a given set of circumstances. These motivations are as follows:

- Expectations: Your expectations are influenced by the likely outcome of your behaviour as well as your belief in yourself. If you believe in yourself as having the ability, then you will achieve your objectives. If you believe that you will fail for any reason, you are more likely to fail, as a result of a lack of confidence in your capabilities and ability to perform.
- Appraisals: If your appraisal of a situation is negative, this can create anxiety in you that exaggerates the problem. In turn, your negative outlook is more likely to lead to a self-fulfilling prophecy of what you fear. On the other hand, a positive appraisal is likely to motivate you.
- Attributions: Your beliefs about the outcome of events will depend on your attributions of your own internal motives, abilities, and efforts. Also, you may make external attributions about certain circumstances that may be perceived as beyond your control. Negative attribution leads to de-motivation in the expectation of failure.

Positive attributions about circumstances increase your likelihood of success, which motivates you in turn.

Self-Defence Strategies

"A defensive strategy (or an ego-defence mechanism) will be an unconscious or partially conscious trait that the client will employ in a feverish endeavour to keep traumatic or conflict-laden psychic material locked up in a secure and impenetrable corner of the mind. The defensive strategy will act in a protective capacity when the client has been faced with an overwhelming or unmanageable psychic crisis." (Morison 2004: 185). By keeping unpleasant memories out of conscious awareness, this gives you the illusion of psychic homeostasis (balance) in avoiding your psychic trauma. The subconscious mind seeks to protect you in this way by keeping trauma out of your conscious awareness. This defensive strategy distorts reality as a survival mechanism for you that leads to self-deception. You may believe that your life can be made simpler by avoiding the pain of facing reality.

Defensive strategies influence your behaviour and motivation, while also influencing your personal beliefs, attitudes, and convictions. They also allow you to conceal the distress, trauma, and self-doubt that have resulted from psychological disturbance. So, in some cases, you may not be conscious of the trauma that has taken place in your life. In turn, you become a victim of your own inability to cope with the external world. Hidden trauma can lessen the effect of your interactions with others in the social world when your subconscious safeguards your self-concept. The following are the various defensive strategies used either separately or in conjunction with each other:

- Repression: Repression can occur when an event has been perceived by you as a major trauma, which will then be placed totally out of your conscious awareness. It will be an unconscious act of burying memories and emotive responses in order to obscure these elements from your conscious awareness. Repression is a means of protecting you from the perception and the reality of your trauma. It ensures continued survival when you cannot cope with the fear or guilt associated with the memory of the traumatic experience. Repression can include all the emotive responses, perceptions, attitudes, beliefs, motivations, and physical sensations that you experience at the original time of the distressing occurrence.

- Denial: Denial and other forms of memory suppression can occur when an event has been perceived by you as a minor trauma and will then be placed partially out of your conscious awareness. You may be able to remember a semi-forgotten experience in conscious awareness, but the recollection will be virtually lost from view until a search, possibly under hypnosis, can be implemented with some degree of resolve.

- Dissociation: Dissociation can be a form of emotional numbing that may indicate that you have undergone a traumatic experience. If you have closed off your emotive expression or physical sensations as a shock reaction, this way of coping with life can then become a in-built tendency later on.

- Conversion: This occurs when you convert the conflict, trauma, or distress into a psychosomatic symptom. Usually the conversion symptom uses the mind's capacity for symbolic representation. In such cases, your mind may be signalling the source of your distress, which can be highlighted in the quest for change for the better.

- Negation: Negation, or minimization, is a means whereby you can deceive yourself into believing something that you regard as socially acceptable and that does not isolate you from the crowd. A negation comes in the form of an unconsciously driven false belief about your past traumatic experiences, and this serves as a cover-up in order to deflect attention away from your reality.

- Rationalization: In this case, you deceive yourself about an obvious fact, with excuses that seek to conceal your own personal truth. By excusing your own behaviour, you can feel a need to justify your actions to others.

- Introjection: Introjection comes into play when you emulate or adopt the values, beliefs, attributions, convictions, or actions of those who have done you harm. These standards of behaviour would normally be unacceptable by you.

- Regression: You may cope with distress by regressing to a former immature psychological state, which allows you to opt out of a situation while getting sympathy. This is like a cry for help from your subconscious. Childish behaviour, flashbacks, and baby talk are forms of regression.
- Acting Out: "Acting out means taking some impulsive action to pre-empt awareness of distressing inner states. One might, for example, go shopping to ward off a sense of grief or depression." (Morison 2004: 202).

Your Journey to Your Authentic Self

In your inner journey of self discovery, you become empowered in finding your own answers through a process of insight and choice. You can examine your freedom of choice in making the most of life's circumstances. You are responsible for your own choices and actions in life. You can be the architect of your own destiny, rather than being the helpless victim of circumstances. You can be free to choose the way in which you interpret events, either by making the most of opportunities or by giving way to despair and inevitability. Through gaining self-awareness, you become active in making your own decisions from your own centre, as you are thereafter less influenced by others. The values of respect, openness, compassion, empathy, and speaking the truth are essential, with regard to yourself and others, in bringing forth your authentic self. Speaking your truth enables you to become aware of where you are holding back, denying, or procrastinating.

Aligning with your authentic self puts you back on track towards your plans and goals in finding your true purpose in life. In the process, you overcome your internal saboteur, which was getting in your way before. You know what you want now. You know you can create what you want. When you know this, you can take the steps towards your purpose after making the choice. In keeping yourself accountable, you maintain movement and momentum towards your goal and destiny. You become empowered along the way in finding your own answers. You learn to have the courage and confidence in bringing out the best in yourself. This includes finding support, encouragement, and championing from those around you. In this way, you foster and maintain commitment towards action.

You can learn skills and techniques that encourage and support self-discovery, awareness, and choice. These new skills propel you forward in attaining your goal, achieving results, and improving your performance along the way. In this way, you close the gap between where you are and what your goal is. You hold yourself accountable for taking action towards your steps to your goal. These action steps are based on the context that there are possibilities for every situation.

You Are Naturally Creative, Resourceful, and Whole

You do not need to be fixed. You already have your toolbox of internal resources, and you can tap into these through your questions of self-discovery. By seeking your own answers, you discover them within. Your answers do not come from the expert on the outside. You are the expert in your own life. As your own expert, you know fully the context of your own life in terms of strengths, fears, limitations, self-defeating behaviour, motivation, and purpose. As such, you can make choices in your thoughts, feelings, and behaviours. Your self-discovery questions guide you to seek answers that may not have been looked for before but were always there. When you come up with your own solutions, these are usually more effective. This is because you are more likely to follow through with the action required, using your own resources under your own steam in gaining self-satisfaction. In this way, your locus of control comes from the inside, and as such, it is more powerful for you. At the same time, you can remain objective while leaving your personal issues out of the picture.

Your focus determines your results. For this journey inward, it is good for you to create a safe, comfortable environment for yourself. This is achieved by focusing on being calm, being confident, quieting the mind, stopping the internal dialogue, and having a blank slate. In moving inward, you unlearn your conditioning along the way. Be aware that the world reflects back to you what you project onto it. What is on the outside comes from within.

Keep your language clean so it does not contaminate your thinking. Non-judgement and thinking without assumptions or opinions fosters an inner locus of control towards self-empowerment. Your inner locus of control allows you freedom of expression without any threat of judgement from others. What others think is not linked with your identity of who you really are. This is what allows you to explore new areas and stretch your boundaries. As you grow and evolve, you expand your boundaries even more, as well as the possibilities for yourself. With expansion of thought, everything else in your life expands. As your mind map expands, so your world expands in terms of your reality and what is possible for you.

Your beliefs about your self-image are formed as part of your conditioning from your experiences since birth into this world. Your belief systems have also been formed out of others' expectations of you, what you were taught by role models, and also by your experiences with family, friends, and society. Your self-image is your reference point for your actions. Your beliefs influence your feelings and your actions in turn. What you believe in your own head is your own reality, and this influences your perception of the world. Somebody else may have a completely different perception which is true for him or her. There is no one truth; there is, however, only one true way. This may sound like a paradox, but it isn't.

Who were you when you were a baby? Are you the same person? Of course you are. A human's natural state is to be at peace and joyful. Babies that have been born blind and deaf can still smile and laugh. You are the person that was born into this world in a state of peace and bliss. The only thing is that after you were born, your conditioning in life led you to forget the magnificent being that you truly are. Once you move towards your authentic self, you start remembering once more, as your knowingness merges with your conscious self from the subconscious. In this way, you become more integrated within your self as a whole, being at one. Therefore, the things that have happened to you on the outside since birth do not define who you are on the inside.

According to Dr. Bruce Lipton PhD, the first six years of your childhood are spent in a subconscious state that renders you fully open to the maximum impact of suggestion, influence, and lasting impression. In his article, "Are You Programmed at Birth?" (www.healyourlife.com), Dr. Lipton states "The predominant *delta* and *theta* activity expressed by children younger than six signifies that their brains are operating at levels below consciousness. *Delta* and *theta* brain frequencies define a brain state known as a hypnogogic trance, the same neural state that hypnotherapists use to directly download new behaviours into the subconscious minds of their clients." In the first six years, your subconscious mind is powerfully programmed by your life experiences that are perceived according to your temperament and psychological disposition. Your subconscious mind, during childhood, can be influenced in both direct and subtle ways by others, by social pressures, or by the media. This leads to a conditioning that is not conscious.

Therefore, you as a child become a product moulded by your environment in terms of your personality, which is usually formed by the age of seven years. You are not your personality. Some especially potent experiences – whether brief and traumatic, repetitive, or continuous and painful – can be repressed and blocked from consciousness. These repressed complexes can exert a determining influence on mood, behaviour, perception, and relationships into and through adult life. According to Karl Jung, a complex can occur with conscious knowing of the cause. It may also be an unconscious phenomenon, or a partial consciousness wherein you may be partially aware of the complex but not its origin or nature. The source of a negative complex may result from a life experience, perception of reality, or reaction when a disturbing event occurs.

The way in which a complex forms will be determined by way of reaction to a disturbing experience. A child has a natural tendency to conform to social and educational pressures in order to adapt to its environment. Sometimes much of what rightly belongs to your personality is suppressed or repressed in order to make it conform. The tendency to repress emotions or aspects of ourselves can be so effective that we may actually believe we are exactly as we appear to be. This compromise between ourselves and society can lead to a social mask or persona being formed to hide our real self. Jung's aim in therapy was to balance the conscious and subconscious elements of the mind. You are and always were the same. Your self is not defined by your ego, which identifies with possessions, achievements, or materialism. By thinking outside the ego, you can return to the source of your being once more.

You Set Your Own Agenda

You always set your own agenda. Keep your agenda in mind when going through the process of self-discovery and awareness. It is not for others to advise, tell, or be seen as the expert outside of you. It is good to surround yourself with people who support you in formulating your dream, in clarifying your purpose, and in achieving your goal, with your agenda in mind at all times. In this way, you move towards fulfilment, balance, and process in your life. Self-management involves leaving others' agendas outside of yours altogether. Those that are neutral to your agenda have your best interests at heart. Your big-A agenda is a the big picture of what you want to make your life more fulfilling, balanced, and with better process. The little-a agenda involves specific issues that you may want to discuss or work through along the way. Your ability to link up the little-a with the big-A promotes movement towards your goal or outcome at all times.

Everything is used for feedback to learn from. You do not compromise who you are meant to be for the sake of other people's opinions and beliefs. You should not concern yourself with what other people are thinking. If you do, you are handing over your power to them. If what other people think concerns you, then this can affect your state of being. They are they, and you are you. Their stuff is their stuff, and yours is yours. Everybody has access to his or her own authentic self, which is connected to source. You can realign your self with your authentic self through your intention.

The power of your authentic self is blocked when the ego mind determines your choices. Ego beliefs do not define who you are; they define only who you think you are. That's the illusion. These ego beliefs are based on material possessions, achievements, reputation (in terms of what others think of you), separateness from other people, and separateness from God. When you realize that your ego mind does not define your authentic self, you begin to let go of these former beliefs and wake up to who you really are, always were, and always will be. With this realization, ego's hold over you is weakened and you can be free to move towards where your purpose lies. This journey of faith and trust brings new adventures and companions along the way. It is made possible by relinquishing ego thoughts and realigning with your inner knowing, your real self. When you align with your authentic self, you start to feel your way through life instead of thinking your way through life. Your authentic self knows that you are always loved, cared for, and appreciated. In order to love others, you need to be able to love yourself first. Love is never outside of you; it is within you. To be ready for love, nourish your heart, and feel and be love. Be open and receptive to what is around you. Decide what you want to experience in life. Your external reality comes from your internal reality. As you experience greater and greater love, you experience more and more the truth of what is.

By using your intuition, you can dance in the moment. This means you can change direction in an instant by listening with intuition about what is important to you. Your skill in this context depends on having awareness. With awareness, you can sense when and where it's the right time to spontaneously change direction, tread lightly, or keep going in the same direction. It's all about accepting yourself unconditionally and where you are. Dancing in the moment is about being flexible and unattached. It involves staying curious about the flow and adjusting instinctively using intuition. Humour can be a great tool for dancing in the moment. How humour is used depends on its effectiveness.

Through your journey to self-discovery; you learn to address your whole life. This means you recognize that different aspects of your life are all interconnected as a whole. Any decisions or choices made in one area can have a knock-on effect in other areas of your life as a whole as well. A financial choice can affect work, play, or health, and vice versa. When focusing on any one area, always hold in mind that it is a part of the whole. Changes in one area can lead to changes in other areas at the same time. The same goes for choice. Making decisions in one area of life can affect other areas. Be flexible in addressing each area of your life while viewing them as interconnected in your whole life. By following the principle of fulfilment, balance, and process, you guide yourself towards aliveness and a life truly lived.

Fulfilment

Know what you want to achieve in order to have a fulfilling life. Initially, your idea of fulfilment can evolve from talking about external things to becoming aware of internal values and what really makes your heart tick. Living by your values makes for a fulfilling life. By knowing and following your values, you can steer yourself towards a valued life. Knowing your values allows you to make choices or decisions according to them, in living a more satisfying life. It is important to learn what your values are. This process can take months in itself. Once you become aware of your own values, they provide clarity and focus when making decisions about what's important to you. Living according to your values leads to a happy and fulfilled life.

Balance

When your life is out of balance, with no change, you may have a view that your options are limited. Becoming self-aware allows you to widen your perspectives and therefore increase your options available in terms of choices. In feeling able to have more choice in life, you gain more balance. Even though it may be challenging when saying no to some things, this provides space to allow the things you can say yes to in your life. If you say yes to everything, then you can feel overwhelmed. Balance in life is ever-changing, so it's important for you to know whether you are moving towards or away from it. Balance is ongoing and not a goal as such in itself. Balance can help you to get more from life and to live life fully.

Process

Process in itself is about the actual journey in terms of flow. The flow of life can be smooth, rocky, turning back, or rushed. As Heraclitus said, "you can never step into the same river twice." The flow constantly changes, and when you can detect this, you recognize where you are in the process. In being aware of the process, you can champion yourself by celebrating success, or else challenging yourself where appropriate. Being in the flow occurs when you feel yourself moving forward in life with ease and grace. Everything seems to be happening for a reason, moving you towards your goal. When tuned into the flow, you can dance in the moment. Your aware-ness in the now guides you in the direction you should take. Aligning with your authentic self allows you to tap into your personal power. You create an environment that supports your agenda and needs. You can commu-nicate and express what you want effectively. You create relationships that are mutually beneficial. You have control and are able to choose. In having control and choice, you learn to make the changes needed within a safe and courageous space. In this way, you are co-creative, as you make choices and take action from your own empowerment. Therefore, you are not codepen-dent on others.

It is important not to use your word against yourself. In knowing that you always do your best with the resources you have, you can now focus on the rightness of you. In accepting yourself, you know that your self always has your highest intention in mind. You are doing your best, and your best is good enough in this moment. It is not any more or less than; it just is. Being and doing your best does not mean you are comparing yourself to other peo-ple. It means that you are comparing yourself only to the best that you can be. This is not about ego. You are whole already. You do not need anything from the outside, because you already have all that you need on the inside, at your source. This is where your authentic self lies at your core. You are a magnificent being in reality. When you express your magnificence, you are expressing your true self. When you acknowledge this truth about yourself, you allow others to do the same. How they are in themselves comes from them and not from what you think about them. What you think about them is a reflection on what you think about yourself. When you love and accept yourself unconditionally, you can love and accept others unconditionally also.

Similarly, if you hear others using their words against you, you know that this is a reflection from them and that it is not about you. It is a reflection of the thoughts behind the inner workings of their mind. When you know this, you don't take it personally. If people appear to be against you, know that this allows you to tap into your strengths in overcoming the problem. In this way, you realize your own determination and courage, which you can use with fortitude in accomplishing your own goals. With this courage, you can follow your destiny in realizing your own dream. In overcoming others' objections, you clear the way so that your inner light shines forth, seeing you forward. When you know you have the courage to move towards your desire, this will be reflected back to you from your experience of reality on the outside.

In staying connected with your purpose, mission, and vision, your inner talk must match up with your intention for your goal. Any negative thinking must be immediately corrected with a positive statement that is in alignment with your authentic self. Be aware of the saboteur, or inner critic. The saboteur may try to sabotage your plans before they come to fruition. This reinforces the illusion you have been living in, which does not serve you in any way. This illusion is not reality, though it may seem like it. While the illusion keeps everything the same around you, it can also keep you stuck. If you think about what's missing in your life, then that is what you attract. To counteract this, you must state your intention for attracting unlimited abundance into your life in the form of an affirmation.

Your circumstances are what you have created up until now, believe it or not. Take responsibility for your own life. This means letting go of judging and blaming others for your perceived problems. That's right; all problems are problems of perception. If you focus on the solution instead, then there won't be a problem. The more you move towards the solution, the more you move away from the perceived problem. Every problem has a solution, just as every coin has two sides. The glass is either half full or half empty, depending on how you see it. In relation to challenges, you can either choose to let them get the better of you or choose to look at them as opportunities to grow and evolve. All challenges are opportunities if this is what you tell yourself. There are no mistakes; there is only feedback. Feedback is something you can learn from also.

By reframing in this way, you change how you look at things. In the process, the things you look at change. Focus on the here and now. Let the past go, and don't worry about the future. That way your attention is in the present. When ruminating on the past or anticipating the future, you are not present in the present. The past and the future do not exist; only now exists. Pay attention and stay focused on what you intend to manifest into your life. This includes being mindful of your inner talk. Change your focus from thinking about other people's opinions of you and living up to their expectations. Instead, focus your inner talk on your goal for creating and attracting what you want into your life. This requires commitment on a continual basis, and reminders to yourself if you slip back into old self-defeating habits.

Other people do not control your life if you are aware that you are following the inner voice of your authentic self. What other people think is not your concern. You should concern yourself with your own thoughts only. Everything on the outside is an illusion. What is real is what you think is real. What reality do you want to create? Reality is not a given, meaning you have a say in what you create around you. Your indifference to other people's expectations of you allows you to focus on yourself as a result. When people realize that their judgements have no effect on you, they will simply stop trying to control you. In the same way, when you become indifferent to your internal saboteur or inner critic, it will simply fall away into the distance. Instead the internal voice of your authentic self takes over, now that you can hear it. Your authentic self has been talking to you all along, but you were not tuned into it – that is, until now. As your thinking becomes more positive, your energy level becomes more heightened. Self-defeating thoughts become fewer and have less influence over you. Eventually they just fade away out of your mind. As you let go of the monkey mind, you realize that you are letting go of your former illusions about your world also. After clearing your mind of these appearances, you can use your energy towards creating the life you want. You can now replace your illusions with what you want in your life instead. Set an intention for what you want, have no judgement, and expect your life to change.

Your own perception makes things right or wrong. With this awareness, you can interact with others without making them feel wrong. You can honour who they are, but at the same time, you do not have to accept their behaviour. If they say something you do not agree with, you can respond without disagreeing. Your awareness brings about a response based on your inner connection, instead of a reaction based on your emotions. You can acknowledge what they have said or done, without agreeing with it. With awareness, your response always is neutral and non-judgemental. That way you have nothing to regret and you may have broken an old pattern of interaction that did not serve you before. Also, you are not giving your energy to an unhealthy process in this way.

When you are making beneficial changes in your life, it is important to let others know that you are setting the boundaries of mutual honour and respect. When you give respect, you receive it in turn. By honouring others, you are honouring who you really are. You deserve to be honoured and respected for who you are. Sometimes, your habitual way of being can bring up the same obstacles in life. However, by following your own path, you can pave the way forward for yourself. It is by taking the road less travelled that you move forward in life with freedom.

When you follow your true path, every step is on solid ground and there are no surprises. You know what to expect, and you are ready for what may arise. What once was, you can now walk past. Even better, you can take a different route to the same destination. Many roads lead to the same destination. You are never confined to one way of doing things. You can utilize your energy for your greatest potential through your own choice. The less complicated your life is, the simpler things become. It is we humans who sometimes make things complicated for ourselves. In reality, less is more. How you see things is how they appear to you always. What are you saying to yourself about what you see? Become aware of your inner talk. Is it for you, or is it against you? Let go of what does not serve you. That way you get to keep what is for you and what does serve you. When you are living in alignment with your true self, you are living life based on who you are and not on the conditions in your life.

It is by changing your perception of your life conditions that you make them work in your favour. When you change your perceptions to be life-enhancing, your life becomes enhanced in turn. You can think of yourself already as to how you would like to be. For instance, whatever your heart's desire or dream is, you can look on yourself as having already achieved that. Hold this thought every day until it becomes part of your feeling about yourself. Then you will find that it becomes a part of your being. After doing this, you do not need to think it any more, because what you want is who you are. From the place of who you are, you are living life on a more authentic level when you are one with it in your being. By having faith, trust, and belief in your self, you know that your inner guidance is always around you.

When you come to know your authentic self, so you come to know the love that is always there. As you move closer to your authentic self, so you move closer to the loving presence of your heart. Love has the power to transform you and those around you. By opening yourself up to your deeper aspects of being, you are following your heart, for that is what guides you. When you follow your heart, you follow your bliss. When you do so, you know you are already successful, because you are on the path of what is true for you. You are a magnificent being at your core in reality. You are now choosing to be more of your authentic self and not what your monkey mind tells you. When you do so, you realize that what you thought may have been problems before actually came from your perception only. In fact, there was no problem; there was only what you thought was a problem at the time. With your change of perception, you can now see the good in everything and how you learned all your lessons in life. Nothing is wrong, and nothing was ever wrong. There is a reason for everything, which may not be apparent to you at times.

It is sometimes only in retrospect that you can make sense of a situation. That is why it is so important to be mindful at all times and operate from a place of being in the moment. You are the maker of your Self. What this means is that what you see, feel, and hear in the world comes from who you think you are. When you know who you truly are, as your authentic self, your way of being in the world takes on a whole new meaning. The decisions you make are then more in tune with who you are, because you have a deeper knowing into the ways of the universe. Your knowing gives you access to the doorway of your heart, through which you can manifest your heart's desire. Your heart gives you access to the universal realm and the source of all that is possible. Now you can have access to your own guidance from within, while on the path to your purpose, mission, and vision in life.

How you identify with yourself is important. If your concept of self relates to the body as being separate from all others, then you are more likely to compete than cooperate with others. Ego is the idea of who you think you are, and it prevents you from connecting to your authentic self. You are under an illusion if you think ego is your real self. Choose not to be offended by others' behaviour, as this will only weaken you, attracting more of the same. Appreciate life for what it is and the way it is now. Accept all that is. Everything is as it should be. In this way, you can live in peace. If you identify with ego in wanting to compete and win all the time, this will set you up for disappointment and feelings of wanting, lacking, and wishing. You are not defined by your achievements. It's all right to compete in activities and have fun, so long as competing doesn't take over your thoughts.

We all have access to our authentic selves, so nobody should be labelled as a winner or loser. The illusion of win-lose is born out of a competition mindset. Win-win is brought about through a cooperation mindset. By changing your mindset, you change how you view your results in life and the means to get there. The end result is a means in itself, depending on your views about it. There are no losers. Be objective in your opinions of others, and don't make assumptions about them. The ego mind has a need to be right that makes others wrong. In judging and blaming others, the ego mind can cause conflict in the form of anger and resentment. It is more important to be happy than it is to be right. Let go of your need to be right. Set yourself free from the ego by choosing to live in happiness, peace, and love. Learn from others at all times. Be grateful for the lessons in patience, strength, and endurance. Respect others' models of the world, even though you may not agree with their viewpoints.

Humility is not a character of the ego. The ego instead needs to feel special and superior in relation to others. We are all the same and emanate from the same energy. We are all equal in God's eyes. Don't judge others on the basis of ego that says you are what you have, how you look, and what you achieve. The ego is always in a state of wanting more, no matter what. When you let go of ego, you let go of needing or wanting more.

When you let go in this way, all that you need will manifest effortlessly into your life. By trusting in the all-providing universe, you detach from your wants and needs. Being open allows abundance to flow to you and through you. If you try to hang on to it, you stop the flow. The ego is concerned with reputation and what other people think of you in their minds. Reputation is beyond your control. Know in your heart what your truth is by listening to your inner voice. Know that anything is possible for you. Avoid spending your energy trying to convince others how great you are to foster a good reputation in their ego minds. Stay in alignment with your authentic self by focusing on your inner self and not your outer self. Listen and be guided by your inner voice, with detachment for the outcome. Be on purpose and take responsibility for who you are on the inside. Trust in your inner source; your authentic self, for your strength. Be mindful of your energy levels, and always raise the frequency if your energy drops. Know the link between what you're thinking or doing and the energy at the time. Let ego know it has no hold over you. While ego is a part of you, you do not have to let it control you any more. Think outside the ego in the here and now while being constantly tuned into your authentic self.

Become aware of your internal dialogue and what you associate with in terms of metaphors (such as those found in symbols or the stories you tell yourself). Working with metaphors can be very powerful, as they send a message to the subconscious indirectly. Metaphors are unique and individual for each person. The use of metaphors can be a helpful tool in assisting you to discover more about yourself. When you work with internal metaphors, any change to the metaphor can change how you think. You can expand your awareness by focusing on what your metaphors are in your life and then changing them to empowering ones, if necessary. Metaphors can form the link between the conscious and unconscious mind to bring about healing and change. Your personal metaphors (or everyday sayings) can be questioned according to whether they are self-empowering or self-limiting. In doing so, you are questioning your belief systems and self-imposed boundaries. By reflecting on the answers, you can search for new meanings and discoveries. Speak your truth, and be clear in what you say. This in itself helps you to move forward from a locus of inner-self control and empowerment.

You see in others what you feel inside. "As within, so without," the Emerald Tablet states. Being at peace enables others to be at peace in your presence also, when you view them as spiritual beings. These people, in turn, give back to you in ways that assist you in your purpose. What you give is what you receive, whether it is kindness or love. You can only give what is in your heart, while attracting the same back. Your impact on other people depends on your level of connection to your authentic self. When you see people from your source of authenticity, you give without expecting anything back. All is one and comes from the same source. When you see yourself in others, this means you recognize your connection with them. They are not as separate as they appear to be. Yet you are an individual expression of spirit in this world at the same time. Ego thinking views others critically while creating a need to feel superior to them. In being aware of how you view others, you know why you attract the same positivity or negativity into your own life. In this way, you get to choose your allies towards making an extraordinary life possible for you. If you expect ordinariness, that is the energy you send out and receive back. Know what ordinariness is to you, as well as the high energy levels that can move you to the extraordinary life you can live. Be aware of others' reactions towards you as you tune into your authentic self.

When you are at peace, you instil peace and calm in those around you. People react to you in a more positive light as a result. Acceptance of yourself and others leads to peace and draws people to you on the same wavelength. Opposition to others in ego thinking separates them from you. Your compassion and empathy for others makes them feel better about themselves. They feel understood and can be themselves. When ego dominates, you are egocentric and don't see things from others' point of view. The opposite of this is having empathy for others. Those connected with their authentic selves inspire a win-win situation. We're all on the same side. There is no other side; therefore, there is no need for opposition or defences where hatred and judgement can lead to a win-lose situation in the illusion of duality. We are all one with nature and God. Your connection with your higher self allows you to be at peace while having a sense of forgiveness and understanding. Those around you are more likely to trust you and want to open up to you. They will do what they can in assisting you towards your goal.

On the contrary, ego thinking, which has a low energy vibration of distrust, superiority, or judgement, makes others feel less likely to help you towards your goal. This is because a win-lose situation has been set up, which involves competitiveness and conflict against what you really desire. It's a two-way process. What you send out is what you receive. An open mind allows you to learn and ask questions. A closed mind means you think you have all the answers or are afraid to learn anything new. A closed mind is shut off from the truth being revealed of what is guiding you through life. Then your life just becomes a daily routine with no room for growth and evolvement. Challenges are avoided when you hide from the truth of who you are. Change is resisted as a result, leading to being stuck in a rut in your movement towards your authentic self. Nothing is permanent in reality. In reality, change is the nature of nature. It is how the universe operates. Life and reality operate in cycles of change. Open your eyes now. Wake up from the illusion you have been under. See with clarity what is really going on inside and around you. Life doesn't just happen to you; it happens through you! Anything is possible in potentiality. Your knowing tells you this when you tune into your authentic self.

Exercise: Journaling

Journaling is a way of jotting down your thoughts, feelings, and emotions onto paper. Daily journaling is as important as meditation. If you find that you are unable to do this on a daily basis, even weekly journaling will have remarkable benefits. Journaling helps you to clear your mind of clutter and to see what is really important to you. You can put anything in your journal, from perceived problems to any positive thoughts on things. This allows you to question yourself and focus your mind to find your answer ultimately, in an easy and effortless manner. Journaling allows you to ask yourself powerful questions that reach deep within. Once you put your thoughts on paper, you can leave them there. These can include thoughts of fear, anger, jealousy, or resentment.

When you put on paper that which is bothering you in your life, you can look on it from a place that is removed from the actual experience. In journaling you become the silent witness of what you were caught up in before. By writing it down on paper, you remove yourself directly from the experience. When you read what you have written, you can view your life circumstance from a detached position. This happens automatically, and you do not need to do anything other than write down your thoughts. You can also include a list of what you are grateful for in your journal. What you are grateful for brings more of the same. When you journal what you are grateful for, you are using the movement of your body, your sight, and your inner hearing to reinforce what you appreciate in your life. When you use your body's senses in this way, you are powerfully attracting to you that which you are grateful for from your very being.

At the same time, you are letting go of your denser feelings and thoughts on paper through journaling. The more you journal, the clearer your mind becomes. You will be pleasantly surprised by how much easier life becomes for you with persistent journaling. This happens automatically on a sub-conscious level. You are not aware of this happening until you find yourself reacting differently to certain situations or people than before, or thinking differently than before. You become more removed from anything that does not serve you, while at the same time being drawn to what does serve you. You become aware of an inner strength and resolve that you did not feel before. You can access your own answers much quicker than before also, as your indecision becomes a thing of the past. You become more certain of what steps to take in any situation with regular journaling. This is because you become more certain of your self and what you want. In essence, journaling allows you to grow and evolve on your spiritual path. On paper, with you as your own witness, you have the courage to question, explore, and challenge your self-beliefs. You can observe from the outside and be open to experience, even if it means being vulnerable. Is it not better to live with courage and an open heart than to live in fear and just exist? Isn't it much better to thrive rather than survive? You know the answer, don't you?

PART 2: SELF-EMPOWERMENT

Our task must be to free ourselves – by widening our circle of compassion to embrace all living creatures and the whole of nature and its beauty.

—Albert Einstein

CHAPTER 5

YOUR PURPOSE, MISSION, AND VISION

What is your purpose here on earth? What is your soul purpose? It is not what others tell you to do. It is not others' truth, either. Your inner feelings are your guide to what is true for you. While others can offer guidance and support, only you discern what is true for you. You can learn to find your true path in life by sitting still in a quiet place, reflecting, and meditating in silence while asking universal intelligence or God to show you the way forward. Your soul purpose is about finding and coming to know your own truth. By expressing your own truth, you set yourself free in the process. Your feelings are the language of your soul. Learn to listen to them. This includes negative emotions. Become aware of when and why emotions arise. With awareness, you can choose to transform your emotions before reacting to any situation. You can train yourself to notice and change your emotional state into one that leads to a satisfactory outcome for all.

All thought is powerful, as thought is linked with creation itself. You are a co-creator with the universe, meaning that your thoughts affect your outcome by bringing into being that which is in thought. It takes time to transform your negative thought patterns by choice into more positive ones. In turn, you learn to switch off your autopilot response to certain triggers, and instead you cultivate more life-affirming responses. In the process, you learn to transform yourself in your conscious evolution. Your purpose in this lifetime is to self-actualize and align with your authentic self. This means remembering once more who you truly are in your essence. Self-realization can be achieved only by working on yourself in order to grow and evolve. As you transform through growth and evolement, you merge into the loving, positive being that you already are. In this way, your authentic self emerges from within to integrate with your way of being in the world.

Before you came to earth, you chose certain goals to achieve, and these became part of your soul contract. After birth, the veil of forgetfulness prompted you to search for the meaning in your life. In your search for meaning, you learn to discover the truth of who you really are. If you knew your soul purpose from the beginning, then it would be too easy. The things in your life that you most love to do are connected in some way to your soul contract. You can choose to experience as often as possible these things that make you happy. It is from these experiences that you have come here to learn.

It is also important to look at all the negative experiences that seem to show up in a repetitive pattern over time in your life. These will more than likely be linked with your soul contract also. Look to see the pattern of recurring challenges or issues that you have been struggling with. There is a message here for you. What is the lesson you have not yet learned? These are no doubt also linked with the lessons you came here to learn in your soul contract. These same issues and challenges will keep presenting themselves to you over and over again as opportunities to learn about yourself and how you are being in the world. When you realize this, you can consciously choose a more positive behaviour instead. As you recognize these challenges in the patterns of your life while working on them in a process of change, you ultimately transform your character and way of being in the world. In the process, you increase your level of vibrancy, and so you resonate with a higher way of being in mind, body, and soul. The challenges and issues that you experienced previously now seem to have disappeared from your life. Occasionally, they show up to test your learning and to make sure you haven't forgotten once more.

Your purpose here is to realize your self. In becoming aware, you learn to work upon yourself in becoming that loving being once more, in every way. Your triggers for reacting negatively to certain situations are brought into the light of your consciousness through self-understanding. Through enlightenment, you overcome your previous reactions by consciously choosing to replace them with more positive ones, such as care, love, appreciation, or compassion. You now understand that everything happened the way it did to bring you to this place in your life. If it had been any different, then you wouldn't have learned the lessons that you now understand. Life can be full of tests. It is these tests that challenge you. There is always a lesson to be learned. Every challenge presents an opportunity to learn. All is in divine order. You are right where you are meant to be.

If you are not living your life's calling right now, have you ever thought why this might be so? What is holding you back? Is it your fear of the responsibility this may hold, or is it because you believe it's going to be a struggle and hard work? Your concept of work may be keeping you from your purpose in life. Your purpose is what you have passion for, and this is not the same as work. The rules of the daily nine-to-five work routine do not apply to carrying out your soul purpose in any respect. Can you imagine how easy it would be doing what you love while knowing you were helping other people? It takes more courage and strength to do a job that you know does not suit or serve you. Wouldn't you rather answer to yourself than to a boss whose values are not in alignment with yours? When you are fulfilling your own values and not others', this is the path to true happiness.

Carrying out your life's purpose means you are being in service to other people in some way. At the same time, you are following your heart and not the rules set by others that kept you feeling trapped and constricted in the past. By following and expressing your own voice, you are freeing yourself of the old way of conforming to a system that does not support your well-being. By carrying out your life's work or calling, you are creating a new story for yourself, because you have let go of the old story. By remaining true to yourself, you have let go of conforming to be accepted by others. You are here for a reason, and when you know what it is, you will do whatever it takes to carry it out.

If you are genuine about seeking out your mission and purpose in life, ask for help and the answer will be revealed to you gradually when you are ready to receive it. Whenever you ask for help from the universe, you will always get an answer in some form or another. Be patient. Be alert to any signs that may show up about the next step to take. Such signs may appear in the form of something you read, what somebody says, or synchronicity that arises. Once you are open to your purpose and have taken the mission on board, you will be helped in ways you cannot even imagine. All it takes is belief and action. You may be divinely guided by your hunches or gut feelings when making decisions. Your intuition will sharpen in time, as will your discernment about what is best for you. Your vision of what you want to achieve will become more apparent to you as you move along the journey of your soul purpose.

As you travel along the path of your life's calling, you pick up speed when you surround yourself with like-minded people, as well as people who have already achieved what you are aiming for. You will be amazed at how doors open for you and that you can spot opportunities as they arise. By creating a dream team for yourself to carry out your purpose, you will be lifted up in the collective consciousness of this group of people. You will be supported and encouraged in your quest for helping others, and that is because you support and encourage them also. This is part of your life's calling when you are in service to others. Being around the people who have your best interests at heart accelerates your progress in carrying out your life's purpose here on earth. When you are around successful people who have already achieved the same as your purpose, you pick up on their energy and soak it up over time. You become immersed in their world, their thoughts, their language, and the way they express themselves.

A successful person that you admire can act as a role model for you to aspire to be like and learn from. He or she can be a mentor for you also, either directly or indirectly, but this is not essential. Successful people have strategies for success. That's what makes them successful. Strategies include thoughts and beliefs about how to do things and how to view the world. When you can imagine the vision of your soul purpose in your mind's eye, the more you do this, the stronger your vision comes into being. When you surround yourself with people who inspire you, you remain enthusiastic, motivated, and passionate while carrying out your life's work. Your energy and spirit remain high, and this gives you a magnetic effect which attracts to you more of the same. When you surround yourself with the right people, you see your purpose as already possible. As Einstein said, "Imagination is powerful. It is the preview of life's coming attractions." As you expand, evolve, and grow, so does your purpose in life.

When you are in alignment with your authentic self, your life path will bring synchronicities (non-accidental coincidences) that show up in divine timing and divine order. Synchronicities are referred to by some as "messages from God." Things are not as they appear. There are many possible future events that can be seen in the present. When you step into your true path of calling, you are fulfilling your desire and your purpose. As you step into your true calling, everything just falls into place through the shifting and rearranging of the universe. When you express your authentic self fully in the now, while following your true path, you are already living your dream life. You can step into it right now and start truly living according to your authentic self. This is your destiny.

When you set a goal for your life, you are setting an intention at the same time. What you intend for your self comes from what you think. Your thoughts are very powerful, so it is good to be mindful of them. Thought is energy, and what you think about carries energy. This energy, which comes from you, moves into the universal field of possibilities. Whatever is on the same wavelength is drawn to you, according to quantum physics, whether it is people, places, or events in your life. Your intention is your purpose or aim, with a determination to produce a desired outcome. Your purpose is in alignment with your authentic self. When you have this focus, your never-give-up attitude and strong will just won't allow anything to interfere with achieving your dream or inner goal. Your inner representation of the world and how you choose to think about it directly affects your perception of the objects, events, and people in your life. In this way, your intention helps you to recognize and take advantage of any opportunities that may arise, thus maximizing your potentiality. Your intention is not ego (mind) related; nor does it include will itself.

You can tune into your authentic self by aligning yourself with the peace and harmony therein, without any distraction from the outside. This can be achieved by slowing down the monkey mind during meditation, relaxation, or guided visualization. In this way, you can tap into your own power when carrying out your intention for fulfilling your goal. In this empowered state, your level of energy vibrates at a higher level and speed than the lower energy which is brought about by self-defeating beliefs. At this higher level of vibration, you are in the flow. When you are in the flow, somehow, miraculously, the right people and opportunities seem to come into your life at just the right time. Some people call this luck, but in reality there is no such thing as luck. What might appear to be luck is actually you being ready for an opportunity to happen, and that's why you can recognize it as such. When living on purpose or when you have a calling to purpose, your intention allows you to be driven with inspiration while being in spirit. In this way, you learn to solve problems in a spiritual manner.

You can learn to follow your gut feeling and inner voice in making decisions. Feelings are linked with how you think, what you contemplate, and your inner dialogue. Your authentic self seeks to express itself through you with confidence. Your feelings point the way towards your inner potential and destiny. The spirit that is you, once remembered, expresses itself through you. This link is strengthened by the continual growth and evolvement towards your real self and your purpose in life. Your intuition guides you in this way, leading you down the path in life and helping those around you. Your authentic self is actually your connection with spirit, which exists in infinity whether you choose to see it or not. It is timeless and has no space to occupy, with no constraints, in a material sense. Your authentic self always was, is, and will be. It is infinity; it is spirit and exists in the same realm as God. Everything that is created is manifested through intention into the physical world. Your intention has the power to co-create with the universe.

According to the first law of thermodynamics, energy is neither created nor destroyed, but it can be transformed from one form to another. When you tune into your authentic self, this transforms your life and what you attract to yourself. Your authentic self guides you towards your soul purpose. Just as an acorn already has the oak in it, your authentic self has everything you

YOUR PURPOSE, MISSION, AND VISION

need already. It just needs the right conditions to evolve and grow. By nurturing and caring for yourself, you allow your true nature to come forth. It is not selfish to care for yourself. In fact, you need to be spiritually selfish sometimes, because if you neglect yourself, your purpose may never be realized. It can be too easy to become distracted by what is going on around you in the outside world. It is only natural to care for yourself. In this way, you can care for and serve others. Nature is in harmony with the universe. When your purpose is to serve others for the good of all, the universe will conspire to help you a hundredfold.

Intuition

Intuition can be described as your sixth sense, a hunch, a gut feeling, or just knowing something to be the case without hard proof. Intuition allows you to listen at a depth beyond words with a knowing that is always present. Intuition is a skill of receiving input from people and the world outside of yourself, and it can be practised and developed. It can allow you to pick up on more information and feelings than can be consciously explained. In knowing where you are in relation to what you want, you can then work on closing the gap with your agenda in mind. For intuition to work at its best, you need to have a clear, quiet, empty mind. This takes discipline, but the more it is practised, the easier it becomes. Intuition is a skill that you can develop and expand on by relaxing fully in the moment. It's about being in a gentle, open space and allowing "what is." It's about trusting in yourself as well as in the universe. Intuition is about listening and allowing for whatever is received, while accepting it as it is. Holding back doesn't help intuition. By letting go, you let God. In being unattached to needing to be right or worrying if it is right, you will find it easier to take risks using intuition. Using intuition brings with it a willingness to fail, and humour, which allows you to bow out and continue with a freedom that remains unchanged. Your intuition redirects you to your purpose, goal, and vision when you find yourself wandering off track. Your intuitive direction saves you from wandering off the point, keeping you focused to get back on track. Intuition can be used to clarify or speak your truth. By tuning into your own intuition, you can learn to trust your gut feeling and take action as a result.

Curiosity

Curiosity is essential for ongoing learning, and it helps you to remain objective. There's always more to be learned. When you think you have all the answers, that's when you stop asking questions. In asking the right questions, you can become aware of any perspectives beyond the boundaries of your normal thinking. In this way, your curiosity can help you to expand in terms of your self-development. Courage is needed for you to delve deeper inside while remaining in the moment. Curiosity promotes a genuine interest in your own self-discovery. Your curiosity and listening skills allow you space, openness to talk, and encouragement to speak your truth. Curiosity invites you to express your authentic self when you tap into it. Being curious in a gentle, playful way puts you at ease in learning about your inner and outer life. You are already creative, resourceful, and whole, and as such, you can learn to explore beyond previous self-limitations with curiosity and without fear. Curiosity helps you find a way beyond your own self-limits. There are no limits with curiosity that is genuine and respectful. In this way, you can learn to delve deep and understand everything that has led to who and where you are right now. In understanding this, you can let go of restraints and propel yourself forwards towards your vision, while carrying the lessons learned from that curiosity.

Curiosity creates a pathway for exploration in the now. It has no preconceptions and leads only with your agenda in mind. You can ask powerful questions in a curious manner that lets you know it is safe to speak in the presence of rapport with others. Curiosity, in this way, can even allow you to ask challenging questions, knowing you are in a safe environment. Curiosity allows you to explore your world when asking open-ended questions. It also promotes flexibility and allows possibilities for deepening your own self-discovery. The solution lies within. Curiosity on your part helps you to draw on your own solution and resources, leading to self-empowerment and learning. In turn, this motivates you to change and evolve further.

Curiosity also draws you out in disclosing information, thus building on your connections in your relationships with others. It can involve asking powerful questions that steer the conversation. Curiosity with intention steers you to your own self-discovery and decision-making. You are the expert in your world, and only you know where you fit in with your big picture. Curiosity with intuition allows you to get feedback on your feelings and motivation, in an authentic sense. It can be a powerful process for you to question with curiosity while allowing for silent gaps of reflection. It's important for you to give yourself space and allow the answer to come when you are ready to receive it.

Questions that are simple and short can be the most profound and powerful. This is because they allow you to hear your own answer directly in order to learn from it, without getting bogged down by the question itself and what it means. Closed-ended questions require a yes or no answer only and so do not allow for inner exploration. "Why" questions always require a defence or explanation in response and so do not usually lead to new insight. It is better to ask questions beginning with "what", as this allows for more information in the answer. For example, ask "What can I learn from this?" instead of "Can I learn from this?" In the process of learning how to be curious about your inner self, be mindful to avoid judgement of yourself.

Moving Forward and Deepening Learning

I know you genuinely care about moving forward towards creating your goal, without a doubt. Instead of just talking the talk, know that you can walk the talk. There is a difference. No matter how much you want to do something, sometimes there is something holding you back and you don't know what it is consciously. Through awareness and self-understanding, you become aware of your own self-limiting beliefs that hold you back. You can also hold yourself accountable at the same time, while keeping yourself in a safe, encouraging, and supportive environment. When you know you are safe, your subconscious is more likely to allow you to take the right action. Then you can move forward towards the results you want. By speaking your truth, you move forward in action towards making change.

At the same time, learning itself can precede taking this action which also leads to further learning. Learning deepens your understanding in terms of your inner self, in connection with the outside world. This deepening leads to introspection towards your inner self, while the forward movement leads to evolution of your outer life. The closer you are to your authentic self, the more your life can be truly lived on purpose. By being authentic, you learn what it means to be honest. In knowing what is real, you can take risks in the knowledge of your constant anchor. By aligning with your authentic self, you add to the aliveness in your life. Your courage and commitment are your key to success. You are responsible for learning and moving forward, which means learning and taking action. Learning about your inner self can create momentum for change. Change means taking action. Your authentic self is the catalyst for change for your highest good and the highest good of others.

When you determine a goal, reality, options, and will (or commitment to take action), your foundation for making change can be formed. Goal setting involves focusing on a goal for some particular time in the future, as well as ongoing goals in between. When you take steps in between, the ultimate goal doesn't look so big to you. Setting options can involve brainstorming outside-the-box ideas. This is where you generate ideas for your agenda by tapping into your own solution. You can challenge yourself to move beyond your boundaries of self-imposed limitations. When you believe in yourself, you know you can move beyond your current comfort zone without fear. You can be courageous in moving forward while deepening your learning.

Self-Management

Self-management involves giving yourself space and keeping out of your own way while staying with your own agenda. When you remain objective, your assumptions, judgements, and opinions will not get in the way of what you want to achieve. With patience, you can be neutral, not needing to feel right or look good according to ego's thinking. Self-management means leaving the ego outside the room. In having presence of mind, you can effectively manage your own thoughts or judgements and opinions of self and others. Self-management is essential for trust in yourself, as well as for building rapport within yourself between your conscious and unconscious mind. As Milton Erickson said, "Anything is possible in the presence of rapport."

Rapport and trust are the basis for all communication that takes place. This includes communication between your conscious and your subconscious mind. When you have rapport with your self, you are totally congruent with who you really are. When you are in alignment with your authentic self, you feel comfortable and safe expressing yourself as you are. Alignment can be encouraged by compassion, empathy, flexibility, and openness with yourself and others. At the same time, you are non-judgemental and relaxed, while giving respect to yourself. If you listen to and follow what others tell or advise you to do, you remove the recognition of your own personal power to come up with solutions. Taking in others' advice can contaminate your way of thinking. Giving your power to others in this way takes away from your inner resourcefulness. Instead of seeking your own answers, you become codependent on the opinions of others in this way. Self-management can be achieved when you remain objective, hold curiosity for all things, and accept yourself unconditionally. Remember that humour is a coping mechanism for many situations.

Always hold a state of compassion and empathy when dealing with other people. Self-management involves creating your own safe open place for speaking your truth, in keeping on track with your big-A agenda in mind. Avoid getting hooked on other people's issues. If this happens, you may need to clear your thoughts, feeling, or emotions. In this way, you can be fully present for yourself and remain strong. When you notice any disconnection from your source or your authentic self, your ability to name it and reconnect are included in self-management also. In reconnecting, you become realigned with your goal and your authentic self at the same time.

If you are intensely emotional about something, this can interfere with your direction. In this case, it is good to vent whatever is bothering you, as you do not want to carry emotional baggage that will weigh you down. In allowing yourself to get it out and voice it to someone you trust, you allow yourself to express yourself in a creative way once more. By seeing things from a different perspective, you can reframe situations. Reframing sees the bright side of things and helps you to see that you are on the cause side of your life rather than the effect side. This helps you to make the distinction between facts and disempowering beliefs. Give yourself time to speak your truth and express who you really are at your core in the now. This is essential for closing the gap between where you are and where you want to be.

When you live your life purpose, you are expressing your authentic self from where you are in your life. As you evolve along the path in life, so does your life purpose. With your growth in life, so your purpose also grows. Your understanding of your life meaning in turn gives meaning to your purpose in life. Your purpose is an expression of who you are and what you are in reality. Your self-consciousness determines your awareness of that purpose. Your purpose leads to the vision, is the vision, and lies beyond the vision also. Your purpose creates constant evolution in your life that impacts others ultimately. Your belief in your purpose makes it a knowing deep within that is unwavering. Your calling to this purpose brings it forth through being in service to others in some way. You get to choose the way. Your free will gives you choice always. There is always choice. You are the master of your destiny through free will. Whatever you think is imposed on you is an illusion in reality. You have more power than you may realize. Believe and it is so.

Being who you really are is what it means to be a human being. If you feel that you need to be a "human doing" on the outside, then you lose the connection with your inner being. It all comes from within, where your true source lies. Your life purpose is something that gives you passion. It comes from your passionate desire to fulfil who you really are by being who you really are. Carrying out your purpose is your mission to achieve your vision for your life. It is something you chose before you were incarnated into this life. It is in remembering who you really are that you also begin to remember your soul purpose, which is your soul contract. When you agreed to this mission, you knew you could achieve it. Through your life experiences, you were conditioned and programmed to believe that you were a limited being, and so you forgot who you really are. Your authentic self became hidden be the veil of illusion and the world of appearances. That spark of your authentic self is always present, which expands to become a light that shines brighter with every lesson learned in life. As your inner light of awareness expands, it illuminates the truth of who you think you are and who you really are. There is a difference, for you will never know your authentic self from your thoughts alone. Who you really are can only be known from feeling, experiencing, and perceiving your authentic self when you are in alignment with it. This includes tuning your thoughts by turning the dial to love, care, compassion, and gratitude. Your authentic self can only be witnessed in that space of no thought. For this reason it is important to empty your mind of chatter by tuning into the now when you are looking for guidance as to what step to take next.

Within your being is the whole, and this includes your thoughts also. If any part of your is incongruent with the truth of who you really are, then this will block you from realizing your purpose, mission, and vision in life. The truth of who you really are is your authentic self. Your authentic self holds true empowerment for you and for the higher good of all. You empower yourself when you come to know yourself, because it is only then that you can discern what is right and good for you. Discernment comes from within, where you spirit resides. Judgement is not the same and comes from outside when you compare yourself to other people or things. You cannot be better or worse than any other person in reality. Within your authentic self, you see others as equal, and therefore you do not judge them. When living from the level of your authentic self, you reside in calm neutrality, in peace with all that is. Your power comes from within and not from outside. Therefore, in reality you do not need anything from outside to fulfil your purpose, mission, and vision. All will be provided at the right time when you hold a genuine intention within.

At the same time, you remain undistracted by whatever is going on outside of you. You will meet the right people, receive opportunities, and get hunches, and one thing will lead to another, so you will find. There are no coincidences in life; there are just coexisting incidents that are beyond chance. Be ready with open eyes, open ears, and an open mind.

Your spiritual discernment is the gateway that allows in the true knowledge, while it also keeps out the illusions of the world. Your authentic self is the source of your guidance. When you look within in silence and contemplation, the answer will always be revealed to you from your source. When you look to the outside for answers, you can easily become distracted from your purpose and from the grounding of your authentic self. Stay connected to your authentic self daily. Be mindful of every moment in the present. Ruminating over the past or worrying about the future dislocates you from your presence in the moment. This takes practise and becomes easier with repetition until it becomes automatic in your very being. In your being, you are always present to your innate power to be used in service for the highest good of all. When carrying out your purpose, you are being in service to humanity, doing what you love to create your vision of what you know is possible. Your belief in your purpose is steadfast and unwavering.

You are not deterred from your dream, no matter how outside appearances may seem. It all comes from within first. The outside always follows from the inside, even though you may have been taught different. Your expectations always create the outcome, whether you are aware of them or not. When you consciously co-create with the universe, your awareness of what is determines what you expect, and so it is. Even though you may not see results straight away, just relax, let go, and know that it is on its way to you. Detach from wanting or needing, because this is like saying you are in a state of lack and so you don't believe. Carry out the purpose while holding the vision. Be in service while holding the purpose in your mind for what you are doing and what you know you can achieve. There is no room for doubt. Your purpose becomes a part of your way of life when you know it is a part of the real you at the level of your authentic self. It is knowing that leads to being. You can only be what you know to be so. Knowing how to be at one with your self is what brings you peace, joy, and bliss. How could you be any other way? Oneness is inclusive, loving, compassionate, caring, and accepting of all that is. It is that place of rest that supports you and lifts you up to a complete level of inner coherence, where you set an example for those to follow.

By following your purpose, you allow yourself to continually evolve and grow in fulfilling your vision. This gives meaning to your life. Every single person has a purpose in life, so it follows that every single person has a meaning in life. By carrying out your purpose, you get to contribute your greatest gifts to the world. Others get to witness your gifts, which can bring awareness to their own inner gifts. By sharing their gifts also, they can learn to find their own purpose, and so your gift spreads. This is how you can make a difference in the world. Even small acts can lead to big things. Even if it means sending a smile to a stranger and bridging the perceived gap between you and other people, you begin to realize that life is on your side. There are no sides in reality, as we are all one in humanity. By relating to each other with love and cooperation instead of competition and separation, the world enters a new era that is beautiful beyond imagination.

Believe in and act on your dream. When you are carrying out your purpose, your love is in action. Living from love gives you the life you desire. Your purpose makes you an important link in the chain of events that determine our planet's future and everything on it. Do you accept your mission? When you do, you have already achieved your vision. Your purpose brings it into being. Your purpose never ends, because your vision reaches higher levels of being in an ongoing fashion. There are no limits in reality. How wonderful to know this. When you achieve your vision, it doesn't stop there. You can continually refine and improve on your vision in helping other people on the planet. In this way, you always have a purpose and meaning in life. How good is that? You know the answer, don't you?

As you follow your purpose, you are also following your heart. Your heart is where your true being lies. In discovering who you are once more, you remember that you are more than you were led to believe – much more. When you realize the magnificent being that you are in actuality, you also realize that your place in this world carries more weight than you previously thought. You are just as important as anyone else, and you have a purpose for being here. You have everything you need right now, and you don't need to put it off any longer. Today, take one action, no matter how small or big it is, in the direction of your vision. Energy in motion creates the emotion.

What emotions do you think you may feel when you set your energy in motion for your life's dream? Excited, perhaps, and a little scared? Being excited and scared is good. Know that this means you are moving out of your old story into the new one you are creating for yourself right now. Whenever you feel excited and scared, you know that you are moving in the direction of your soul purpose. While stepping from your old story to the new one, your feet may be in both stories at the same time. For this reason, it may seem a bit confusing at times. By holding your vision, you know which direction you want to go in. You are on a mission with a purpose to fulfil your vision. Your guidance is always present and not in the past. With this realization, you can lift your being from the past and move right into now, from where you create your present story.

Any future is probable. You get to determine your future now. Which probability would you prefer? The possibilities are limitless. When you are able to let go of the old story completely, you are free to move forward in awe at your new perception of everything in the world and what it has to offer you. The way you used to see things was linked with your past. Your perception of your past had tainted your perception of the world you were living in. By disconnecting from your past, you have allowed yourself to remove the blinkers from your eyes. Now you can let the light in. When you are in the moment, you can look at the world with new eyes and a new sense of everything that is. You understand now that the lessons you learned from your past have led to where you are today. You wouldn't have learned those lessons if things were any different. It's like looking at everything again for the very first time and in quite a different way. By being aligned with your authentic self, you can see the light in everybody and everything. Your filter that you see through becomes one of beauty. Everything that you see is then tinged with the spectacle of beauty. In this way, you draw beauty towards you. You attract your beautiful life to you from your own beautiful vibration.

Carrying out your purpose allows you to expand your life in ways you may not have believed before. In the process, your own consciousness also shifts to a higher vibration that allows more knowledge to seep in. As your life changes for the better, you become more aware of how others around you are starting to see you in a new light. This allows them to reflect on their own lives in turn to make their necessary adjustments. Living your purpose is life transformational, because once your start, you will never look at life the same again. It's all good! With each step you achieve, you can then move on to even greater and bigger steps to take. Each time you conquer that scary feeling, your excitement increases at a steady pace. This is because you know you are drawing nearer and nearer to your vision. While there may be challenges, you know that these will only strengthen your resolve to get the life of your dreams. Nothing can stop you when you hold the intention for your purpose in your heart. It is important that you take care of your needs first, be they physical, mental, or emotional, when carrying out your purpose. That way you are in the best state and shape to help others in turn.

If you become tired, depleted, or distracted, you can lose focus. Get plenty of rest. Make sure you get good nutrition in your food. Drink plenty of fluids to flush toxins out of your body. Also, regular exercise keeps you in fit condition. Sounds like you are in training – and you are! What are you training for? You are training your body, mind, and soul to integrate within your very being as one unit. When you are at one with yourself, everything becomes easy and effortless in your life. No longer do you need to struggle to get what you want. By aligning with your authentic self, you can express your truth directly from your source. You are in harmony within yourself, and you can carry out your purpose unhindered. You are giving that genuine part of your self with purpose and passion in whatever form you choose. When you do this, you love your life. When you love life, then life loves you back. That's the law of attraction.

No matter what your vision is, it is for the betterment of you, other people, and the planet. Your purpose is how you carry out your mission on your quest. It is an adventure into the unknown that sometimes takes a leap of faith, courage, and determination. Your innate knowing keeps you on track. Your connection with your authentic self keeps you in tune with your inner guidance. Your inner guidance is what will direct you in the right way, not what other people say. As you use your intuition more, you will learn to follow your heart with increasing conviction. You will know your decisions are right for you the moment you make them, not in retrospect. This saves you a lot of time and gets you to where you want to get much quicker. Your connection and alignment with your authentic self make everything seem so much easier now. Where before there was struggle, now there is effortlessness.

In connecting with your authentic self, you have learned the art of ease and effortlessness. With this comes grace. Grace is an open door for all the presents that you are in reality. Grace involves giving and receiving that which you are. This is a true expression of your authentic self. When you are in the flow of grace, all that you need comes to you naturally. Just allow and receive. Trust and have faith. Everything has divine timing. So, whatever happens, believe it is for your higher good, in spite of appearances. Persist on your path and take the lesson with you. Don't try to analyse what is happening. Just accept what you experience and let go of what does not serve you. Any emotional baggage will just weigh you down, which will only slow your journey.

Decide where you want to leave your baggage to be recycled. This could be in the form of a prayer of thanks, a meditation, hypnosis, visualization, or even by setting an intention and repeating a mantra like "I am emotionally free." You could say this three times a day and feel how it is to be so in your heart. The ancient Sanskrit for this is "Moksha, moksha, moksha." You can use this as a mantra while meditating also. Remember, emotions are energy in motion. So, when you let go of your baggage, in whatever way, know and imagine that it will be transformed into the purest light. Whatever is good for you makes you feel light. When you let go of your emotional baggage, in its place you can allow the light in. What once was heavy and dense has now become light and airy. Letting go of baggage means you are emotionally free. As you continue on your path in this way, you know how it feels to be light on your feet, while airing your views with complete freedom unreservedly.

This is your destiny. When you align with your authentic self, you bring it forth. In this way, you bring the truth of who you are to the world, which needs you so desperately. When carrying out your purpose, you become an agent of change. So now you are an agent and you have a mission. Sounds exciting, doesn't it? It's an adventure into the unknown. In the unknown, you find that which is your birthright. You find that which you forgot about yourself. In the unknown, you find your self, your authentic self. In this way, the unknown becomes known once more, when it is remembered by you at a deeper level. You remember who you really are when you discover your purpose. As you carry out your purpose, more memories start coming back. Everything in your life starts to make sense. You know now that there was a reason for everything happening the way it did. The past has passed. You have let the old story go. It does not define who you are any more. What you do now is defined by who you really are – your authentic self.

Your journey now is one of discovery and empowerment for you and for other people. This is the story of your life that you are creating now. It is a powerful story of empowerment for all. It is not about ego. This power is for the benefit of all and is not concerned with personal gain. It is a story that will lift people's hearts and inspire them to connect with their own inner power. Your life story now propels others towards their dream under their own steam. They know from your example that it is possible. No matter what your background, anything is possible. Most successful people in life have had mountains to conquer to get to where they are. In doing so, they have learned how to move mountains and hence move forward in their lives. You can do this too! You have just as much potential as any other person on the planet. What makes the difference is when you tap into your own potential and believe in yourself. If you give up too soon, what happens to your vision? It is still there in potentiality but is suspended in the quantum soup of possibilities. It is you that brings it into being. It is you that manifests it into being. See the end result already created when you are on purpose. Stick with your purpose, mission, and vision, no matter how long it takes. It is this belief that makes it so. Your commitment to your vision is what drives you, because you love what you are doing. You know you can make a difference in the world. Yes, even one person can make a difference globally.

There is no shortage of people who were in the same position you are in now. Against seeming odds, they surmounted the mountain of their lives to conquer their best life "Everest." It all starts with a step in the right direction and then another and then another. When you are equipped with the right tools, nourishment, focus of mind, a plan, a mind map, shelter, and support, you can conquer any perceived mountain in life. Once you reach the summit of your life, you feel ecstatic! Now you can see from this perspective which mountains to avoid in future. From this peak, you can see your path laid out before you clearly. You also know that your purpose has taken on a higher meaning from this plane of earthly existence. There may be more mountains to ascend, but as you take in fresh, crisp air from the mountaintop, you know your journey will be much easier. That's because you can see more of all that is. You also have more awareness within yourself of what is the next step. Everything is easier now. Mission accomplished, and boy does it feel good! Savour this moment, because now you realize that your mission continues in an easier way. You get to choose the next destination. You also know now that though you thought you were alone on this journey, you can look back and see that you were not alone. There are many other sets of footprints beside yours on the path that leads you to where you are now. Now you can see what you could not see before. Now you know that you were helped along the way by unseen forces. The universe was conspiring in your favour all along. Now everything makes sense. This makes you feel good. It is all in divine order.

Your faith and trust are what fuel your journey. Your purpose is the vehicle to get you to your destination. Your mission is the direction you take, and the vision is the life of your dreams. Your vision is your heart's desire. It means you have arrived. It means you are awake to all that you could not see before. Now you have more certainty than ever before about where your life is going. Your internal resolve has served you well. You are now living your life with authenticity from who you really are – your authentic self. You have more connection with your authentic self now, as you close the gap on who you thought you were. As you close this gap, you allow your authentic self to move forward into your very being. So now how you are is more connected with who you really are. People start to see you in a new light. Now you become a source of inspiration for them. If they look for direction from you, help them to find their own direction. In this way, you serve them best. It is not for you to decide what step or action other people should take in their own lives. They are the experts in their own lives, not you. At the level of their authentic self, only they can know what is ultimately in their own best interests. Just be your self. That is all you need to do. Just be your authentic self! That way you carry out your purpose from your own true source.

Your purpose is always self-directed from your inner being. Being comes before doing and not the other way around. From your place of being, you know now what you are to do in your life. If you are doing in order to be somebody, then you are working in reverse. Doing on its own is external to who you really are. Being is connected to who you really are. Being connected to your authentic self allows you to carry out your purpose with precision. From your authentic self, you automatically know what you must do. In this way, your actions are guided by your connection to your authentic self. A whole series of events takes place beyond your imagination when you are aligned with your authentic self. Synchronicity increases as the universe conspires for your success. It nudges you along in the right direction always.

As you move further along your path, you attract more like-minded people into your life. More doorways of opportunity open up for you now. Your authenticity shines forth as genuine integrity to other people. You are happy because you are living your life on purpose and with purpose. Your passion for what you do is contagious, and other people like being around you. Your zest for life is unmistakable. Your energy is vibrant, and you glow in your appearance. At any moment, your life can be transformed even further along in an instant. This can happen from a chance encounter with a person you meet, at an event, or in a particular location. In this way, you have taken a quantum leap that propels you much further along your path. With this leap, your purpose also takes a leap to a higher level. In your own trans-formation, your purpose has also transformed. The original purpose hasn't changed; it has just become more enriched and expanded. Now it holds more possibilities for you and for other people. Now you also have more choice, along with increased opportunities. By having more choice, so you have more creativity. You can see possibilities now that you weren't able to see before. Your ability to co-create with the universe has become finely tuned from your ability to align with your authentic self. As more people want to help you on your quest, the life you are living with this alignment is proof enough. You know it to be so from your experience of life.

Your external life is always a reflection of what is going on inside you. The world is a mirror for you to look within. When you can see yourself with clarity, you get to know your self better. Now you remember everything you forgot and you realize that you had this internal power all along. By clearing the way between you and how you saw yourself before, you become able to know who you really are. What you see in the mirror is the spark in your eyes that is the window to your soul. You see your own divine spark. Through your eyes you see your authentic self. As you look closer and closer, you get to see more of your authentic self in your reflection of yourself. You can only see your self through your reflection. This is the only way to get to the core of who you really are. As you proceed with your purpose, all this happens – and much more!

As you look at your self more and more, you move closer to the core of your being. The more you look at your self, the more you get to know your real self. Along with your knowing, your inner sight also expands. This inner sight is what allows you to see more on the outside, by which you can discern more in your view of the world. Your knowing also includes the knowing that your purpose is really for you. You are a unique individual on the planet, just like every other person on it. You have a unique purpose that nobody else can carry out. So realize now that what you have to offer to the world is unique. What you have to give comes from your experiences alone and not anybody else's. Your purpose gives you a feeling of accomplishing your mission right now. You can see now where it all leads in your vision. You can feel the excitement in your heart centre in this moment. It is all connected as you connect with your authentic self. You can feel this connection within your being. You are connected to your purpose, and it is connected to who you really are. Now you know you can be true to your self. You have learned the lessons.

What other people think does not matter where your purpose is concerned. Just stick with your inner guidance and you will stay on track. Listen to your own inner voice only. You are your own Master, because now you have the master's in self-mastery. You've taken the course of your life, and have passed all the tests. These tests have become foundational lessons for the life you are now living. The lessons you've already learned mean you do not need to take these tests ever again. Once the lesson is learned, you can move on, leaving the past behind you. Sometimes you can learn a lesson before you need to take a test. This way you avoid the test, and so you can move forward much quicker. In this way, you are one step ahead. By being one step ahead, you can minimize any further tests along the way. Now your life becomes easier as you complete each course with ease. You have now become an A+ student in the school of life. No longer do you need to stay up late studying and preparing for the next day's exam. Now you know your stuff. Now you are showing others how to excel in their lives also by your example. Now you know you can achieve whatever you set out to achieve. Your personal credentials are who you have now become. You speak for your self. You and your self speak as one. In this way, you are a pure expression of your authentic self. Your purpose has led you here, and it is from this place of oneness that you will lead others.

Be patient. All will be revealed. When the curtains draw back, let the show begin! Bring it on! You are the main actor in your life. You can be the star in your life film as you shine forth your light within. As you watch your film unreel, you can now sit in comfort, safety, and pure happiness at what you see. You are now in this place from where you can see all that is unfolding in your life. All that happens is in alignment with your authentic self. You are now being your real self in your life. Now you don't need to hide your self any more (and you never did). Now your life fits perfectly with who you are in reality. It's a perfect match with who you really are. You are one with your own life in this way. Your life has now become heart-centred and heart-directed. You moved out of your head a long time ago.

When you are one with your life, you find that you are one with all in it also. You experience the connection with everyone you come in contact with. Sometimes it's like you've known them your whole life. Your alignment with your authentic self is what attracted these people on the same wavelength. The more you connect with your self, the more prosperity and abundance comes into your life. It is only natural for you to be abundant. The planet is abundant in reality. You may have been taught differently in school or even thought about things around you based on their appearance only. How things appear to be is not necessarily how they are in themselves. As you connect more with your real nature, your birthright becomes yours naturally. Now you can see how carrying out your purpose can enrich your life so much more. You can also see that carrying out your purpose can enrich other people's lives also. You are the authority in your own life, and that's why you look to yourself for direction at all times. You now rely on your inner guidance solely in steering you forward. In this way, your purpose is directed from within. Your inner direction is what guides you towards your heart's desire, towards your vision. Now you know that your dream is not just a dream in your imagination. Now you know you can actually bring it into being, through carrying out your purpose in a relentless manner. By "relentless" I mean you hold the vision in sight always.

Your persistence will reward you with results in your life. In your journey, you have learned the golden keys to success and what it takes to bring your vision into being. These golden keys are your own personal keys designed to unlock only those doors that are for you. When you arrive at the doorway of opportunity, take your key and put it into the lock. You find it fits, because it is the right key for this time. As you turn the key, you realize you are turning a new direction in your life. As you step through the doorway, you know that you are the doorway for the possibilities that lie beyond. You step through with excitement into the light. You have entered a new world of possibilities as you close the door behind you. Here is a place of deep beauty that lies within a source of infinite possibilities. There are many more doors ahead; some you can see, and some not yet. It all depends on which path you take. You have more golden keys to success that have yet to be used. You now know that when you arrive at the next door you choose, the key will fit. Your life is now full of doors that you can open at will. Choose wisely. Each door gives you a better view of your vision as it comes more and more into focus. As you move along the path, you pick up even more keys.

Sometimes another person or event may give you the key you were looking for. Keep watch! When you expect to receive that key, your eyes will be open for it. You will see your key straight away, whereas somebody else will just walk by without noticing what it is. Your alignment with your authentic self and your purpose is the reason you are here at this time. That is why you are always in the right place at the right time. Trust and it is so. Your inner direction gives you the advantage of being able to access exactly what you need at any given time. You do not need to try to figure out what you need or how you are going to get to your destination. By just carrying out your purpose, you are fulfilling your mission in moving steadily forward towards your vision. Your purpose is part of your life plan and is linked with who you really are. When you are carrying out your purpose, you are living your authentic life and you feel it to be so. Every day is an adventure that brings you closer to fulfilling your vision.

On your quest, your adventure also brings you closer to who you really are. May the force be with you on your mission! May the source be with you. Now is the time to live your life with unbridled passion and purpose. Now is the time to fulfil your vision. Go forth and conquer your self. When you do, both you and your self win as you become one. As you become one with your self, so you become one with other people. Eventually, it spreads as the planet itself becomes one once more. With this oneness that the sages have been talking about for centuries comes harmony, connection, peace, and joy. One for all and all for one. As Buddha says, "A wise man, recognizing that the world is but an illusion, does not act as if it were real, so he escapes the suffering."

Exercise: Uncovering Your Beliefs

Are you aware of all your beliefs? The likely answer is no, because a lot of your beliefs are in your subconscious mind. They are hidden from your conscious mind as a result. To learn what your beliefs are, look to your outside world. How do you behave towards the world you live in? How you live your life comes from your beliefs and expectations. When you want to know what your limiting beliefs are, look for what's not working in your life. Then ask yourself, what would a person need to believe about the world for this to happen? A self-limiting belief cannot be removed through will power alone. It has become part of your programming through conditioning. So the only way to remove it is to reprogram your mind, either through hypnosis or meditation. What is the opposite of that self-limiting belief? This is what you need to replace the self-limiting belief with.

CHAPTER 6

QUANTUM ACTUALIZATION (MANIFESTING)

Everything that is created in material form emanates from the quantum field of potentiality. You are here because you were intended here, just like everything else that exists in this world. There are no mistakes in the nature of the universe. There are no mistakes in the source. Energy is the creative force. Everything on earth is composed of energy and particles. Your energy is infinite, whereas your material body is not permanent. We all come from the same energy source, and we share the same material particles that make up our bodies. We receive nourishment from the environment to make our bodies grow. What is in our food is assimilated into our bodies and becomes part of us. You are not your body. Your physical self is not your real self. You are not your personality either. Your personality is shaped and moulded by the conditions of life in the environment, especially during the first seven years. What *is* never changes and cannot be anything else. Your real self never changes. Your free will, or conscious mind, does not define who you are either. It is the means by which you consciously choose and make your decisions in everyday life. Things are not achieved in life just by determined free will. Your imagination, which is linked with your subconscious, is more powerful than your free will. What you visualize in your mind's eye communicates directly to your subconscious mind, which recognizes symbols and pictures instantly. Your conscious mind determines 5 per cent of your behaviour, whereas your subconscious mind determines 95 per cent of your behaviour. When you are aligned with your authentic self, you are aligning your conscious and subconscious mind as one.

For the power of your authentic self to work in harmony with the universe, you must trust in the source or God and let go of doubts. To stay on track, or realign with your authentic self, you must constantly remind your self that other people are not separate from you. We are all part of the same universe and share the same energy, though at different levels. We all come from the same source in our creation. We are not separate in reality, though it may appear to our senses that we are. We are one in the universe, and a universal energy resonates inside each one of us. Ego thinks of itself as separate from others. This line of thinking separates you from your goal and your authentic self, which is full of abundance and has no lack in it. When you see yourself in other people is when you really start getting to know your real self. When you accept yourself for who you really are, you really start having the feeling of belonging.

Everything around you is connected to you; it is not physically separate, as it appears to be. Things as they appear are not necessarily as they are in themselves. Appearances can be deceptive. You have been conditioned to perceive in a linear sense from the outside in by using your five senses. In reality, by using your gut instinct or inner voice, you learn to use your sixth sense to see the world from the inside out on many levels at the same time. Your level of awareness on the inside allows you to see the same level of energy, in whatever form, on the outside. This is when you have an inner knowing about what is going on around you in the moment. Your inner knowing is a feeling that you have about what is going to happen or what somebody is thinking. This inner knowing comes from your authentic self. This inner knowing can also include having a gut feeling of what needs to change. This is how synchronicity, or meaningful coincidence, comes about. You are thinking in alignment with the laws of the universe that exist here, now and in the source. You are the connecting link that brings this energy forward by tapping into it, while you stay connected with it. Your thoughts must be in harmony with the laws of the universe to be on the same wavelength as the spiritual energy, from which everything emanates. By learning to think in this way, you become the co-creator in your life.

Life doesn't just happen to you, because you always play an active role in making it happen. Life happens from the way you intend it, in the energy field of the universe. Time and space do not come into this equation, as they exist in the physical world only. In the quantum field there is only now. The future and the past do not exist in the quantum. Whenever you are thinking of the past, you are actually thinking of it in the now! This is how your brain perceives what it sees. Your timeline as you see it is always in the now. By changing how you view your timeline, or history of events, you can change your perception of past experiences right now. In changing your perception, you change the experience itself. The same applies with anticipating the future. There is only now. Know that whatever happens is for your ultimate good. When you focus in this way, you focus on what is good for you.

According to Lynn McTaggart (author of *The Field: The Quest for the Secret Force of the Universe*), there is scientific evidence of studies done which support the existence of the field of intention. In the field of intention, higher and faster energy can be tapped into by anybody. Anything that is created has intention built into it. If you try to discover the source of life in reverse order, by breaking down the body into molecules, atoms, and particles, you find that there's no particle at the source. The source itself is pure energy vibrating at a speed beyond measure and without form. Your own source is formless energy vibrating at a high frequency. Intention exists in this spiritual field of energy and is present everywhere. Intention determines all creation in the universe, from the non-physical. This brings about manifestation of the acorn by "pulling" forward its growth into an oak tree. Intention exists in the non-physical and physical worlds, according to Dr. Wayne Dyer (author of *The Power of Intention*). It sets in motion the process of growth, once conception takes place. Your intention also includes your thoughts, emotions, and connection with your own soul. Intention lies within your authentic self. It is infinite potential, with regard to your physical and non-physical appearance on earth. Even though you emanate and manifest from this infinite intelligence that is everywhere, during creation you become present in time and space on earth. Your authentic self is always a part of you. It can be tuned into whenever you raise your levels of awareness to new possibilities that before might have seemed impossible.

You can also tune out of the power of your authentic self in the field. This happens if you believe it is separate from you and exists on the outside rather than on the inside. You can follow your destiny to a large degree by taking charge of your inner resources once you discover what and where they are. Things don't just happen to you; you let them happen to you in the ordinary world. By using the power of your authentic self, you can learn how to think about and deal with your self in relation to the world, and not the other way around. Extraordinary living can be possible when you raise your awareness in this way. In doing so, you take charge of your life, while living it on your own terms and not everybody else's.

In the world of matter, objects exist in three-dimensional solidity. In this world, time is linear and everything appears to be separate to each other. Certainty of truth in this paradigm is linked with science's experiments based on observation where something is witnessed to be so. According to this approach, whatever cannot be seen is regarded as the "ghost in the machine." According to science, if something is not observed, it has not yet been proven to be true and therefore is not scientific. Science, then, is always looking for the solution to problems according to this approach. The solution in this case is recognized only when it is shown to be the case from the evidence of experiments and studies carried out. The solution is upgraded or revised only when new evidence is observed that counteracts previous evidence. Newton's method of physics requires a conscious approach only.

The paradox is that Newton's laws are unconscious of infinite possibilities that exist in the quantum field. Newton's laws do not apply to the quantum field. In the quantum field, consciousness itself is the driving force for manifestation and co-creation with the universe. Therefore, potentiality is fluid and not set in solid stone as with Newton. The infinite field of possibilities that exist in any moment of now is what makes potentiality fluid. Quantum actualization is actually responsive to thought and consciousness, either from an individual or the collective consciousness. For this reason, dimensions in quantum physics range far beyond the three dimensions that we are all familiar with. The three-dimensional world view I speak of is linked with density. In the quantum field, higher dimensions allow for expansion of infinite possibilities, without the notion of time or space. The solution already exists now in the quantum, and it flows back from now to bring it into being. It's as if the solution appears simultaneously, without any apparent cause, when an intention is set. Sometimes the solution may not appear till some time later when the conditions are right. In the quantum field, we as humans are all one because of our connection with each other. Everything that exists is connected in the quantum world, because everything is made up of energy that has a vibration.

Quantum physics is now being proven to be valid more and more through the use of modern technology. In fact, it is now considered scientific and undeniable. What the sages have been saying since ancient times is now being proven scientifically, according to quantum physics. Therefore, science now is beginning to agree with spirituality! Now the familiar term has become "science and spirituality." Now we know that the human mind is not separate and self-contained, as was previously thought. Quantum physics shows that consciousness is an interconnected and powerful force for creating both within and outside of time and space. This cosmic, or collective, consciousness is what brings manifestation about.

Humanity has a role to play in this cosmic consciousness. Your mind is linked with your brain yet is independent of it. Your brain, which consists of electrical activity and chemical reactions, does not comprise your whole mind. Your mind also has a consciousness aspect that is connected to the universal realm. The universe is regarded as infinite intelligence, to which your mind has access. In the universal realm is the sea of consciousness, where you can float on the waves of potential. Therefore your mind is connected with your physical brain and the invisible realm of universal intelligence simultaneously. In this way, your mind can experience many dimensions simultaneously. Your mind is a drop in the ocean of consciousness. As such, it is a part of the whole, while being the whole at the same time. As part of the universal mind, you have access to all that is, has ever been, and can ever be in potentiality right now, in any given moment. When you are aligned with the universe, you are tuned into receiving infinite possibilities, according to your needs. You have everything you need already. When you believe this is so, it is so. This is a law of quantum physics. Therefore, your mind can shape your reality and what shows up in it.

An ongoing study called the Global Consciousness Project is being carried out by Dr. Roger Nelson at Princeton University.over the last thirty years (noetic.org/directory/person/roger-nelson). Initially in the mid 1980's, Nelson found that a person sitting nearby who focused their thoughts on a random number generator, could actually affect the numbers being produced by the electrical device. In the late 1990's, with the assistance of his colleagues, Nelson decided to test his theory further by setting up random number generators in various laboratories worldwide. Nelson has since shown that when a large number of people share a state, especially an emotional one, the global network shows deviation from randomness. During the 2008 presidential elections in America, data shows that the numbers generated had a thousand to one odds that they would show up like that, according to Nelson. After analyzing twelve years of his data results, the odds of the numbers that showed up were a billion to one. Originally, Nelson had been searching for evidence of a global mind and global consciousness. His data speaks for itself.

What happens to you now can also change your experience of your past. In the quantum, as I said, there is no past or future; there is only now. Therefore, all is now. Everything that happens is now. Change in the now affects all that is now, even your past. You can change everything in the now through your consciousness and intention using quantum manifesting. You can even change your perception of your past when you change what you believe and think in the now. Time as you know it does not apply to the quantum field. Everything can be instant in the quantum. You do not realize how powerful you are until you self-actualize. Aligning with your authentic self means you move closer to becoming self-actualized. With self-actualization comes mastery of your self. Mastering your self gives you the power to create in your life. This is how quantum actualization takes place.

In reality, we as humans are all created from both physical and energetic components of the universe and so are part of it. You reach higher levels of energy as you can connect to your inner source by aligning with your authentic self. This inner source is the portal to universal energy that's always present to be tapped into. Your subconscious mind is connected to the universal consciousness and the vast wisdom that exists within. You can tap into your subconscious using your imagination. Your imagination is much more effective in linking up with the universal mind than your willpower. Strong willpower on its own is closer to ego. Your imagination allows you to create a picture in your mind which you can then co-create into being, in a physical sense. The higher your vibrational frequency, the higher your "magnetism" for attracting what you desire. While manifesting in this way, you remain in harmony with the universal power of your intention that is pure love in action. Your spirit of intention gives expression to whatever it is you desire.

If you consciously try to will yourself to do something your imagination doesn't see as possible, your imagination will always win. If you can trust and see yourself in your imagination able to be something beyond your body, you begin to feel yourself as something beyond your body. You visualize yourself as stronger than the task at hand. Your inner picture of high intention is linked to serving others in some way. When this is the case, the universe responds on the same wavelength. In this way, your pure intention seeks what is good for you, for others, and for the planet as a whole. So what may have seemed impossible before is possible now. The universe wants to help you to help and serve others. Just allow it to do that, but you have to ask first. When you ask for help, allow and be open to receiving what is coming to you. Be in harmony with your authentic self. In this way, you will be in harmony with the universe and all that it has to offer. Believing it is so makes it happen also. Otherwise, you disconnect from your own self-empowerment. Being open to receive allows the right people to turn up at the right moment. When you are open, you have unlimited potential in manifesting your desires. As Wayne Dyer says, "Abundance is not something we acquire. It is something we tune into."

Become a witness to your own thoughts. Set an intention for the goal you want to manifest. Willing yourself only to do a task is thinking from the ego. Also, anything that is obtained through dishonesty won't bring peace with it. Living in love allows for expansion and abundance to come into your life. Living in fear closes you off from your heart connection and your natural power to manifest. Know that you deserve what you intend. You are connected to it already in your mind, as your vibration is aligned with it. As you think, so are you, so is your life, and so it is.

When you create physical matter or form from energy, your goal must be loving and kind in nature. At the same time, your goal can be practical for everyday life. This can apply to business, social, and leisure aspects of life. What you wish for others comes back to you in turn, in some form. Research shows acts of kindness shown towards another person improves the immune system and stimulates production of serotonin in the giver, receiver, and observer of kindness. Serotonin is a hormone that make you feel at peace and blissful. According to Dr. David R. Hamilton (www.dr.davidhamilton.com), acts of kindness create emotional warmth, which releases a hormone known as oxytocin. Oxytytocin causes a release of a chemical called nitric oxide, which dilates the blood vessels. This reduces blood pressure and therefore protects the heart. Various other studies into acts of kindness have shown different beneficial effects on the body and mind.

Also what you see in your mind's eye is powerful, whether it is in actuality or in your imagination. Your brain perceives both as reality, as shown from brain scan studies done. In May 2001, E.D. Grossman and R. Blake wrote an article "Brain activity evoked by inverted and imagined biological motion" (Vision Research, 41, 2001: 1475 - 1482) after doing brain studies to this effect. These experiments explored the area in the brain called the superior temporal sulcus (STS) which is activated on viewing biological motion. The relationship between neural activity in this region and perception were explored in these studies. Activity levels in the STS were measured in one experiment when observers viewed actual images of movement and another experiment where they imagined biological motion. The study showed that "In both experiments, we found that the BOLD response was modulated with perceptual experience." What this means is that what you see and what you imagine (in this case, movement of an object) can activate the same part of the brain that perceives movement. Your imagination (mind's eye) allows you to think from the end and behave as if what is sees is already here. Imagination has no physical limits and is your connection with spirit.

Buddhism speaks of contemplating loving kindness in our thoughts and actions. Being unkind causes you to block the power of your intention, both in thought and deed, thereby weakening you. By giving, you receive. When your thoughts, feelings, and actions have kindness in them, you are on the same wavelength as the power of your authentic self. In this way, you are linked with it. If you think or act unkindly, you become what you think outside the realm of your authentic self. Be kind to yourself. Be kind to others and your kindness will return to you. Bring your energy into alignment with those who already have what you desire. Others on the same wavelength will help you achieve your purpose in ways you never expected. All of us are connected to each other in the universal mind. How we treat ourselves or those who appear less than perfect to us affects others and ourselves in turn. Feel good about yourself and accept yourself as you are. Be grateful also for what you already have.

What is Quantum Physics?

The entire universe is a vibration. The illusion you live in is a frequency at a particular physical level. It is said by quantum physicists that currently you experience 2 to 4 per cent of what is actually around you in the universe. According to the physicists, your brain processes this amount of incoming information from the external world. Your conscious mind processes incoming data at a much lower rate than the vast capacities of the subconscious mind. While the conscious mind processes forty bits of information per second, your subconscious can process twenty million! Your subconscious mind recognizes patterns, symbols, and visual images instantly in your environment. Your conscious mind, on the other hand, processes specifics, while analysing the situation in a sequential manner, using left-brain logic. Whatever you experience is the level you are vibrating at. Everything is vibration. This original essence that things arise from comes from the understanding and observation that everything in the universe is energy. Energy has infinite intelligence that exists in every dimension at every level of being, even in the physical world. Your vibrational energy allows you to perceive, become, and feel in a more heightened way when you increase your focus on who you really are. The deeper you get to know your self, the higher your dimensional state. The more you can "see" yourself, the more you can increase your own particular vibration, as well as your experience of life. In this way, you consciously evolve your way of being in this world. Your vibration matches your experience. If you are not happy with your experience, then you can adjust your vibration. When you raise your energy, your experience also changes. In the presence of the moment, time does not exist. When you are not in the moment, you limit yourself. Being separate from what is creates the illusion of appearance because you are looking for something other than what is now.

If you become too comfortable with your current state of being, familiarity with your life conditions can bring reluctance to change. Resistance to change means you block yourself. When blocking yourself, you may think you understand all there is to know about yourself, and so you withdraw to the outside world. Without awareness of this blockage, you cannot unblock it. Your awareness is the key that loosens your blocks before opening the door to abundance. Your perceived blockages create a wall of separation, preventing you from moving towards your inner self. This happens when you impose images from the outside on your own experience of who you think you are. Any disconnection from your true self can lead you to experience things less directly, as they become less connected to you. So how you perceive attracts conditions that testify to your experience, even when you are out of touch with your authentic self. When you are out of touch with your Self, you may try to fill the holes of emptiness in your life without success. Your misperception of your inner truth can cause suffering, which is a falling away from love. Sometimes you may forget who you are when you look to the outside for answers. Knowing who you are at your core gives you connection to all things and ways of being, in any moment. Your experience of your self gives you information and power. With a higher vibration, you know more about who you really are. With self-awareness, you can disengage from the illusion of life you were living up till now. In this way, you eliminate all barriers and so allow things to be as they are. By not allowing, you do not accept that everything is in perfect divine order, in perfect timing. By allowing, you know you are one with all that is.

What has the quantum field got to do with actualization or manifesting anything into existence? The answer is everything! Everything exists in the universe as an ill-defined wave-particle duality. What we see and perceive as solid reality is not actually solid at all. Everything exists as an oscillation or ill-defined wave of energy. This wave of energy remains the same until a particle is observed, where it changes from being in a wave state to being solid and existing in a definable place. In quantum physics, it is known that a particle can exist both as a wave and a particle at the same time. In order to achieve anything in your life, it has to go from the unformed, ill-defined wave state of ideas (dreaming, wishing, or desiring) into a solid state (through belief and conviction). By collapsing your limiting beliefs, self-denial, aversions, and resentments, you align with your authentic self at your very deepest level. At this level, there is no lack, no unfairness, and no discrimination. In this way, you flip over and away from the insecure, ill-defined wave state that blames and judges others for where you're at in your life. Instead, when aligned with your authentic self, you know that abundance is yours already. Everything you desire is yours already. In collapsing your self-limiting, self-defeating beliefs, you open yourself to co-creation with the universe. This change of mindset directs your subconscious to open the door to creating all the abundance you can possibly imagine. All points of abundance, where points in our limited three-dimensional reality show up, are solid particle states, not ill-defined waves. So, to make manifestation work for you, your limiting beliefs need to be put aside by whatever means. In becoming centred and aligned with your real self, you align with the solid symbols of abundance. Success breeds success. Make note of what you want to bring into your life as a co-creator with the universe. Write it all down. When you believe and know you can create everything you want, you can follow through until you get the results you desire.

The universe has no limits. You can believe that you can be, do, have, and create everything you desire for your life. You can imagine being a magnet that attracts all you desire to you. In order to make your feelings aligned with this, you maintain agreement with all the abundance around you. If you disagree by being angry or resentful of others' abundance, then you exclude yourself from the same thing. You deny your ability to create the same thing, by excluding it from others, even when you think this in your mind. You create the same as what you focus on. What you experience in your life right now is a result of what you have been focusing on consciously or subconsciously. The ego mind can block your creative force with feelings of envy, judgement, or lack of self-worth. It is by identifying with abundance that you become one with it. The authentic self is already abundant. By aligning with your authentic self, you are already abundant. You feel and know this to be true. You are neutral in your feelings about abundance because it is a natural state for everybody. Becoming aware of the abundance around you lets you know that this is true. Your self-worth is not linked to your material possessions. Your personal power and abundance already exist on the same level in the now.

Positive affirmations can work when repeated over periods of time on a daily basis, but they can take a long time to work. Meditation or hypnotic trance is usually a more direct route for getting into the state of manifesting. Using affirmations with emotion, though, can help your subconscious mind to manifest your visualizations into reality. What you shape as your inner reality through visualization and affirmations will manifest as your outer reality when you believe it is possible. This happens when circumstances around you shape themselves to suit what you've come to expect from your visualizations. You are what you think and what you believe. Therefore, if you are saying affirmations while having conflicting self-limiting beliefs, these can prevent your affirmations from coming into being. If you think of scarcity, then you will be limited by what you can have. If you think and believe in having abundance now in the present tense, then you manifest for yourself a life of abundance, happiness, and wealth. As Napolean Hill says, "what the mind can perceive and believe, the mind can achieve."

Break free from the old ways of limited thinking, doubt, and fear. When you change your thoughts, you change your world and your life. What you experience comes from what you place your attention on. Your attention and intention are the life force that brings into your life what you focus on. Know what you don't want, and focus only of what you do want. Know that you are perfect and that everything is in perfect divine order. Be open and receptive. Commit to yourself and you will be living according to your true values. Commitment means taking action towards your goals. By becoming more flexible than you've allowed yourself to be in your past, you can learn to let go and release what does not serve you. In letting go of self-limiting beliefs, you clear the way for abundance, or what you want to attract to come into your life. In this way, you allow the natural process of moving towards what you want. Set goals that contribute to your ultimate dream. Achieve these goals one day at a time in motivating you nearer to your vision. Resist procrastination in postponing or delaying the achievement of your dreams. Do not settle for less. Take action and do it now.

Expectations can be formed with your emotions. If you can develop emotional excitement about potential physical constructions, such as events, then you will find it easier to manifest that which you desire. When you reach a level of being able to feel this emotional state in your mind intensely enough, while focusing on your heart's desire for long enough, you permeate the quantum field with this desire. The intensity of your desire in the being and feeling of your body acts as a magnetic resonance for the universe to bend and transmute the potential of your desire into its actual existence. Other people who are in fact connected to you on an energetic level can help this shift to come about also. The universe always conspires in your favour. You are in the universe, yet the universe is also within you. Your consciousness on an individual level is connected to the collective consciousness of humanity as a whole also. Other people's actions can directly or indirectly fulfil your intention in this way. You are in nature, and nature is in you. Your connection with nature means you are a part of that whole too, as it is a part of you. In this way, nature can also conspire to bring about the fulfilment of your desire, leading to a synchronicity of events in the natural world in your favour. This happens as long as you believe in your heart's desire as coming into being right now. If you look on it as wishful thinking, wanting, or waiting for it to happen, then it will not materialize in this way. Your heart's desire is already manifesting, if you believe this to be so.

The intensity of your belief is important. Beliefs are the method by which you create your experience. Your events, your life, and your experiences are caused by your present beliefs. Change your beliefs and your life changes. Events are not things that happen to you; they are materialized expressions formed by you according to your expectation and belief. You are in control of your personal experience when you are in control of your beliefs. If you do not like your experience, then you must change the nature of you conscious thoughts and expectations. By learning the power of thought and emotion, you can free yourself from being a slave to events or circumstances. You are constantly receiving a stream of inner data that is in line with your personal expectations. Expectation of your desires causes their manifestation into reality. Expectation also manifests the things you don't want, if you actually believe they will happen. It is always best to focus and build on what you want for this reason. The more you focus and build on your heart's desire, the more real and believable it becomes. Expectation triggers inner data into physical actualization; from psychic reality into physical reality.

All physical objects are constructions of energy. The fact that a physical object like a chair appears to be solid is created by your senses. The matter in the chair is switching on and off too fast for your senses to perceive the change. The space between the individual atoms of the chair is vast. Quantum physics shows there is almost no solidity in the chair, as it is mainly empty space with the illusion of solidity. The basic energy of matter is always there; it manifests into your physical world in patterns which have been prepared by your individual consciousness or mass consciousness at the subconscious level. When your conscious desires are in alignment with your subconscious expectations, along with sufficient emotional yearning, this allows for your subconscious to follow the desires of the conscious mind. This can happen quicker during alpha or theta meditation states. If there is conflict between your conscious desire and your subconscious expectation, then it is unlikely to bring about manifestation of the desire. The combination of thought, expectation, emotion, and desire creates form. This form is created by your subconscious manipulation of the basic energy units of the universe, when that combination is present. Alignment of your conscious and subconscious mind brings about balance where manifestation becomes easier. Alignment of the conscious and subconscious mind also brings about whole-brain thinking, which means you can receive and process information more efficiently than before. By aligning your mind with your body and soul, you come to realize how powerful you truly are. In this way, you can tap into the genius within.

Einstein's equation of $E = mc^2$ is the same as saying energy is equal to mass multiplied by the square of the speed of light. Therefore, energy and matter are interchangeable. Matter as we know it is merely energy units converted into solid perceptible items that we can perceive via our physical senses or measure with using scientific instruments. This matter is not permanent as we understand "permanent" but switches itself on and off at a vibration rate so fast that we cannot perceive the off state (which is antimatter). Scientists know this to be the case. Matter spends as much time in the antimatter state as it does in the positive matter state that you perceive with your senses. Matter is not permanent; it just appears to be so. All matter is constantly being created. So what appears as physical growth of a living creature is not growth at all; instead it is a constantly updating reconstruction of the structure to a newer slightly updated pattern or form. As the psychic energy diminishes, then this form loses its initial sharp focus and the body deteriorates. This is what we call ageing. As the initial psychic energy weakens, this causes the physical pattern to blur.

In 2003 the Human Genome Project (HGP) decoded only approximately three per cent of the total DNA in humans. The remaining ninety seven per cent was then termed "junk DNA", because it had no known biological function and could not be coded. This means that our decoded genes reside in only three per cent of our total DNA. "Junk DNA" does not contain any known genes. Also, the HGP found that there are fewer than twenty five thousand genes in the human body. The original prediction was that there would be one hundred and twenty thousand genes to account for all their theories on genetics. Finding only twenty thousand genes in human DNA was a shock for the geneticists doing the study. This was because there is not enough coded genes to account for the complexity of human life or of human disease. The other ninety seven per cent of our DNA is a mystery to scientists and so is not generally talked about or referred to by them. If more attention were to be placed on "junk DNA", then we may need to re-evaluate our whole concept of genetics and inheritance. Genetics is not a fixed science as demonstrated by the unaccounted for DNA that we have within our blueprint.

According to David Stern, a Princeton professor in the Department of Ecology and Evolutionary Biology, scientists now believe "junk DNA" is crucial for turning the information encoded in genes into useful products by means of switching them on and off as needed. New findings from a Princeton-led team of researchers claims that "junk DNA" contains additional copies of instructions for maintaining stable gene function, even in a variable environment (www.princeton.edu/main/news/archive). This, he claims, is so that genes produce the right output for organisms to develop normally, be it a fly, a mouse or a human. In a way, it makes sense for us to have an inbuilt system that helps us to deal with whatever arises so that we can develop normally. From Stern's studies on the fruitfly, the "shadow enhancers" ("junk DNA") seem to activate when they are needed in adverse environments that the organism does not usually experience. This shows how our environment, "junk DNA" and our known DNA can interact together to produce the best outcome in our genetic expression physically! It also supports the view that our genetic expression can change over time depending on our environment. There are many more questions to be answered. More importantly, there are many more questions to be asked in relation to genetics. One of these questions could be "does your perception of your environment play a role in how your genes express themselves?"

Dr. Candace Pert, Ph.D., a prominent researcher and pharmacologist is the author of *"Molecules of Emotion"*. From her molecular research on how the body processes emotions, Dr. Pert has proven that neuropeptides (specific chemicals triggered by emotions) are actually thoughts converted into matter. Her research also shows how emotions reside in the body and physically interact with cells and tissues. The importance of the connection between emotions and health is significant, according to Dr. Pert's research. So it would follow, that by changing your perception, you are changing your emotions. By consciously changing your perception in this way, you affect how your feel emotionally. The neuropeptides produced in your body are a reflection of the emotions you feel, according to Dr. Pert.

Another researcher, Dr. Bruce Lipton, the author of *The Biology of Belief*, has studied the link between perception and health. His research highlights how our perception of our environment comes from our beliefs and that this can affect our physical body. "When the protein receptors on the outside of individual cells receive the information via neuropeptides, they send a signal to the cell nucleus, where the messages are encoded. From that encoding, the protein creates the DNA for a specific cell so that it will adapt to its environment. The nucleus of the cell, according to Dr. Lipton's research, is in fact the reproductive system of a cell - it is the centre of a cell's ability to regenerate." (Emoto, 2004: 131). Furthermore, Dr. Lipton found that the cell's brain resides in its protein receptors on the cell membrane and not in the nucleus, as previously thought by cellular biologists. According to Lipton, genes by themselves cannot control the vast range of physical expressions in the human species.

Epigenetics is a new field of biology that shows how the environment influences cell behaviour, without changing the genetic code of DNA. Epigenetics is now finding that the chromosome's proteins have a vital hereditary role to play, just as much as DNA. According to Lipton, "in the chromosome, the DNA forms the core, and the proteins cover the DNA like a sleeve." (Lipton, 2005: 37). DNA cannot express itself physically, unless the protein sleeve is uncovered from the DNA. According to Lipton, environmental influences like nutrition, stress and emotions can modify (uncover) these genes without changing their basic DNA blueprint. Interestingly, epigeneticists have found that these modifications can be passed down to future generations. This has vast implications for how we can view genetics from now on. We may have to rethink our whole approach to genetics. It seems that originally, genes were viewed by biologists as having a fixed inherited trait that cannot be influenced from the outside! Now, research like Lipton's is showing that genes can express or not express depending on the environment and your perception of it. For Lipton, "Genes are not destiny." Interesting concept!

Dr. Masaru Emoto, noted for his water-crystal research, has shown how perception of the external environment affects the molecular structure of water. This includes water that is in the human body also. Emoto's studies on frozen water crystals show how water molecules change according to vibrations in the external environment. These vibrations include words, pictures, sounds and music. Emoto claims that even an intention of thought like love or thanks can influence the molecular structure of water and he has photos to show this. For him, the words "love" and "thanks" produce the most beautiful water crystals.

Matter is the result of molecular composition. The molecules are converted from pure energy by psychic pressure, triggered at a subconscious level by expectation, emotion, and desire. Be mindful of the pictures of your mind and imagination. Your inner expectations give rise to your environment and the conditions of your life. Your inner psychological state is projected outward into physical reality. By knowing this, know what your psychological state is and change your conditions for your own benefit. Your attitudes form the nature of what you see. In order to know what you think of yourself, see what you think of others to get the answer. True self-knowledge is vital for health and vitality. When you recognize the truth about how you behave in the world, you are finding what you think about yourself subconsciously. What you see in others is already within you first. Otherwise you would not see this. What is it you would like to see? Know that the truth about your authentic self is good, and build upon this. It is important to have aims and goals in life with determination, but the illusion is that ego, willpower, and your body achieve these. By realigning with your authentic self, you gain the power to create anything in your imagination. Be confident in your imagination on a continual basis for materializing what you want into reality. Banish all doubt.

Being creative means having trust in your destiny and purpose. Being consistent means holding your vision in the background of your daily thoughts and actions. After writing your goals down, you may place them in a place where you are bound to see them, such as your mirror, for instance. While repeating your goals, get into the feeling of having them already. How would you feel if you had your goal now? What would you see, feel, and hear? Use your senses in your body to make it present now. This is how you draw to you what you see in your mind's eye. In focusing on your goal in this way, without effort, you create an energetic link with the universal mind within. Through repetition and practise, the information eventually goes into the subconscious mind, which then links up with the universal energy. At the same time, you are detached as to how your goal comes about. The universe looks after the how. The universe has no limits. It is ever-expanding and infinite. By aligning with your authentic self, you allow yourself to expand and grow as you evolve intellectually, emotionally, and spiritually. This means letting go of the way you used to think. You are created from abundance and can experience the expression of abundance in your life. It's already a part of you. Instead of thinking in terms of limitations, you can raise your awareness to knowing that your potential has no limits. Live without limits! The people and things you need to fulfil your purpose are already here. By tuning into your authentic self, your supplying resources are manifested. It is also never a question of resources but always a question of resourcefulness! Your resourcefulness gets you what you need, and this comes from belief in yourself. Your inner knowing of this unlimited abundance allows you to think with unbending determination. Any thoughts of lack will block your connection to your authentic self.

I want = lack
I need = lack
I should = lack
I ought = lack
I must = lack

I allow = co-creation with the universe
I have = co-creation with the universe
I am = co-creation with the universe

As thoughts of abundance become your way of thinking in relation to your goal, your authentic self works in harmony with you in bringing your desires forth. Be grateful for all the good things in your life. By making gratitude a daily practise, you open up your heart centre to receive more of the same from the universe. When you have a connection with your authentic self, you are always receptive to bringing forth your dream by means of creative visualization. Never worry about the how. The universe takes care of that. Once you set your intention, then you detach from it and let it go off into outer space. By letting go in this way, you let the universe take over in actualizing it physically. This may not happen straight away, but when it does, you will know it instantly. Allowing your dream to become a reality takes patience, courage, and trust. It means you are at peace with yourself, with your mind at ease. It is effortless, because you know that everything is taken care of. At the same time, it doesn't mean you just sit back and ignore what is going on around you. In fact, the opposite applies. Keep your eyes and ears open for any signs, opportunities, and people that come your way. By recognizing your intuition, or gut feeling, about something, you can make the most of everything that comes your way. Success builds upon success. Take action where you feel it is appropriate. Successful people are the ones who are prepared to do the things that unsuccessful people are unprepared to do. By letting go of ego, you can have patience and be at peace while following your dream. In this way, you manifest your desires into your life through your connection with your authentic self. Meditation is the key for finding peace within and for tapping into your authentic self. When you quiet your mind, the inner silence allows for growth of awareness to take place. The more you become aware of yourself, the closer your connection to your authentic self. This is where you true power lies – deep within yourself, at your core.

Every thought you have affects you and others around you. This is because every thought has its own vibrational frequency. By correcting yourself immediately whenever you have a weakening thought, you can change to one that raises your energy level. In keeping your energy high, you keep your spirit high also, as well as your connection to it. By having high energy, you attract the same to you also, according to the law of attraction. You raise your energy levels to be what you desire. Like attracts like. You become what you think. Also, be aware of the sounds, music, and food that you surround yourself with. Everything that exists carries a vibration according to its make-up at the level of subatomic particles. As vibrations resonate with each other, you can understand why you want to be surrounded by high energies. Whatever has a high vibration can uplift you to its level. As Oprah says, "The more you focus on words that uplift you, the more you embody the ideas contained in those words."

This is the same for the people in your life. Avoid whatever is toxic for you, including toxic people. Low energy attracts like energy and cuts you off from your authentic self. This can even be in the form of drama where your attention is captured, even momentarily. Avoid drama in your life. It just takes from your energy. Welcome what is uplifting for you. Surround yourself with positivism and positive people. Be aware of the energy levels of those that surround you. You can raise your energy through being in close proximity with those who radiate higher consciousness. Higher energy transmutes lower energy. Aim to be around higher-energy people, places, and events. This will allow your self-limiting thoughts or beliefs to fade away, only to be replaced by your focus on your dream once more. Higher energy brings with it clarity of mind, peace, and harmony. It's when you are in your zone with laser-sharp precision that you come to know the next steps you need take. To keep you in the zone, you can say affirmations daily in reaffirming your intention, in keeping your energy high for actualizing your goal. Your thoughts can be inspired, or they can come from outside of your authentic self. Outside of spirit, your ego dominates. Be conscious of the activities you do and the actions you take. Open your mind to possibility. Impossible is nothing! Possible is all. All is possible. It's all one and the same. Open your mind to your authentic self. That's where everything is possible.

Manifesting Abundance

You can become a magnet for creating abundance in your life by focusing on creating and delivering value to others on a consistent basis. Manifesting is about alignment with the law of attraction and the laws of quantum physics. Alignment with the laws of quantum physics is affected by your thoughts. Positive or negative thoughts attract their vibrational match. What you focus on with intensity and emotion will set the universe in motion to bring that into your life. Conscious and subconscious alignment is also important in manifesting abundance or whatever it is that you want to actualize into your life. Your conscious desire and your subconscious intention must be in alignment for this to happen. If your conscious mind wants one thing and your subconscious mind wants something else then it's impossible to create what you want. This is because of the incongruence between the conscious and the subconscious mind in relation to what you want. Deliberate creating comes about through aligning with your goal automatically, thereby attracting the results you desire. Conflict between your conscious and your subconscious mind can hold you back. Conscious and subconscious agreement means that you design your destiny by choice. Where there is conflict, your limiting beliefs (unconscious) or unexamined negative habits lead to an automatic life by default. Your expectations, even if they are subconscious, lead to your results in life.

You can become aware of your inner critic (which is unconscious) by keeping a journal and writing down your thoughts. In this way you become aware of your self-limiting beliefs and tap into the power of your innate wisdom. This internal critic is not deliberately sabotaging your life. It is a programme set up from your experiences in life, especially the early ones, in order to protect you. It may have served you in the situations in your early life, but now that you are an adult, this old programme actually now holds you back from moving forward. Success does not come about by just setting a goal with intention and emotion. When you use daily positive affirmations to cover a lifetime of negative expectations, this is like putting a Band-Aid over a deep wound. The root cause is merely hidden from view in this way. Therefore, limiting beliefs and negative habitual patterns can still hold you back from creating the life you desire. The wound does not heal in this way. The only way to heal is to go deep into the wound, dig out the root of the pain, and allow healing to occur from the inside out. This means leaving the wound open, trusting, surrendering, and believing it will heal and is healing already. By understanding what caused the wound in the first place – the root cause – true understanding of the self comes about. In this way, the root cause can be released, and so the wound heals automatically.

By uncovering and releasing these unconscious obstacles and habitual patterns, you can become free to take control of your life. You can collapse those self-limiting beliefs and unconscious habitual patterns that stood between you and what you want. Once you are conscious about what is really happening in your life and why you don't have what you want, you are destined to live a life free of fear, doubt, and worry. Instead, you can be happy and live with peace, love, and joy while knowing that you are meant to thrive and not struggle. With peace, love, and joy, you can have unlimited possibility instead of limitation and unfulfilled desires. By allowing things to be as they are, you can be open and receptive. In this way you move through the following stages.

- Unconscious incompetence occurs when your subconscious is not in alignment with your conscious mind and therefore resists the thoughts you get from your conscious mind in relation to what you think you want. At the same time, you do not really know what you want to achieve.

- Conscious incompetence occurs when you know what you want consciously but cannot seem to achieve or actualize what you want. Here there is not enough self-awareness in acknowledging any incongruence within yourself, according to what you want.

- Conscious competence occurs when you start becoming aware that the blockages exist not on the outside, but rather on the inside, of your mind. In gaining self-understanding and insight, you start learning how to overcome the unconscious conditioning and programming in order to unlearn what you have believed up till now. This is when you realize that you have been living in an illusion where your reality may not be as it appears. This is also when you start tapping into your own power and start controlling your life from the inside. By empowering yourself, you can co-create with the universe for all that is in alignment with your true soul purpose in this life.

- Unconscious competence occurs when your conscious and subconscious mind are in alignment with pinpoint precision for whatever you want to achieve in your life. When you consciously co-create with the universe, you are in alignment with what your subconscious wants also. Then you will be guided by the right people, circumstances, and conditions that are in alignment with what you truly desire. You become a magnet for everything you desire, easily and effortlessly. The right people, opportunities, and events happen for you at the right time and in the right place. There is more synchronicity in your life for all the non-accidental "coincidences" that take place. When you are in alignment like this, you are in tune with your authentic self. Your real power lies within your core for drawing to you whatever you desire in life. Trust your subconscious mind. You do not have to go searching or looking for it. It will come to you. Your purpose comes to you. All you need to do is relax, be patient, believe, and expect it to happen at the right time. Once you do this, then just get on with your life and things will happen when you least expect it. That's how synchronicity works. Some say that synchronicity is like a message from God or your higher power.

Choose to be consistent in knowing and acting, while knowing that your subconscious and the laws of quantum physics are at work at all times. By reclaiming your own power, you can choose to be a part of the flow of whatever you desire. Believe in your own power and act on it. You may have set goals before and not achieved them, even though you thought you'd followed the steps properly. The reason for this is that in your subconscious mind, you wanted to avoid failure or disappointment instead of getting what you want. Be willing to release limiting beliefs. Get out of the way of what isn't love, and instead focus on what is love. You get what you are and not what you want.

You always have a choice. You can either avoid losing by playing it safe and living a stressful life, or else you can play to win in the game of life. By doing what you know gives you passion, you will get to experience a life full of joy, abundance, and creating anything you desire, regardless of your current situation. When you do what you love, you love what you do. This is when you never have to "work" ever again. This is the natural state of your authentic self, where everything comes to you effortlessly and easily. Your authentic self is your gateway to source from the physical plane. By becoming conscious of your authenticity, you can vibrate at a higher level of frequency than ever before, as it puts you in the flow of a higher reality. The universe creates those conditions that make this possible for you. Your authentic self is the deepest sense of who you really are. If you build your purpose by identifying your authentic self with what you desire, then you become more expansive in your being. In knowing who you are, you can declare your desire as part of who you are already. Knowing your self affects the way you think, speak, and act in relation to your desire. You know you have it already because it is a part of your very being.

There is a difference between knowing and doing something. All learning and change takes place in the subconscious. The subconscious mind can resist change if it is not convinced that change is possible and safe. As the conscious mind is logical in itself, it is the critical censor and on its own tends to analyse all incoming information. As Karl Jung said, "Until you make the unconscious conscious, it will direct your life and you will call it fate." Permanent and lasting change comes about only when the logical conscious and emotional subconscious minds are in alignment with each other. In this way, they are as one. When you are as one with your authentic self, you understand that you are already perfect as you are. By understanding this, you can always create. The world flows from you and not to you. Even the negative is there for a positive reason. The more you allow things to be, the less you impose your values on the moment. When you can be directly aligned with your experience, then nothing can be unfulfilled in that moment. In this way, you can decide how you want to experience things ahead of time. The more you align in the moment based on love, fulfilment, and joy, the more you understand that things are sent to you based on your desire. It will come to you first as a thought and then become physical. You align yourself with what you desire by saying "I am" with what you desire. You are it already when you identify with what you desire.

In your journey to self-discovery, you are continually moving inwards towards self-understanding and your authentic self. Self-actualization is the state that Maslow represents at the top of his pyramid of human needs. Your purpose in life is to remember who you really are, express your truth, and serve others in alignment with who you are for the greater good of all. What you send out will ultimately return to you. So your purpose is also for your benefit. Treat others as you would like to be treated. Even though you are not giving to receive, this is what happens according to the laws of the universe. Acts of altruism never go unrewarded, but the funny thing is that altruism means giving without expecting anything back in return. When you give in order to receive something back, this does not carry the same energy. The intention you have is where your energy lies. Your energy is the vibration that emanates from the source of your being. Your being lies in your authentic self. Your true power of co-creation with the universe lies in your authentic self. Your authenticity reveals itself through honesty, respect, reciprocity, and expressing your true self. You life force is invested in that moment where you speak your truth. Being authentic with others means not interrupting, suspending judgement, and absorbing what they are communicating. Every little act in the microcosm of your life affects the macrocosm of the cosmos. A human being is a small universe. Even though you may think of yourself as small in relation to the universe, in the spirit dimension there is no space or time. You can have a bigger impact on the universe as a whole than you realize. You are made of the same stuff that the stars and the universe are made of. It is all different forms of the same energy. You are part of all that is. You are in the universe, and the universe is in you. Believe that your purpose "is" already, and it is fulfilled.

At your source is consciousness. Consciousness creates and directs everything. The universe is made up of conscious, living, and intelligent energy that is mind. Mind controls everything in reality. Mind is reality. Reality is mind. The power of your mind creates and influences the reality you live in. For your vision, working on the process instead of the outcome is the key to success. Hold the vision while working on the process. Conflicting truths can exist in harmony when they are viewed as existing at different levels. An enlightened consciousness is inclusive and not exclusive. The more enlightened you are, the more you can perceive the truth about reality. Everything has meaning and can be used as a clue to your chosen destiny, from your highest self and the universe. By understanding reality from a higher level, you have more power to change it. Give and it shall be given unto you. This is the ultimate secret of the universe. By increasing your consciousness, you will create a better reality, which affects others' reality for the better because all is one. The best way to receive God's blessing is to be a blessing through service to others and expect God to bless your works also. True wealth is a communication with others. To manifest wealth, you must begin with living as though you are already wealthy in a way that makes you truly happy. Work on creating and transferring value to others in exchange for value that you desire to receive from them. This path creates an increase in life for everyone together. As Einstein said, "Strive not to be a success, but rather to be of value."

Miracles come from love, are created by love, and are attracted to you through love. When you open your heart to loving yourself and others, life will always be a miracle. The more you are open and loving, the more miracles come your way. This happens when you are willing to receive and give love. A state of love is a state of receptivity to the abundance of the universe. Manifestation comes about through the law of cause and effect and the law of attraction. In creation, a state of being is at cause when one says

"I am" or "I have". This opens a portal to the unified field. When belief is present, whatever words you attach to "I am ..." lead to thinking, speaking, actions, and receiving. When you know it is so, so it is. This gives a signal to the universe to bring about the conditions for manifesting it into form. Through being, you allow the process to flow from your highest self. The universe responds to the frequency you vibrate at. Through being, thinking, and speaking of what you desire, you are compelled to take action in doing whatever it takes in order to receive it. The effect is the outcome of what you have materialized through your being. You create your conditions from your state of being. Happy conditions don't make you happy necessarily. Your state of happiness makes for happy conditions. Likewise, your state of unhappiness makes for unhappy conditions externally. So whatever it is you desire, it is important to be in that state, as though you are or have what you desire already, with conviction. You can state what you desire to experience, as in "I am wealthy." Your internal state of being is a decision. Your internal state of wealth is a decision. Love is a decision. It's not about having things in the outside world. It's about a decision that you make now, when you become it. Your point of power is always now. You don't need anything outside of yourself to make this decision. You can change your life with very little effort in this way.

Once you make a decision to become happy, you become happy. You can only be a state. You can't do a state; nor can you speak a state. The object is to be happy and be in love right now. There are no conditions attached. You can experience unconditional happiness and love right now just by making that decision. When that decision is made, you do not need to redetermine yourself. You experience from internal to external. You act on the external; the external does not act on you. If you are internally happy, then the conditions for happiness must follow. Your vibrational being is the attracting factor. It is the vibratory magnetism of who you are. It's your deepest sense of yourself. When you know who you are at your authentic self level, your depth brings what you desire much quicker than before. Your attraction for what you desire is based on your love of yourself.

Avoid thoughts of self-criticism and those who criticize you. Have solid relationships based on understanding, involvement, and mutual power in which appreciation, commonalities, and acknowledgment are present. In being authentic, you get to think and feel about yourself in the best possible way in relation to respect, sharing, and reciprocity. Through self-acceptance you can be in the moment and feel fulfilled, with your mind at ease and your body at rest. Encourage and live your life in the best possible way. Understand your "I am …" body sensation in creating reality by feeling that corresponding body sensation when manifesting in a relaxed state. By pulling that body sensation into you with your "I am", you can co-create anything that you want at a much faster rate. This is also enhanced when you add emotions of love, joy, or happiness to the equation.

The external is only a reflection of what is on the inside. Once you internalize a state of being, the external must follow suit. You manifest through your body. Desire comes through the heart. When your heart's desire comes about, it is because your heart is much stronger and more powerful than your brain in terms of its magnetic energy. This magnetic field of your heart can be measured up to as far as twelve feet from the body, as shown by Heartmath studies. Research by the Institute of Heartmath (IHM) in California shows that your heart's magnetic field is five thousand times stronger than that of your brain (www.heartmath.org). Heartmath research also demonstrates how your heart's electrical field is sixty times stronger than that of your brain. Both the magnetic field of the heart and the electrical field of the heart can be measured by different electrical devices.

In his article "*The Energetic Heart: Bioelectromagnetic Communication Within and Between People*", scientist, Dr. Rollin McCraty of IHM, states, "The heart is a sensory organ and acts as a sophisticated information encoding and processing centre that enables it to learn, remember and make independent functional decisions." (www.heartmath.org/articlesoftheheart). The heart's electromagnetic field contains a coding, which researchers are trying to understand, that is transmitted throughout and outside of the human body. IHM researchers have also discovered that intentionally generated positive emotions can change this information coding. The article *"Heart-Brain Synchronisation between Mother and Baby"* was published after research by IHM showed that the electromagnetic signals generated by the heart have the capacity to affect others around us. In this study, researchers found that when a mother focused her attention on her baby that was lying in her lap, she became more sensitive to the electromagnetic field of the baby's heart. This was demonstrated as the mother's brainwaves synchronised with the baby's heartbeat! This research is ongoing and it has fascinating implications for our understanding of the power of the human heart.

Emotion is linked with your heart centre, which is the seat of your soul. You are more likely to manifest that which you desire with emotion, rather than by pure thought. By increasing the intensity of emotion with your desire, you increase the power of the intention in the universal field. The only thing that separates you from your desire is your resistance to it. All emotions are in the moment and are by choice. You can accept and let emotion flow fully into its full expression, like water in a river that comes and goes. Otherwise, you can resist or suppress it. When you do this, you can become entangled with the emotion and lose presence in the process. This is because the un-released emotion becomes entangled within you. Emotions can be released only in the moment, in any moment of now. Unexpressed emotions lead to emotional blockages that can keep you from what you desire. By holding on to emotions, you are holding yourself back. So in order to manifest or create what you want, you need to clear yourself of emotional baggage. This means that just by being objective to the baggage, you can observe it as if from a distance. It doesn't belong to you if you are viewing it from a distance. When you do this, you're getting out of your own way.

When observing your emotions in this way, do not try to block what is currently happening. You do not get to experience what you want to man-ifest when there are blockages. If your energy is blocked, this affects your current experience because of the old energy that is stored in your body. If any emotion is denied or refused expression, then it is stored in the body as a blockage until it is welcomed, accepted, and embraced. By staying neutral, your silent witness can see and stay with the "what is." In accepting what is, there is no resistance. As a result, your unwanted emotions fall away, as they have served their purpose. See the divine within, as in all of life. You can help to clear your energy blockages by correcting your perception of the outside world, since the blockages were formed by a misperception in the first place. What you may see as a problem is just your perception of it.

What if there really is no problem? If you're not experiencing what you want, don't judge or create limiting conclusions. Instead, accept what you're experiencing, as this leads to a new vibratory experience of being okay. By allowing your emotion to come into the moment, you allow yourself to be free by being non-intrusive. You let your emotions pass through you as they are meant to. Once cleared of negative emotions, you can then consciously choose what emotion you want to use in co-creating with the universe. Clarity of mind brings about pure expression of what you intend into the physical world. Now you can tap into the energy field of total fulfilment, where you can manifest what you desire. All energy is meant to flow. The whole universe is made up of flowing energy. Being in the flow in terms of what you attract to yourself comes from corresponding energy flow in your body. When you feel something to be the case, as in "I am wealthy", then this is what you become in the moment. Being wealthy is the person you become. Being wealthy is an inner job. Everything that you are has a feeling of being that already. So just feel what you would like to become now, and it is yours already. Believe it with your whole heart to be so, and so it is. Integrate your desire into your very being. In this way, you become what you desire.

There is nothing wrong with having nice things, as these make life more comfortable for you. When you have what you desire, you are living your soul purpose and helping others in the process. Who you are and how you are in the world affects all of life by the actualities of your daily practise, in a resonant effect with others. The universe is more likely to assist you in creating what you desire when it benefits others also. By giving what you know, you walk your talk. Your interconnection with everything means you are "inner connected" with all things in the universe. When you cannot manifest your dream or desire, it is because you are disconnected from your source in the field of intention. This disconnection leads to suffering, because you know you are living a life different to what feels right.

What you do is what you are and who you are. See the beauty around you and become one with it. You are meant to live a life of joy, peace, and abundance, ever expanding and evolving. Celebrate your very perspective of life. When you love yourself, you draw loving things to you. You don't need to seek love. By giving love you receive the same in kind. You can be a magnet for your desires by feeling and giving appreciation in the moment. Being present brings fulfilment. Also, your sheer desire, unwavering belief, and total expectancy fuel your energy for manifesting what you want into reality. Recall a time when you had that sheer desire, belief, and expectancy to get in that state of mind now. Make the goal believable, and have the big goal in the back of your mind. Imagine believable goal steps towards it. Be congruent with your desire and accept the outcome you want or something better. You can actively meditate to create an internal focus with a deliberate purpose in mind in a very conscious manner. This can be achieved through self-hypnosis or listening to meditation CDs. Your experience of reality comes from your subjective physicality and your spiritual nature as a human being. In the creation process, you can access information from your subjective body and its surroundings, while you can be inspired from the source of your being, which is your authentic self. Quantum actualization is your ability to manifest from your alignment with your authentic self. In self-realization, your connection with your true self is the key to co-creation with the universe. When you are true to your self, your life flows according to your desires with ease and grace. In mastering who you are, you master the art of manifesting with the universe also. This is because you know that you and the universe are the same in the oneness of everything.

When you are at one with your intention, you think and speak of it in allowing it to become what you desire. When you are compelled to act on your dream after it starts to come into your conversation, the momentum has begun. You actively participate in the creation process through action and receiving. By having a positive attitude towards what you want, you increase your vibration of yourself and your embracement of all that is in the world. When you experience it in a way that pleases you, then that feeling is yours. It will start to come to you. You no longer have to do anything else. By being congruent with your emotions in mind, body, and spirit, this leads to the flow that makes it all happen. When you understand the way of allowing the flow to happen, you can step into the ease and effortlessness of manifesting your desire. Now you know that it is you, by becoming one with it. Therefore, it is only natural for you to have it. You don't have to keep redefining you for it to come about. Just become it. You don't have to keep trying to get it. By clearing your blockages, you come to know that you deserve everything. Nothing is denied to you. The universe is abundant. You have it already. To create is to pay attention to the abundance of what you want. The more you become familiar with it, the more it comes to you. The true state of anything is abundance and pure love. The more you love yourself and others, the easier everything becomes, including manifesting.

Exercise: Creative Visualization

Creative visualization is a simple technique that can be used to add juice to the manifesting process. First, get into a relaxed, peaceful state and make a statement beginning with "I am …" or "I have …" Create an image inside of your mind of what you desire to manifest. Create as much detail as possible and make it compelling. Make it bright and colourful. See yourself in the image as if looking from your own eyes. Feel the sensation in your body of what it is like to be in the image. See what you see, hear what you hear, feel what you feel. You can use taste and smell as well. Hold that body sensation along with the image. Your image is a part of you on the inside. Feel the intensity of love, joy, excitement, and eagerness incorporated into your desire. Examine it more and more. Bring it closer to you until it's inside your body. Draw it into your body so that it integrates with your own vibration of being. Then allow it to come to you, and it will, or something better. Be willing to receive and accept whatever it is with gratitude. Gratitude opens your heart to receive more of the same.

Your imagination can create anything you desire. Your belief and clear energy channels keep the emotions flowing towards what you desire. Your belief can also keep your desire from you if it is self-defeating. Through knowing who you are and where your beliefs come from, you can accept and express your truth and live authentically. Your highest self pushes blockages to the surface at times, in order to be released and cleared in resolving them. If you ignore or deny these blockages, they become repressed once more, only to surface again another time. Every experience brings thought and emotion. When you can feel an emotion with full awareness, the lesson is learned, thus leading to the flow of manifesting power. When belief and emotion are on your side, there is nothing between you and what you desire. Feelings and beliefs lie in the subconscious, whereas analytical thinking resides in the conscious mind. What you analyse, you paralyse. What you believe and feel, you create into your reality. By visualizing the evidence of your heart's desire in a photo or a film reel, you can detach from it by seeing yourself in the photo. This is proof of your end result. It exists now because your mind can see it now. That is all you need to know. It is already!

CHAPTER 7

RETRAINING YOUR BRAIN

As you know, everything in physical reality is made up of atoms, including the brain. Every atom comprises a nucleus with one or more electrons spinning around it. If you can imagine the nucleus increased to the size of a grape, then the electrons would be the size of mustard seeds. At this size, the distance between the grape and the seeds would be two miles. The atom is 99.9999 per cent space! This is a scientific fact. How you perceive reality is an illusion created by your five senses. So the solidity you see in physical objects is not as it seems in reality. The true nature of reality is referred to as a hologram, and this includes your brain. The universe is holographic. What this means is that what exists in particular also exists in the whole. Your brain and cells are holograms for what already exists in the entire universe. The one is in the whole picture, and the whole is in the one. Therefore, the universe exists in you also. Hence, it is known as the holographic universe.

Scientists used to believe that the space in an atom was empty, but now they know differently. The current thinking is that within this space in the atom lies infinite intelligence and energy that exist in the universe itself. What appears to be physical is, in reality, mostly space, as shown by quantum physics. How could this be? The paradox is that everything feels so solid. The answer lies in the limits of your five senses, beliefs, and expectations. Quantum physics now proves that what you expect affects the physical result of what you observe in reality. What you expect in life affects your perception of reality. You can only experience that which you are open to experience within the realm of your beliefs. Does this mean that you can change your experience by changing your expectations and beliefs? Absolutely! Your logical mind, which involves left-brain thinking, is programmed to predict events in a linear, sequential manner. In the right brain, your creative mind sees the multidimensional big picture in any one instant, where infinite possibilities exist in any moment. Your right brain allows for expansion outwards and is the centre of your intuition. Also, your right brain holds your beliefs and memories of all previous experiences since birth. Your perception of your experience affects how you expect things to be. In this way, you filter what you allow into your experience of life.

What has this to do with your brain? It is now known that your brain is neuroplastic. Neuroplasticity means that your brain structure, neurological networks, and brain cells themselves can change over time. What determines these changes are your thoughts, beliefs, and feelings on an ongoing basis. How is the nature of your mind related to your brain in this way? Your mind can use your brain for its purpose or intentions (even though some people may think that the brain controls the mind). Your brain is essentially a tool you use to carry out your tasks in life. The old way of thinking in science was that your brain remains unchanging once you reach maturity and that, in fact, you lose brain cells as you get older. Now current science has evidence to show that your brain makes new cells all the time and that it can become fine-tuned depending on what you focus on. This actually means that you can tune, mould, and shape your brain and its networks based on your specific thoughts, feelings, and emotions.

Whenever you create a new habit, new brain cells form in a neural network inside the brain with repetition of that habit. After about three weeks, the network is usually complete and ingrained in the physical brain. A habit becomes normal and easier to do after three weeks, because of the brain's plasticity in this way. When the habit's neural network is formed in the brain, the habit itself becomes automatic and can be performed without conscious thought. A belief is a habit that also and has its own associated neural network in the brain. According to Dr. David R.Hamilton, "Everything you see, hear, touch, taste and smell changes your brain and every thought causes microscopic changes in its structure. In a sense, thoughts leave physical traces in the brain in much the same way as we leave footsteps in the sand. As you think, millions of brain cells (neurones) reach out and connect with each other, moulding the actual substance of the brain just as an artist moulds her clay" (Hamilton, 2008: 43). Hamilton has researched numerous brain studies that demonstrate the neuroplastic nature of the brain. Hamilton describes the map of the brain just like a network of roads that link towns. According to him, certain "towns" of the brain map can expand, depending on the neural network that is being laid down. "For instance, if you used your right hand for a few hours without using your left, the "map" for your right hand would expand as several new roads (neural connections) were forged in it. In this way, as we go through life our brain maps are in a continual state of expansion and contraction." (Hamilton, 2008: 43).

The brain is essentially a tool that can be sharpened by you to perform better in any area you choose, whether it is memory, concentration, performing a skill, changing beliefs, or even carrying out your life's purpose. Your intention becomes realized in your body's actions when your mind acts on your brain. In research, brain activity cannot explain how one thinks, reasons, or makes decisions. No evidence has been found by neuroscientists to show that mental states, such as thoughts, intentions, or beliefs, are actual neurological processes of the brain. The view is that your mind acts on the brain to bring about neurological activity. Also, with this neurological activity, new neural networks of brain cells are being formed when there are new intentions or beliefs. Your mind is a continuing essence, or medium, which develops during your life, continually evolving and growing. Your mind is a form of energy, which can be understood through advancements in the nature of energy in physics (quantum physics).

To explain further, lightning and an electrical discharge refer to the same thing. While you can perceive lightning through the senses, you cannot perceive electrical discharges, even though they exist. In the synapse between each brain cell (neuron), there is a gap. When a message goes from one neuron to another, there is a "spark" in the gap that carries this message across. How can energy flow from the non-physical to the physical body? Our conception of energy is that it is invisible, yet quantum physics shows that energy can transform itself into either wave or particle quanta (quantities). In short, this energy, just like your mind and body, shares wave and particle characteristics, but it does not share the same rules of time and space as we know them. This energy can act as a wave or particle depending on the situation. The power source of your mind is the driving force that operates at a level beyond that of your five senses. Decisions and intentions of the mind cause behaviour, which is the end result. The mind can be thought of as the use of the brain to channel energies in achieving its intention or will. Our physical senses can never perceive, in this sense, the mind as it is.

Quantum physics has shown us that discrete units of energy can penetrate a physical object in either a wave or particle form and that these forms can change from one to the other in an experiment; hence the term "quantum leap". Perhaps, by analogy, radiation of energy is the link between the mind and the brain in terms of physics of the soul. What radiates comes from within and, therefore, cannot be viewed from the outside until it is expressed. By expressing your authentic self, you are expressing your energy vibration from the very source of your being into the world. It is this expression of who you really are that shapes and moulds you according to your growth. Your spiritual growth and new learning, in this way, even leads to the evolvement of your brain in an ever-changing fashion, as shown by science.

With new insights, you learn to see things in a new way that opens up more choice and possibility for you in life. As your brain is moulded by your experiences under your direction, you learn to program yourself for what you want to achieve in life. When you get to know more about the nature of quantum physics and energy, similarly, you may learn more about the nature of your soul (mind) existing in relation to your body. In this way, both science and spirituality can work together in aiding you to reach the goal of finding the link between your mind and your body (via your brain).

By understanding the world as it is through only our five senses, we are led to the material illusion of our reality. Our illusion serves us, however, in our daily living. Einstein claims that results of observation depend on the realm we live in, in terms of the methods used. Understanding the truth between the mind and brain depends on your realm of awareness. When you change your focus and viewpoint from looking out to looking in, beyond time and space, you begin to discover a whole new world and ways of looking at things. This starts happening when you tune in with your authentic self at the core of your being. As you do this, your inner focus becomes incorporated into your physical being via your brain, which is your tool for success. You can achieve anything in life just by changing your focus and point of view.

There are about two billion bits of information coming at you every second. If you took in all this information in one go, you would not be able to function normally, according to your present brain. Your filtering system for what you process in the outside world is situated in your reticular activating system (RAS), which lies at the base of your brain. This is the oldest part of your brain and it is known as the "reptilian brain". Your filtering of information is affected by your values, attitudes, memories, beliefs, and concept of time and space. In actuality, you allow only about 146 bits of information into your experience per second. Your internal representations of this information affect your perception of the experience itself. This means that you represent the information to yourself in terms of meaning. All meaning is context related. Also, your learning style affects your perception of the information processed. You learn principally through one of the following processes: seeing, feeling, hearing, smelling, tasting, or by speaking to yourself. How you represent the world to yourself comes through your five senses. You make sense of it according to your filters and primary form of learning. In all your experiences you will use a mix of visual, kinaesthetic, and auditory processing, but the level of each will vary from person to person. What does your brain have to do with all this? Well, the answer lies in you having more choice in your life when you know how you can influence the function of your own brain. This is achieved through retraining your brain, which is in fact a tool designed to get you what you want. It is well known from current brain research that the brain itself is neuroplastic. This means that the brain is moulded and shaped by your experiences, and this includes your own thoughts and feelings. Every thought you have has a simultaneous effect on your brain. The more you think the same thought, the deeper the "groove" becomes in the physical network of brain cells related to that thought. When the groove gets deep enough, that thought is firmly established within the brain itself, and it becomes automatic. In other words, it becomes a habit that actually affects your behaviour. This usually happens subconsciously without conscious awareness.

Have you ever noticed how a lot of your daily thoughts recur from day to day? When you become aware of your inner voice, you realize what you have been telling yourself for so long. A lot of what you have been telling yourself is habit, and this includes your beliefs. The same thought repeated over and over again eventually becomes reinforced, leading to a belief. This belief is the programming that automatically affects your behaviour subconsciously when you are on autopilot. You can reverse this pattern, though, to create different results in your life, starting from the inside out. By changing your beliefs, you can automatically change your thoughts and your experience of life. It is possible to change your beliefs. This is achieved by consciously deciding first what you want to believe in for creating a better life for yourself. Then you just program your mind with the beliefs you want. Your brain is the hardware of the computer mind. What you program into your brain is the software that you choose from your free will selection. You can program your mind by using self-hypnosis audio, meditation audio, subliminal message audio, brainwave entrainment audio, or guided positive affirmations in a deeply relaxed state.

Once your brain becomes hard-wired with what you want, you have created the physical aspect of your brain cells that make your programming automatic. The more you program yourself for a single belief, the more it becomes hard-wired. The more a belief becomes hard-wired into your brain, the more the opposing belief you may have had begins to fall away. When you want to replace a self-defeating belief with an empowering belief, then you take your focus off the former. When you do this, the self-defeating belief loses its hold over you as it continues to fall away over time. While this is happening, the limiting belief's physical counterpart in the brain also falls away at the same time. In other words, you lose those brain cells associated with the old belief when you pay no attention to it. Now you know you can focus on wiring your brain in ways that serve your highest good. The Solfeggio harmonics is one example of this.

The Solfeggio Harmonic Frequencies

Solfeggio is an ancient sacred music scale that was included in ancient Gregorian chants and ancient music. This scale is known to be in harmony with how the human body works. Solfeggio resonates with the same frequency as the body on a number of different levels. The Solfeggio scale can be traced back to a medieval hymn to John the Baptist. The first six lines of the hymn start with the first six notes of the scale. Therefore, the first syllable of each line was sung to a note one degree higher than the first syllable of the line that preceded it. In this way, the music had mathematical resonance, and it is said to inspire mankind to be more "Godkind." The hymn to John the Baptist translates as "In order that the slaves might resonate (resound) the miracle (wonders) of your creations with loosened (expanded) vocal cords. Wash the guilt from (our) polluted lips." It is known that the Solfeggio harmonics were originally decoded from the Bible, where they were found in an encoded form. They had been there for over three thousand years!

Ancient musical instruments that have been excavated have been found to be tuned according to a Solfeggio frequency, 432 hertz. The frequency of 432 hertz resonates inside the human body, where it releases emotional blockages and expands consciousness. In the process of listening, you become tuned or attuned as you gain access to the knowledge of the universe around you in a more intuitive way. You become one with the universe as you resonate with the same vibration. The more you listen to this music, the more your energy and vibration are calibrated to coincide with that of the universal realm. Music played on instruments tuned to 432 hertz brings peace and well-being to you.

Musical instruments that are tuned to 440 hertz are disharmonic to the human body. The frequency of 440 hertz causes stress, negative behaviours, and unstable emotions. Interestingly enough, most musical instruments are tuned to 440 hertz nowadays. In fact, laws were passed to standardize the tuning of musical instruments in Great Britain to 440 hertz in the 1950s. Why is this so, and what is the benefit? Think about it. Who benefits when people are stressed out and have unstable emotions? Do these stressed people feel empowered and in control of their lives? Do they feel powerful enough to make the changes they need in their lives? What do you think? Are they easier to control by the powers that be? Similarly, the 440 hertz tuning scale has been standardized in music in America as well. Interesting, eh? By changing the notes, humanity's well-being and increased levels of thinking were subdued and suppressed. These changes in thinking also affected conceptual thought in how we give meaning to things. A higher level of thinking has its connection with source that lies within – an "inner authority", so to speak. Any perceived authority on the outside has meaning only in terms of your perception of it. When you look to the outside for answers, you are at effect.

In reality, you are your own authority and so it is natural for you to be at cause in your life. When you use them regularly, the Solfeggio frequencies will help you to harmonize once more with your own power and guidance from within at source. These are called the sacred frequencies because they bring you home to your sacred self within once more. At this source, you get to experience your authentic self at your core as you fully remember who you are in reality. When you do, you cannot be controlled from the outside any more. Have you ever heard of the Mozart effect? Mozart's music is said to exponentially increase your brain's capacity for functioning. His music was tuned to 432 hertz! Mozart did not follow the crowd. Vivaldi's music was also tuned to 432 hertz, as was Bach's and Beethoven's. Most other musicians of the time tuned their music to 440 hertz because they conformed with the system.

What has all this got to do with the human brain? Well, music emits vibrations of various frequencies. When these frequencies are in the environment of a human being, depending on the frequency, they can directly affect the physical and genetic make-up of an individual. Frequencies and vibrations can pass through the human body. Electro-magnetic waves and thoughts are included in these frequencies and vibrations. Dr. Bruce H. Lipton, PhD, a renowned cell biologist, claims that the biochemical effects of the brain's functioning show that all the cells of your body are affected by your thoughts. In his book, *The Biology of Belief,* Lipton describes the precise molecular pathways through which this occurs. Using simple language, he describes how the new science of Epigenetics is revolutionizing our understanding of the link between mind and matter and the profound effects it has on our personal lives and the collective life of our species. According to Lipton, "cells possess a uniquely "tuned" receptor protein for every environmental signal that needs to be read." He describes how some receptors respond to physical signals from the environment. Interestingly, Lipton also describes how "receptor antennas can also read vibrational energy fields such as light, sound and radio frequencies. The antennas on these "energy" receptors vibrate like tuning forks. If an energy's vibration in the environment resonates with a receptor's antenna, it will alter the protein's charge, causing the receptor to change shape." (Lipton, 2005: 53). Lipton's research shows how cell receptors can read energy fields and because of this, the previous scientific belief that only physical molecules can impact cell physiology is outmoded, according to him. "Biological behaviour can be controlled by invisible forces, including thought, as well as it can be controlled by physical molecules like penicillin, a fact that provides the scientific underpinning for pharmaceutical-free energy medicine." (Lipton, 2005: 53).

From studies done on the heart by Heartmath (www.heartmath.org), it has been shown that there are about forty thousand cells that resemble brain cells. These cells can have memory and experience, independent of your brain. They can function independent of any connection with your brain. In a human embryo, it is the heart that forms first, before the brain. The human heart, as previously mentioned, has been found by scientific studies to have a magnetic field five thousand times stronger than that of the brain. The planet earth itself also emits an electromagnetic signal or vibration of 7.8 hertz from its core that can be measured by instruments. The frequency 7.8 hertz is the fundamental beat of the "h-earth" of the planet, and this is called the Schumann Resonance. The earth – or Gaia, as it is known – has this heartbeat of 7.8 hertz. This heartbeat, or the Schumann Resonance, is the earth's electromagnetic resonance or pulse of vibration.

Data was obtained to this effect from the Global Coherence Monitoring System in Boulder Creek, California, at the Institute of Heartmath Research Centre. Radiation from the sun ionizes part of the earth's atmosphere and forms a conductive plasma layer, the ionosphere. The ionosphere surrounding our planet is positively charged while the earth's surface is negatively charged. This creates an electrical tension within the space between the earth's surface and the ionosphere called the "Schumann effect". It has been noted by scientists how the Schumann resonance is similar to that of the human brain. "A new field of interest, measuring earth's magnetic fields, is related to short-term earthquake predictions. Schumann resonances also have gone beyond the boundaries of physics, into medicine, where it has raised interest in the interactions between planetary rhythms and human health and behaviour" (for more detail, see www.glcoherence.org/monitoring-system/commentaries July 7, 2009). Many studies at Halberg Chronobiology Centre at the University of Minnesota have shown that there are important links between solar, Schumann and geomagnetic rhythms and a wide range of human and animal health and wellness indicators.

During hypnosis or meditation, your brainwaves slow down from the beta state (14 to 21 hertz) to the alpha state (8 to 13 hertz) before dropping down to the theta state (4 to 7 hertz). In the deep theta-wave state that resonates with Gaia's heartbeat (7.8 hertz), the two hemispheres of your brain become synchronized to function as a whole. When this happens, you have whole-brain thinking, where your brain works infinitely better than normal and experiences a greater flow of information. At this level of brain functioning, solutions to problems can be accessed readily and creativity is at its highest. The frequency of 8 hertz can activate the full and overall activation potential of your brain. The 8 hertz frequency is also the frequency of the double helix in DNA replication. At this level of awareness, DNA can actually repair and regenerate itself. During this state, you are deeply relaxed and fully aware at the same time, when you are in hypnosis or meditating.

You also enter the theta state every night when you have good-quality, restful sleep. In the morning, as a result of your deep sleep, you feel refreshed, relaxed and recharged, ready for a new day as you jump out of bed. During the theta state (4 to 7 hertz), you experience an inner bliss and peace deep within, where you feel disconnected from your physical body. In the theta state, you may feel like you are floating in quantum space also. Theta state occurs before you drop deeper into actual sleep at 4 hertz or below. Sleep in the delta state is between 0.5 hertz and 4 hertz. Sleep in the delta state never drops below 0.5 hertz normally.

At 8 hertz, the hormones melatonin and pinoline are produced in the brain, and these enable DNA replication in the body. At different frequencies, different hormones are produced in the body according to the level of the vibration. Hormones control the organs in the body. So it follows that by using beneficial frequencies, such as the Sofeggio frequencies, your body's functioning benefits also, as does your general state of being. As a result, you have well-being within yourself and in the world. You can activate your full potential at an accelerated rate by tapping into the power of these Solfeggio frequencies. This includes your brainpower. Using these frequencies can sharpen your brain to make it a fine tool that can do a lot more than you think. You become sharper in your thinking and behaviour, as your intuition increases at the same time when you develop your heart–brain connection. So what are these Solfeggio frequencies? These frequencies are waves of potential that can activate physical manifestation of their effects in the human body. What are the effects of these Solfeggio frequencies in the human body? It is said that the Solfeggio harmonics heal the body, mind, and soul. The following are six of the main frequencies and the areas of their effects (even though there are more frequencies):

1. Ut: 396 hertz – liberating guilt and fear
2. Re: 417 hertz – undoing situations and facilitating change
3. Mi: 528 hertz – transformation and "miracles" (DNA repair)
4. Fa: 639 hertz – relationships and connecting with your spiritual family
5. Sol: 741 hertz – expression, solutions, clearing, and solving
6. La: 852 hertz – returning to spiritual order

It is said that the famous Tibetan bowls resonate at 528 hertz, the frequency of love. Also, you can get tuning forks, each in one of the six different frequencies. Some kinesiologists use these tuning forks to bring about balance in the human body. These tuning forks can also be targeted at certain organ areas in the body depending on the frequency used. You can also listen to Solfeggio frequencies that play in the background of music. You will notice their effects on your life when it changes automatically, as does your behaviour.

Current research has also shown that in the last few years, the Shumann resonance of the earth has moved up from 7.8 to 13 hertz! 13 hertz has become the new baseline for this resonance. What are the implications of this on the human brain? Current measurements of the Schumann resonance by scientists show spikes of up to 50 hertz daily, from the baseline of 13 hertz. This was not the case before the last few years. In the past, the norm of the earth's resonance was 7.8 hertz. The frequencies in your environment have a pivotal role to play in how you are and how you act in the world. Frequencies in your environment affect your biology and how your brain works, according to Bruce Lipton. By listening to the Solfeggio frequencies, you learn to lose fear and guilt automatically without effort as you move easily to expressing your true self. You become more your self in the process. As you become more balanced and harmonized within your being and body, you realize that you are living your life with more authenticity. The result is increased self-confidence and more trust in your self. You believe anything is possible as you start seeing the world through what and who you are in reality.

At the ordinary level of thinking, the waves of the human brain lie between 14 and 40 hertz. This beta state involves only certain types of nerve endings belonging to brain cells mainly within the left hemisphere of the brain. The left side is the logical side, which focuses on problems to be solved and the analysis of situations. In the beta state, the main activity is in the left brain. If your brainwaves are moving from 14 hertz upwards, the higher they go, the more stressed you can become. The slower your brainwaves go below fourteen hertz, the more relaxed you feel. It is known from research that meditation is one of the most effective methods for reducing stress and also increasing well-being because it helps you to produce more alpha and theta brainwaves. Studies have shown that those who meditate regularly spend more time in the alpha state, which leads to more creativity. People who are stressed tend to have more beta activity in their brain, which can lead to depression, anxiety, or stress-related diseases. Brainwave audio technology allows you to reach deep meditative states much more quickly than when using traditional meditation on its own. The more you go into trance, the deeper and quicker you go each time. Brainwave entrainment (BWE) can be achieved by putting on headphones connected to your mp3 player, smart phone, or pc and listening to specialized audio.

When you are in the alpha state, any mantras, intentions, or positive affirmations you say can go into the subconscious mind much more easily. This is because your conscious mind is more relaxed than when you are in the beta wave state. By repeating these mantras, you can reprogram any wired negative beliefs that hold you back from your desires. Usually there is a voice to guide you while the music plays with the BWE audio in the background. Currently, there is a lot of brain research being carried out, and new findings are being discovered all the time. Recent findings have shown just how much the different frequencies and vibrations can impact on the brain's functioning. Scientific research also shows that the brain constantly changes over time in an ongoing fashion, depending on your thoughts, beliefs, and emotions. In this way, the brain is called "neuroplastic", as its neural networks are formed on a continual basis based on your habits, beliefs, thoughts, and emotional experiences in life. When a habit or belief is reinforced continually, this keeps the associated brain neural network intact. When a habit is discontinued, the brain network linked with it just falls away. Similarly, a new habit brings a new physical structure into place in the brain via a new network that is formed. Beliefs can be changed. Habits can be changed. New habits can be created. All of these have different physical implications for the brain. BWE can accelerate changes in your brain and, therefore, in your life.

What is Brainwave (BWE) Entrainment?

Brainwave entrainment involves changing the frequency of your brainwaves deliberately. Its beneficial effects are now being recognized in the scientific field, from research and studies carried out. Binaural beats involve two different frequency tones being played at the same time that cause your brain to entrain to a different brainwave frequency. You can actually change your brainwaves in order to optimize your brain and body's functioning more efficiently. When used regularly, brainwave entrainment brings changes in your brain's wiring and circuitry. Rewiring your brain in this way affects how it functions as a whole. Entrainment of the brain is made possible over time by listening to specific brainwave entrainment audio programs, binaural beats, or any other brain-altering frequencies. The more you practise training your brain, the better the results.

Whatever you do to train your brain, know that you can entrain it to give you what you want. When you want to move from a state of feeling stressed to a state of feeling relaxed, you can play the frequency that induces alpha brainwaves. New information is more readily received into your subconscious when you are using BWE. This new information, in the form of positive suggestions, once received, becomes part of your programming by choice. Using this technology, it is much easier to reprogram your own beliefs and way of being in the world. While listening to the binaural beats, you can watch positive images or use positive affirmations at the same time to magnify the effects. With the entrainment of alpha or theta brainwaves, these positive images and affirmations are more readily received into your subconscious mind. Therefore, it is possible to programme positive images and affirmations into your subconscious using brainwave entrainment in this way. This is because your conscious mind is not on alert when it is in its safe place, and so your mind's defences are relaxed. Brainwave entrainment changes how you operate from within in many ways. In optimizing your brain, you are optimizing your life.

Your brain weighs about three pounds and is made up of billions of nerve cells. There are more neural networks in the brain than there are telephone wires in the world! Brains are electro-chemical organs made up of billions of neurons (nerve cells). These neurons communicate with each other by means of electrical signals that cross between the gap (synapse) of the neurons involved. An electroencephalogram (EEG) machine can detect this brain activity in the form of brainwaves. There are five types of brainwaves that represent five types of states:

Gamma (22 to 38 hertz): Gamma waves are present during high-activity behaviours that require concentrated effort. An example would be when an athlete is competing in a marathon. Buddhist monks have been known to meditate with gamma brainwaves present. While they meditate, their awareness is concentrated with pinpoint focus. Gamma waves are relatively new on the scene in terms of being discovered and studied.

Beta (14 to 21 hertz): Beta brainwaves are present when you are wide awake or when you are engaged in mental activity linked with the left hemisphere of the brain. The left brain deals with rationality and is reality-based in terms of its analytical and logical approach. In the beta state, you are goal-orientated, with an increased focus and ability to think quickly. You perform at your peak when you are in the beta state. The beta state enables socialization with others also. If the beta wave becomes intense, the brainwave speeds up and you begin to feel stressed. As a result, the left and right brain become less synchronized in their function. In this case, you have left-sided thinking and so are cut off from the creativity and imagination of your right-brain hemisphere. The saying "What you analyse, you paralyse" is quite true. In analysing, you become focused on the problem instead of the solution. The right brain allows you to see the whole picture, while the left brain deals with specifics.

Alpha (8 to 13 hertz): This lower frequency of brainwaves leads to a relaxed state in which you are not engaged in focused mental problem-solving or task-executing activity. When you daydream in the alpha state, you can still carry out routine tasks, such as taking a shower. At the beginning of any meditation, you enter the alpha state first, before going deeper. Similarly, you experience the alpha state before going to and waking up from sleep every day. In the alpha state, your thoughts are not concentrated and wander freely. Relaxing activities can induce the alpha state. The alpha state enables relaxation of the body and mind. In this state of relaxation, your immune system also becomes strengthened. The alpha state itself increases receptivity to suggestions made, as beta activity with its reality-checking focus is not present. Alpha waves strengthen creativity and creative visualization, as the left and right brain hemispheres become naturally synchronized with each other. Whole-brain thinking enables super learning in turn, as information is readily processed and integrated into your understanding spontaneously in the alpha state.

Theta (4 to 7 hertz): This lower frequency induces deeper relaxation into a trance-like state that may feel like sleep but is not sleep. Daydreaming or meditation can lead into this state, where you may lose track of time. What may feel like five minutes is actually twenty minutes in this state. In theta, you get to experience an inner deep state of being in serenity and deep peace, where you become aligned with your spiritual connection. Your visualization and creativity are increased even more, as your mind is very relaxed, and your receptivity to suggestion is increased also. The theta state lowers any anxiety, stress, or neurosis, as you experience deep relaxation and well-being in this state. Whole-brain synchronization that occurs means you have whole-brain thinking. Therefore, your brainpower in the theta state is increased significantly. Solutions to previous problems may just automatically show up in this state without any effort, due to your advanced problem-solving skills in theta. The theta state occurs in sleep when you are dreaming and you get rapid eye movement (REM). Theta waves are important during sleep cycles for you to process information that has not been laid down in memory yet. As in a computer, information cannot be stored unless it is processed first. It is the same with your brain. Information that is not processed becomes free-floating and can show up in your feelings, dreams, daydreams, and even flashbacks. Now you can see that the theta state allows you to empty your mind of clutter, as healing of the body and mind takes place naturally during this state. A clear mind has the ability to learn more and process quickly, leaving you ready for a new day.

Delta (0.5 to 4 hertz): This is the slowest brainwave that occurs in deep dreamless sleep, and so it is the deepest state of relaxation. In this state, your body recharges by restoring and healing itself. The delta state is an advanced state of healing of the body and mind, as your immune system becomes highly enhanced during it. In this state of extreme bliss, you get to experience perfect intuition because your connection with your subconscious is at its highest. Your level of connection with your subconscious in delta means you also experience a high state of empathy. During delta, anti-ageing hormones are produced in your brain. This is why you look so good after a good night's sleep. If your sleep is not of a good quality, you may not be experiencing enough delta waves during the night and so you wake up tired. Good quality sleep leaves you revitalized and replenished when you wake up the next morning.

How does BWE work?

BWE tunes your brainwave frequencies in order to achieve specific states. Specific brain rhythms are associated with specific emotional and cognitive functions in the brain. For example, at ten cycles per second (hertz), the hormone serotonin is produced in the brain, which induces well-being. BWE works by bathing the brain in specific frequencies to get a specific outcome each time. When the brain hears those frequencies, it adjusts its own frequencies to entrain and match with those coming from the outside. This brain entrainment happens only at certain specific frequencies. The effects of the frequencies used in BWE have been researched extensively, which is why it can be used to get a specific outcome each time. The benefits of BWE include increased whole-brain thinking; increased verbal skills; increased memory; stabilization of emotions; raised mood; regulation of sleep cycle; release of beneficial brain chemicals, such as DHEA and serotonin; and laying down of new neural paths and growth of nerve cells, leading to increased brainpower.

With long-term use of BWE, your brain develops increased processing speed as you increase your level of brainpower from whole-brain thinking. Your higher mental ability means you have increased creativity and innovation for new ideas. The hormone DHEA reduces the effects of ageing and is said to actually reverse ageing. It also reverses the effects of the stress hormone cortisol. With increased blood flow to the brain, your perception and awareness are also increased as a result of an increase in the number of neural pathways. Therefore, your ability to recognize opportunities increases also. Over time, BWE enhances your mental and emotional state of being also, as a result of the increased supply of beneficial brain chemicals (neurotransmitters) that bathe your brain. At the same time, fewer non-beneficial brain chemicals are produced, owing to BWE, and so their effects are decreased. Subliminal messages (SBM) also change your beliefs and brain functioning by directly accessing your subconscious mind through bypassing the conscious mind. The difference is that SBM does not involve changing the brainwaves.

What are Subliminal Messages (SBM)?

Subliminal messages are not audible to the conscious mind and so go directly into the subconscious mind. What you may hear in SBM audio is usually just music. Your conscious mind cannot hear the subliminal messages voiced behind the music, but your subconscious mind can, and it readily accepts the suggestions. SBM works better with regular use over time. It increases your energy, focus, and motivation while modifying your perception and beliefs as well. As a result, you experience behavioural changes also. With SBM you do not lose control and you remain fully conscious throughout the audio experience. SBM helps you to achieve goals you are focused on. There is no trance with SBM, so you can listen while on the move, while at study, or when you are exercising. Driving while listening to SBM audio is not recommended, however, because of possible suggestions for relaxation. SBM contains only positive messages (which you can pre-check in writing if provided). With SBM, the result is not automatic, as you still need to take action, armed with your increased energy, focus, and motivation from your SBM audio. Therefore, SBM supports your pre-existing goals by rewriting your self-beliefs, ways of thinking, and even behaviour patterns. This allows you to make life changes, allowing you to overcome any challenges that may have held you back before. SBM bypasses the conscious mind and, therefore, your resistance to change which held you back previously. Your ability to change increases exponentially with SBM, as it directly affects your subconscious. Your increased focus gives you a higher level of concentration and clarity in thinking. SBM also increases your determination and persistence to fulfil a goal. Your increased motivation determines your desire to succeed, along with continued commitment. SBM also increase your positive self-beliefs and decreases long-term limiting patterns of behaviour. SBM increases the conditions for your success as you follow your dream towards your heart's desire. Some tips for using SBM include the following:

- Have a clear and concise goal.
- Expect your own success
- Be consistent when using SBM as in how you actually listen and how it becomes your daily practise.
- Visualize yourself as already having achieved your results and success. Your visualization could be of a film in which you see your future successful self while you are listening to the SBM audio. Imagine your virtual surroundings, as well as how people relate to you when you are successful.
- Use SBM as much as possible so you become immersed in the audio and what it contains, whether it is for happiness or health. You can even play silent audio during sleep, with the encoded SBM therein.

As you practise using SBM, or any of your preferred methods for retraining your brain, you are bringing the success of who you are to your endeavour in realizing your goal. As your brain retrains under your direction, it transforms itself to become a tool that propels you forward at an accelerated rate. As a result, you and your life transform in ways you could not have imagined before. Hypnosis can have a similar effect on the brain, though in quite a different way. What do you know about hypnosis? What do you think of it? Hypnosis may not be as you think, and what you think you know about it may not be accurate. See what you think after you read the following section on hypnosis.

What about Hypnosis?

The trance state of hypnosis is not new. All hypnosis is self-hypnosis and is perfectly natural. Methods of producing altered states of awareness have been known in all ages and to all people. The knowledge of such methods date back to the early ages of history and records of antiquity. Ancient civilisations, such as the ancient Hebrews, used breathing exercises and eye fixation, which produces a state of ecstasy. Ancient Egyptians used "sleep temples" for the same purpose. Egyptian hieroglyphics describe hypnotic induction procedures similar to those used today. Galen, a Greek physician, discussed the influence of the body and the mind upon each other. Sigmund Freud was the first to use hypnosis successfully with psychotherapy. Milton Erickson, the father of modern-day medical hypnosis and the founder of The American Society of Clinical Hypnosis, brought about the use of naturalistic techniques in hypnosis. Milton contributed massively to the field of hypnosis. Another contributor to the field of hypnosis is Dr Jack Gibson, a surgeon who performed over four thousand operations without any conventional anaesthetics using just hypno-anaesthesia alone. Many of these operations were of a serious nature, and all patients were relaxed and pain-free with the use of hypnosis alone. However, he derived the most satisfaction from helping people with illnesses such as asthma and acne, and dispelling phobias about flying or creepy-crawlies. He also helped people to rid themselves of pain, post-operative trauma, smoking, and overeating. Dr Gibson claimed that self-hypnosis has to do with mind-strengthening and not mind-bending, as is the illusion in manipulative stage entertainments. According to him, control of one's own mind, as in the subconscious mind, is the answer to many of today's diseases.

What Is hypnosis?

"Hypnosis is an altered state of consciousness and heightened responsiveness to suggestion" (Keaney, Lesson 1, 1999: 35). This altered state of consciousness involves a process whereby your brainwaves slow down to the alpha or theta state through guided relaxation. This involves listening to the voice of the hypnotist as it lulls you into a deep state of relaxation. Trust and rapport with the hypnotist is important for this reason. Hypnosis is self-induced and leads to increased use of mental imagery. All hypnosis is self-hypnosis, in that you always hypnotize yourself from within. Hypnosis can come about by listening to either a guided audio visualization or to a hypnotist. The more often you go into trances, the easier it becomes each time. Hypnosis can also be induced using a pre-conditioned cue that leads into a deep trance automatically, such as the words "sleep now".

Hypnosis is natural to all human beings and occurs on a daily basis. You can be hypnotized as long as you are motivated to do so. You are not asleep during hypnosis, but you have a heightened sense of awareness instead. In hypnosis, you are either in the alpha or theta state. During hypnosis, your attention is focused on internal events, with a decrease or loss of interest in external realities. During hypnosis, your awareness is increased. Hypnosis is not a therapy in itself but is a tool of therapy with which capabilities already existing in you can be used in new ways. You can reject hypnotic suggestions if they go against your own personal or moral ethics. You can also respond to hypnotic suggestions in your own unique, creative way, according to your own personal understandings, experiences, and abilities. During hypnosis, your conscious mind, or critical factor, is put to the side while your unconscious mind becomes more active and influential. Hypnosis can be used to obtain post-hypnotic responses from suggestions made during hypnosis, an example being "You have increased confidence."

During hypnosis, suggestions are given to you either by a guided audio track or a hypnotist, which you readily accept when your brain is in the alpha wave or theta wave state. These suggestions go automatically into your subconscious when you are deeply relaxed. At the same time, your conscious mind is off-duty in its safe place. Normally, in beta state, your conscious mind acts as a sentry, allowing in only the information you accept according to your existing beliefs. If you do not believe in something, then it won't get past your conscious mind, because it will seem unacceptable. Hypnosis can change your beliefs to ones that are empowering, if it is performed in the presence of empowering positive suggestions that are relevant for you. Suggestions used in hypnosis bypass your conscious mind and go directly into your subconscious mind. During hypnosis, you are in control at all times and you cannot be made to do or say anything that you do not agree with. You always have free will to open your eyes and leave the room if you so wish. Belief in hypnosis is important for it to be effective. Remember, your beliefs are powerful and create the reality you live in. The formula for hypnosis to take place is as follows:

Misdirectected attention + expectation + belief = hypnosis + imagination

Your beliefs make what is possible, possible. If there is no belief in hypnosis, then there is no expectation for it to happen, and resistance to it can occur because of this. Imagination on its own will not bring about hypnosis without belief. If you do not believe in hypnosis, this in itself can impede hypnosis. Some reasons for hypnosis not working are fear, lack of knowledge about what hypnosis is, misperceptions about hypnosis, and of losing control or being under someone else's control. For these reasons, it is very important to clear any misperceptions first so that these do not interfere with the hypnotic induction and hypnosis itself. If you still don't believe in hypnosis, then it will not be effective. During hypnosis, you always abide by your own morals, ethics, and free will, even if a suggestion infers otherwise. You always have free will during hypnosis and will follow suggestions when they are in line with your own morals and ethics.

Common Misperceptions about Hypnosis

Do not be influenced by what you see in hypnosis stage shows. There is no need to be afraid of remaining stuck in hypnosis, as you have free will at all times during hypnosis. Hypnosis is meant to be a calming, relaxed, enjoyable experience for you. First, you can learn what hypnosis is about and also the process of trance induction. That way any misperceptions about hypnosis can be dealt with, and so you are more relaxed before going into hypnosis, as a result. If you are in a state of fear before or during hypnosis, this could lead to resistance and a block to relaxing fully. If you are going to a hypnotherapist, you need to feel heard and to have your concerns clarified. In this way, you feel valued and can trust the therapist. For this reason, the introductory talk between the therapist and you is vital in conveying genuine care for you and making you feel comfortable. The reason for the introductory talk is to convey a sense of safety, build credibility, and encourage involvement. The hypnotherapist is a guide and does not control you in any way.

Even though hypnosis varies from person to person in its depth as a state of relaxation, you can open your eyes at any time, if you so choose, and become fully aware. The paradox is that hypnosis heightens your sense of awareness more than when you are in the fully conscious state (beta). Hypnosis is a natural state occurring daily in every person's life. It is important for the hypnotherapist to treat you with unconditional, positive regard without judgement so that you can feel relaxed and free to express any concerns. This creates positive expectancy. The anticipation of success heightens your involvement in the hypnotic process. You should be left with a feeling that you are the one in control when in hypnosis and that the therapist is your guide in this therapeutic alliance.

Stage hypnosis gives the false illusion of the hypnotist controlling the participant to perform bizarre behaviours for entertainment. This can instil awe and maybe fear in the audience in relation to hypnosis. In this way, hypnosis is perceived to be a powerful force outside you that allows things to be said or done to you. The fact that it is being used for entertainment devalues its therapeutic component, which most people may not be aware of. Anyway, this is also due to lack of education about the benefits of hypnosis and hypnotherapy. Similarly, stage hypnosis tends to be sensationalized by the media. Hypnosis is not magic or mystical. If people realized that hypnosis is a natural phenomena occurring everyday in their own lives, they would learn to view and use it differently in a more beneficial way. The media's lack of true insight into hypnosis leads to publications of innuendos and judgements that take away from the practise of the hypnotherapy profession itself. Similarly, hypnosis is not to be used in the area of paranormal study, as this could give a false view to the general public about what hypnosis is all about. If people associate hypnosis with stage shows or the paranormal, this can instil fear and turn people away from hypnotherapy itself.

In Ireland and worldwide, the hypnotherapy movement is striving forward to be recognized fully for its worth and potential benefit to humankind. Hypnotherapy has a lot to offer to humanity, who has not yet learned how to tap into the vast resources within. Stage shows and the paranormal only give fuel to critics when they associate them with hypnosis. In turn, they could also criticise hypnotherapy as a result, if their knowledge or views of hypnosis are tarnished by their previous associations of it with stage shows or the paranormal.

Any previous experience of hypnosis, self-hypnosis, and the number of hypnotic inductions you have received can affect how quickly you go into trances thereafter. Your ability to trust and let go without analyzing or questioning is important. Those who are less critical and analytical tend to be more accepting of hypnosis to a deeper state, as the conscious mind is less active during hypnosis. Also, your motivation to go into a trance affects the trance itself also. Your belief and expectation in hypnosis also have a part to play as they become like a self-fulfilling prophecy when it comes to the level of hypnosis experiences. As people are individuals with different neurologies, then it is fair to say that every experience of hypnosis can vary from one person to another. However, the majority of people are capable of trance, as it's a natural manifestation of the mind at work. During hypnosis, any hypnotic phenomena that are suggested to you may also deepen your hypnotic state. These phenomena include deep breathing, eyelid flickering, watering of the eyes, flushed skin, a feeling of lightness or heaviness in your limbs, muscle twitching, or deep relaxation. When in hypnosis and listening to the hypnotist's suggestions of the phenomena, you can imagine having these in anticipation, which in itself can bring on a trance state and its phenomena.

With your eyes closed during hypnosis, your inner frame of reference is increased, while your outer reality checking is turned down. When in hypnosis, your conscious mind is in a restful alpha- or theta-wave state, which the hypnotherapist utilizes to deliver positive suggestions. If you go into delta state, that means you have fallen asleep, which is not hypnosis, but your subconscious can still hear the suggestions. It is the therapist's skill in gauging your hypnotic phenomena that determines success in suggestion therapy or analytical therapy. When the hypnotherapist feeds back your experience of your hypnotic phenomena while making positive suggestions to you during hypnosis, this can heighten your engagement in your own perception. Therefore, your own experience of hypnosis can become your own convincer.

While suggestions in a light trance (the alpha state) can be beneficial in all cases, it is best for you to be in a medium trance (the theta state) when receiving suggestions. Hypnotic phenomena can deepen your hypnotic state by compounding as truisms, or true statements, in deepening techniques used by the hypnotist. A hypnotic phenomenon such as deep breathing can by used as a cue to induce relaxation during hypnosis during a suggestion. For instance, "the deeper you breathe, the more you relax. The more you relax, the deeper you breathe." A deep state of relaxation can be imprinted as a resource anchor when you are asked to hold the index finger and thumb together while saying "Calm, confident, comfortable, and relaxed" during hypnosis. Once it is imprinted, when you use the anchor after-wards, you automatically feel the desired state. The more this is practised, the more effective it is as a resource anchor. At the same time, it becomes more enmeshed in the brain circuitry the more it is used. In the future, with repetition and practise, when you hold your index finger and thumb together, then you automatically feel calm, confident, comfortable, and relaxed. This is because your brain has been trained to become conditioned to this cue as a result of your neurological re-patterning. In this way, you have retrained your brain.

We hypnotize ourselves naturally on a daily basis. One instance of this is when we daydream. When you forget that you've just driven through a town, you have been in a mild trance. When this happens, your subconscious mind automatically takes over the driving through a reflex action. You are actually safer when the subconscious is on autopilot than when you are consciously driving. When reading or watching television, your brainwaves automatically slow down to the alpha state, which means that you are in a mild trance. During this trance, you are more open to suggestions. Be mindful of what you expose your mind to when you are in an alpha or theta brainwave state. Can you imagine how many people are being hypnotized when watching the drama and sensationalism of the daily news? Drama and sensationalism can evoke intense emotion in a person, which adds to the hypnotic effect. Advertising, the news, and the movies you watch are forms of social hypnosis. Be aware of the power of persuasive information. Be aware also of persuasive authority figures in society. You are your own authority. You can consciously make your own choices without being influenced by others. Open your mind to that which is positive, expansive, supportive, inclusive, and nourishing for your body, mind, and soul. Restrict that which instils fear, encourages defensive action or mistrust, and which encourages your need to feel protected.

You are already safe if you believe you are safe in your mind and heart. When you feel safe, so does your body as it functions optimally in a growth phase. If you feel or live in fear, your body enters a stress mode that your brain puts into place for your protection and survival. In this way, your energy gets used up in your body for readiness to escape the potential danger that never actually happens. Over time, this chronic stress becomes built into the neurology in your physical body, as your brain and organs communicate with each other in a cyclic defence mode. Your digestion slows down as the blood supply is sent to your legs and arms to escape perceived danger or threats. Over time with chronic stress, you lose the ability to absorb some of the vital nutrients for the efficient running of your cells and organs. After a while, you wonder why you are tired and become fatigued, as this cycle does not switch off, because you are still in fear. Yet you do not know you are in fear, nor are you aware of it consciously, when you get caught up with the stuff of life. This is because you do not realize that you have become socially hypnotized.

Are you living in love or are you living in fear? Are you living in a world of love or are you living in a world of fear? What does your mind think, and what pictures has it been fed? Think about it. When your brain sees a visual image, whether it is in your imagination or in picture form, this leads to chemical reactions in your body, as if the images were real. This has been shown in brain studies using brain scans. So what you see around you and what you visualize can have effects on your perception of the world. What you perceive comes from and also directly affects your brain at the same time. Your brain is constantly recreating itself every moment in terms of what cells regenerate and what cells "fall away." You become what you think in your physical being. Become aware of what kind of environment you surround yourself with. Move towards that which expands and empowers you. Move away from that which constricts and disempowers you. Only you know what that is. Go by what you feel. Your feeling will always guide you right.

Most people experience natural hypnosis several times a day and also on entering and leaving sleep. As hypnosis is an altered state of consciousness or awareness, at all times you remain awake and aware of what's going on. Hypnosis is not an unconscious state; rather, it is a heightened state of awareness. Even though you are more relaxed than ever before, you are not asleep during hypnosis. However, you will usually feel deep peace, serenity, and well-being with this deep relaxation. The conscious state in hypnosis can be compared to a see-saw. In the waking state (beta state), the conscious mind is at the high end of the see-saw and the subconscious mind is at the low end. Under hypnosis, they reverse, and the subconscious mind is at the high end and the conscious part at the low end. Hypnosis is a natural state of mind with an extraordinary quality of relaxation in which there is an emotional desire to satisfy the suggested behaviour. There is a heightened and selective sensitivity to the stimuli being received by the five senses also, and this is accompanied by a softening of the conscious mind's defences. When hypnotized, you feel like following the suggestions that are made, provided that what is suggested does not conflict with your belief system.

During hypnosis, normalization of your nervous system comes about in terms of your body and organs coming into balance during homeostasis. Homeostasis is a state in which the body enters the relaxed growth phase, in which cells and organs function optimally. When your body is in balance, you get to digest food properly and your energy is used for growth and evolvement instead of trying to escape a perceived threat. Hypnosis can be the means of activating this parasympathetic response in the nervous system of your body, where you are at ease within yourself. In the process, it shuts off the stress response. When you feel safe in your safe place of hypnosis, there is no need for protection or the defence response in your body or its cells. Instead of maintaining a state of defence, your energy can now be used for nourishment and growth in your physical being. In this way, you can learn to switch off the stress response during hypnosis as your body experiences a state of deep relaxation. You can train your brain in this way to bring about balance in the body and rid yourself of stress and its effects. Therefore, balance and relaxation become your new habit, as the old habit of stress just fades away. You can be at peace within yourself no matter what is going in the outside world. It is possible for you to be calm in the eye of the storm by retraining your brain.

How Does Hypnosis Work?

All trance in hypnosis is about learning to go into a trance state. For this reason, if you learn and understand what hypnosis is all about before going into a trance, then any misperceptions about hypnosis can be allayed. This enables you to go easier into a trance and to know what phenomena to expect. During hypnosis, the conscious mind, or critical factor, is put to the side, while the unconscious mind becomes more active and influential. Some hypnotic phenomena include slowing of breathing and heart rate, watering of the eyes (lachrymation), flickering of the eyelids, a feeling of heaviness or lightness in limbs, flushing of the skin, a deep sense of relaxation, increased awareness, and a heightened sense of hearing focused on the hypnotist's voice. "There is nothing mysterious about hypnosis. Its application is based solely on the known psychological relationship between the conscious and the subconscious minds. "The subconscious, having no power to reason, accepts and acts upon fact or suggestions given to it by the conscious mind." (Keaney, Lesson 1, 1999: 31).

Using hypnosis, suggestion therapy can help to deal with problems like smoking cessation, weight management, nail-biting, exam nerves, or improving confidence, as examples. Psychoanalysis can also be done in hypnosis, where the root cause of problems can be found and released. With this release, the psychosomatic symptoms associated with the cause also tend to disappear. Hypnosis is not sleep. Whatever sleep is, hypnosis is not. Hypnosis is an altered state of attention which approaches peak concentration capacity.

Normally a post-hypnotic suggestion (PHS) is repeated a few times during a hypnotic induction in order to strengthen and maintain it. Repetition of a suggestion increases its effectiveness. If you try too many changes at once, this can confuse the subconscious if it becomes overloaded. Suggestion therapy usually takes one to three sessions and is used for smaller problems. Psychoanalysis under hypnosis is used for deep-rooted problems whose causes are hidden subconsciously as a result of repression, and this can take from eight to ten sessions.

What Is the Conscious and Subconscious Mind?

The conscious mind is the critical factor, or critical censor, that allows in only certain information. When in hypnosis, the critical factor needs to be distracted so that positive suggestions can go directly into the subconscious, as in suggestion therapy. During hypnosis, your subconscious comes to the forefront while the critical factor steps aside. A medium trance in theta state is most beneficial for hypnosis to be effective. During hypnosis, it is always ideal for your conscious mind to have a safe place to go to so you feel relaxed. When post-hypnotic suggestions are given during hypnosis, they are accepted directly by the subconscious as the critical censor is kept occupied elsewhere. Also, when your emotional state is at the height of intensity, this is a good time to give post-hypnotic suggestions.

Your conscious mind is the logical, analytical, questioning factor of your mind. Your subconscious is the seat of your emotions and accepts everything that is allowed in by the conscious mind. Your subconscious can influence your conscious mind in terms of beliefs and behaviours. Your conscious mind also affects your subconscious in terms of what it allows in at the subconscious level when it is distracted. Your conscious mind is responsible for 5 per cent of your behaviour, while your subconscious mind is responsible for 95 per cent. Your subconscious mind can process twenty million bits of information per second, whereas your conscious mind processes only forty bits at the same time. Your subconscious is a powerful information processor that observes your environment, both external and internal at the same time. It automatically reacts to situations without conscious thought and puts into action previously learned behaviours. These learned behaviours have become programmed as conditioned reflex responses to particular stimuli. Therefore, your behaviour can be the result of a knee-jerk reaction to a trigger or stimulus when it is automatic.

You are not usually conscious of your behaviour, and this is because it is automatic 95 per cent of the time. Behaviour can be changed, however, through conscious choice. Your subconscious is non-linear, all-encompassing, and all-inclusive, and it is designed for survival to keep you safe and protected. Through integration and adaptation of your previous experiences in life, your behaviour is shaped by your subconscious to achieve the best results for you. Your subconscious works according to your beliefs, experiences, memories, attitudes, values, and concept of space and time in its function. When you change any of these within, the way your subconscious works also changes. How you are on the inside affects how you behave towards the world. Your subconscious, which is a part of your make-up, has access to the universal field of source.

When you optimize moving closer to your authentic self, you optimize how well your subconscious works for you, with you, and as you. Optimal function of your subconscious occurs when you have whole-brain thinking. This happens when your previous left-brain dominance blends and balances with your right-brain hemisphere. With synchronization of the two hemispheres of the brain, information processing takes place in the whole brain at once. Left-brain dominance leads to an overanalytical, logical, linear, specific view of the world. This kind of left-brain dominance leads to constriction in thinking into one specific way only. The right-brain, being all-inclusive, leads to expansion in thinking, where many possibilities exist in any instant. While both the left and right brain serve a purpose, more can be achieved when they work together simultaneously.

Your conscious mind is the means by which you program your subconscious mind. This programming happens through repetition of a pattern over time, until eventually it goes into the subconscious mind, once learning takes place. Programming occurs when a behaviour becomes automatic and you can perform it without thinking about it consciously. This process allows you to move on to learn new behaviours. Also, if there is any conflict between your conscious and subconscious mind, your subconscious always wins because of its programming.

Your subconscious mind prevents you from becoming overloaded when your conscious mind performs its specific tasks on a daily basis. An example of this is driving without conscious awareness. Your conscious mind can then focus on other tasks, such as your shopping or what you plan to do next. (This happens while you daydream when carrying out the task). In this state, your conscious mind is relaxed and lets your subconscious take control of your behaviour. In a relaxed state, you are not on guard when you feel safe and at ease. When you relax deeply, as in meditation, your conscious mind goes into its safe place, where it rests. During deep meditation, your brainwaves slow down to alpha and theta waves. In the theta state, you can experience whole-brain thinking, where your left and right brain hemi-spheres function as one integrated whole. During whole-brain thinking, solutions, ideas, or inspirations come to you automatically and you can see all the possibilities for a situation at once. When your brain functions as one whole, you can tap into the genius within as information flows effortlessly from the universal realm. Your ego no longer blocks this information, as it has become integrated and unified with your whole being as one. When you are at one with your self, you are at one with source. The more you meditate, the more you get to experience whole-brain thinking. Over time, with repetition, oneness becomes your way of being in the world. For this reason, it is important to meditate daily for even five to twenty minutes. As you do this, you tap more and more into the power of your subconscious; and as it blends with your conscious mind, both begin working together as one in balance with each other.

There are many benefits to training your brain. Think of it as the hardware of your computer. You can increase your memory power and your intelligence, and you can also speed up your thinking processes. With this training, it is also possible to input new "software", or programming, just by listening to certain frequencies. Hypnosis has the same effects on your subconscious as brainwave entrainment, while it does not use frequencies to alter the brainwaves. The difference with hypnosis is that a hypnotist talks you into a gradually deepening state of relaxation in which you become receptive to positive empowering suggestions that are made. In the hypnotic state, you become highly aware while speeding up your capacity to "download" information.

You are not just a physical being. You are also an energetic, vibrational being that responds to the vibrations and frequencies around you. When you bathe your brain in the brainwave frequencies that bring the results you desire, training your brain becomes effortless. All it takes is daily practise that becomes a ritual, such as brushing your teeth. How do you know that training your brain is working? Over time, you will notice the changes in how people respond to you more favourably, and in how you respond to situations with more ease and calm. You experience more peace within, and you feel in harmony with your self. Your direction comes from within as you become less influenced by outside events or people. You learn to follow your own inner guidance more and more with brain training. You automatically feel more confident and joyful with a willing-ness to take more risks in life. No matter what challenges may lie ahead, you feel excited about your life path. You recognize the opportunities that you are attracting, which propel you forward to grow and expand even more. Your outside world begins to change in ways that follow from your inner world within. Your environment and way of life itself become the effects of your brainwave entrainment. You also start to remember more and more who you really are. It is in this remembering that you become more your authentic self.

Exercise

Check out these techniques and use this technology that is available to you now. Experience one or all of these techniques to see which is your favourite. Then continue to practise it on a daily basis. When you prefer one method, stick with it, because then you are motivated to continue using it in retraining your brain. When you use this method regularly, you will be more successful. You will be amazed at the changes in your life as you transform yourself from within and so your outside world changes in turn. You can check out the Solfeggio frequencies at www.mindpowermp3.com and the subliminal messages on Louise L. Hay's CD *Stress-Free* at www.hayhouse.com.

CHAPTER 8

MASTER YOUR EMOTIONS

From scientific tests and research, it is known that negative thoughts like anger, fear, and resentment can actually weaken your muscles. On the other hand, positive thoughts like forgiveness actually strengthen your muscles. Your body has its own intelligence that can be tapped into using muscle testing. This is how kinesiology works. Anybody you perceive to have wronged you in the past should be thought of with forgiveness in mind. Forgiveness benefits you in strength and helps you to let go of the habit of negative thinking. The human body has its own intelligence separate from the brain. Each cell in your body has its own memory also, and this is referred to as cellular memory.

What does this memory refer to? Actually, every thought, experience, situation, and event that's happened in your life up till now is stored in the memory of each cell of your body. Scientists have now acknowledged this very fact. Even the brain's memory is stored in all individual cells of the body. This memory includes every thought and emotion you have ever had. This is the nature of the holographic universe. Every part in the universe has the whole in it. While each part makes up the whole, each part is also the whole. As in a hologram, each part has the whole in it. If you split up a laser hologram of an apple into parts, for example, each individual part has the totality of the apple's appearance in it, exactly matching the original. Your thoughts and emotions can become stored in this way at a cellular level. This memory can affect the functioning of every cell of every organ in your body, down to the molecular level. Cellular memory includes self-defeating beliefs also, which can cause emotional energy blockages in your body. Your body's energy system is normally flowing at all times. Any emotional blockage can affect the flow of energy in your body. When there is a blockage, your energy can become stuck around a particular part of your body. If this blockage is not released, then the way your organs function around that part of the body can become affected when your organs start resonating with the blocked energy, thus creating symptoms in the body.

When you suppress emotions, they can show up in the body as symptoms. Through suppression, you actually hold on to your emotions in the form of denial of or resistance to feeling certain emotions. The best way to release your emotion is to welcome it while allowing yourself to feel and go through it. At the same time, observe the pictures and images that come up. You can consciously let it go there and then. When you know and understand this, you will realize how easy it is to let go of emotions by processing them in this way. When you hold on to emotions, your subconscious takes over in this processing, in order to protect you. The subconscious mind is not accessed as directly as the conscious mind.

When releasing a deep-rooted suppression, you need to access your alpha or theta state, because your subconscious mind is more open to accepting suggestions. Your suppression can show up in your dreams, your daydreams, and your automatic behaviour towards other people when your conscious mind is switched off. Suppression can also show up as physical manifestations in your body, such as pain or an uncomfortable feeling in a particular area of the body. Your subconscious hints at what the problem is in the area concerned, which may be symbolic, because it is trying to protect you. It communicates in pictures and symbols, as well as in feelings. For this reason, it is good to keep a dream journal when you are trying to interpret what message your subconscious has for you. In order to do this, keep the journal on your bed, and when you wake up, record your dream within a few seconds of waking up. If you wait longer, you will forget the contents of the dream, as your state of mind will go from alpha to beta brainwaves on waking up. This change of state usually takes place over a period of seven seconds, and that is why you quickly forget your dreams on waking.

The more you write down your dreams, the more you will remember and retain them in your mind. It is only you who can interpret the meanings and symbols of your own dreams. Nobody else can give meaning to your own experience in life. Become aware of what feelings you have during the dream and what symbols show up. What happens in a dream is not usually to be taken literally, because it is usually full of metaphors and symbolic images. Symbols and feelings are the language of the subconscious. When you dream, your subconscious is communicating with you in a coded form. Only you can decode it, not anybody else. Dream interpretation gives you insight into your own beliefs of what is happening in your life. Dreams in themselves are naturally therapeutic, and this takes place while the dream is happening. Any problems or traumas you may have had in your life previously can be released and resolved spontaneously during a dream. This is because you dream during the theta state, and as you know, the subconscious is more open to solutions and possibility in this state, in alignment with the universal realm.

Trauma release or finding solutions can happen automatically by the actions you take in your dreams to bring about a good outcome. If you become aware in the dream state, as in lucid dreaming, you can intentionally act in the dream to bring about the best outcome for yourself. Just before you go to sleep, you can pre-program your mind so that you remember your dreams when you wake up. You can say something to yourself like "Sleep, dream, remember, rest fully, and awaken revitalised and refreshed." This actually helps you to remember your dreams the following morning, and it becomes more effective with practise. It is important to say "rest fully" so that your subconscious allows you to sleep deeply while knowing that you will remember in the morning. The subconscious takes instructions literally. The more you do this, the clearer you dreams will become and the easier it will be for you to remember. When you write down your dreams and what they may mean to you in your journal, this sends a message to your subconscious that you are focusing your energy in this direction. The process of dream journaling becomes easier over time as a result, and also you may find that your dreams become more vivid.

Emotions are not meant to be held on to. They are there to be felt in order to bring about understanding and resolution in any situation. Release of emotions is important in moving on, without any extra baggage to carry. Some people do not know how to let go of emotions, which then become repressed in the subconscious behind the veil of conscious thought. Repression of emotions happens when you suppress what you are feeling by way of denial or rejection. In this way, you do not actually get to process these emotions and so they become stored in the body. The subconscious does this automatically in trying to protect you. Suppression allows you to function normally in your daily life for a while; otherwise, you may become overwhelmed by the emotions you are carrying. This may work for a short while as you function unhindered, but after a while, the emotions can weigh you down like baggage. The subconscious then allows for processing of these emotions in its own way as it filters the emotions through the veil in the form of daydreams, dreams, or even flashbacks. Emotions surface in order to be observed and released. If you resist emotions, they become suppressed once more behind the dam, which can burst open at any time. These pent-up emotions can lead to over-reactivity to situations that act as triggers for the original event in your mind. These triggers remind you in some small way, subconsciously, of the original situation in which you felt the trapped emotion. This can set up a pattern of behaviour that is subconscious. You are not consciously aware of your habitual reactions to the same situations or people. This pattern comes from your subconscious until the program is changed.

With conscious awareness, it is possible to detach emotionally while viewing events from an observer stance. In this way, you become aware of your own behaviour instead of being caught up with events unknowingly. By disciplining your thinking patterns, you develop a new habit of trained thinking and mindfulness that eliminates negativity in the form of judgement, resentment, fear, anger, and hatred. In this way, your thinking is not biased by your own assumptions. You set your own life agenda from within. You can now view your self without judgement also, with the belief that you have all the resources necessary to solve a problem. Your authentic self guides you towards finding the source, where anything is possible. Trust in the process. You learn, in this way, to solve problems by tuning into your real self, which most of us have forgotten exists at all times. Your authentic self helps you to remember who you really are, so as to prevent you from living in the illusion of who you thought you were. You can live your values and your life on purpose. In this way, you constantly evolve to new heights of awareness in carrying out your purpose here on earth.

Clear Dense Thoughts and Emotions

Emotions carry energy. For this reason, it is good to clear any negative emotions you may be carrying. First you need to become aware of them. A dense thought, if not erased, can lead to a dense condition. Say to yourself when feeling a dense emotion about something, "That is in the past. Now in this new moment, this new present, I am already beginning to change for the better more and more each day." It is best not to deny or repress dense thoughts, such as fear, anger, or resentment. Recognize and become aware of them. Face these dense thoughts and emotions. Allow yourself to feel them. Then, using your mind's eye, imagine them disappearing and dissolving out of your body like puffs of smoke moving into the light of the universe to be transformed. Next, see this transformed light entering your body through the crown of your head, filling every cell in your body all the way down to your toes. Keep your connection with the earth while focusing on the ground below your feet. By dismissing these thoughts and emotions after recognizing and facing them, you are allowing yourself to be aware of them in order to let them go. You can imagine removing any dense emotion by its roots while consciously replacing it with a positive feeling. You are not defined by your emotions as they flow through you. Emotions are felt, and then they disappear. By holding on to them, you cause them to build up over time, leading to emotional baggage. Your authentic self is independent of your thoughts and emotions. You have emotions and thoughts that are used in your mental make-up. By trusting in your own spontaneous nature, you allow the flow of emotions with an order that is present in all of nature. Therefore, your body remains healthy when it is in balance with itself. Balance coexists with stability and allows for optimal functioning within your body.

Physical symptoms are communications from the inner self that you are making mental errors of one kind or another. By changing your mental attitude through self-discovery, the root cause of your problem is brought to the surface to be cleared and released. With emotional release, the problem is no more. You can measure your progress in this regard as your symptoms subside. By accepting life on your own terms, even the emotions you feel, you can know that you trust in your own immunity to whatever arises. You do not need to protect yourself in reality. Your stamina and robustness prevent any perceived problems in the first place. Wisdom means preventing problems or solving problems at the roots while being at cause and not effect. If you want the best, go straight to the highest level – your authentic self. Doing so brings you to the deepest part of your essence and core, where you true strength lies. In doing so, your mind, being, and actions become aligned with each other.

Learn from the wise actions of others. You can use the success of others as a template for your own life. Choose a role model to learn from in the area you are interested in. By integrating all truths, you have complete truth. If you have conflict of reason, intelligence, or wisdom, know there is always a better way of seeing things. Avoid energy drainers. Associate with like-minded people. This raised collective energy gives you positive introspection as to where you can use your skills, attention, generosity, and appreciation while sharing your ability to give and receive love. This in itself is positive energy. Utilize your natural talents. Through developing your leadership qualities by personal reinvention, you can be a catalyst for personal and global transformation. Your positive expectation makes it so. In this way, you become a role model for others to make powerful changes in their lives also.

Perceived wrongness in yourself or others can lead to "wrongness" in your ability to perceive. If you hadn't picked up on the "wrongness" of yourself or others, how would your life be different now? In reality there is no such thing as right or wrong. It's a conditioned way that we have been led to think in the duality of our world appearances. In relation to the polar opposites of right and wrong, there is, in fact, only one reality in being. In reality, no person is right to make somebody else wrong. No person is wrong to make someone else right. We are all equal, and we are all connected. There is no point in comparing yourself to another person, as we all emanate from the same source. While you are a separate part of the whole universe, the whole universe exists in you as an individual. You are made of the same material that exists materially and energetically in the universe. The only difference is that each spark of divinity expresses itself individually.

What physical and energetic actualization of the whole of you are you not acknowledging? Any perceived wrongness can block your life, your living, your reality, and your future Through the power of your mind, you can delete this perception through consciousness and understanding. Wrongness does not belong to you and never did. It is what you learned from others. Say to yourself, "I am perfect. I am magnificent. I am strong. I can do this." Really feel this as you say it. By focusing on everything in your life that is good and beautiful, you attract more wonder and awe into your life. That way you let go of judging yourself. You are open to receiving so that you can be all that you truly can be. By allowing in this way, you create and receive more than you could ever wish for. In doing so, you start to realize the greatness of who you really are, as well as what you can choose in every moment of your life.

What you choose to think, be, and do can change your reality in any moment of now. When you change how you are being, you also change your expectations of life. Your expectation of life determines what shows up in your life. As your self-affirming beliefs become merged with your expectations, your life flows in an easy and effortless manner. In order to receive, you become that which allows receiving into your life. By making a change in your life, you change your world at the same time. In changing your world, you change how you are in the world. This is how you can become the gift and the change that our world requires Your world view has the power to change others' view of their world also. What's true for you is what makes you feel lighter. Always choose what makes you feel lighter. What makes you lighter comes from your inner guidance.

Now it is possible for you to become a light that will allow the world to see itself in its own reflections. The world needs you and the truth of who you are. Show yourself off to the world, and you will see your reflection in all that is around you. Your own true light will shine back on you when it leaves its impression on others. Being in service to others is how you find meaning and purpose in life. Whatever you do to help others comes back to you a hundredfold. Helping others is what makes you feel good about being you when you see the positive impact you can make on others. That way your mind becomes removed from any perceived stress you may have when you become focused on helping others. When you take your attention away from any perceived problems, you stop giving them energy. Anything that loses energy tends to dissolve and fade away over time. That way, you can focus your energy on the solution. Becoming solution-focused means you are tapping into the right side of your brain, where your creative abilities reside.

Stress

It has been said by some experts that stress causes 99 per cent of illness and disease. Some would say that stress causes all disease in the body. Also, stress causes dis-ease within the mind. Stress comes from incorrect beliefs and misinterpretations when you are disconnected from your authentic self. Stress comes about when the outside world is viewed as being dangerous and threatening. Your perceptions of the world, in this way, come from your memories and beliefs associated with experiences from your past. So, in this way, your perceptions and beliefs may be self-limiting according to your conditioning up till now since your childhood. While the stress response is there to ensure your survival in this world, it is meant to be short, acting only during emergencies in which your life may be threatened.

During an emergency, adrenaline is produced by your adrenal glands, which lie on the kidneys. When this happens, extra blood is sent to your legs and arms so that you can run faster in order to escape threat or danger. Your re-action time is sped up also, as conscious thought is not involved in this case. If you feel threatened all the time, then you can become chronically stressed. Chronic stress leads to hyper-vigilance and an automatic overreactive stress response in the body. This response is not voluntary when it becomes conditioned into your neurology. A conditioned stress response happens through repetition of the same thoughts, feelings, and visualizations in association with a perceived threat.

It is always possible to see a situation or problem from many different angles or perspectives. If you have a habit of looking at things in the same way over time, then you have only one way of looking at things and this becomes your reality. Tunnel vision, can lead to a stress reaction becoming reinforced in your body when the body believes it is under constant threat. The good news is that when you are open to other possibilities or points of view, then this too can change how you view everything. When you expand on your world view and the possibilities therein, you can also change the neurology in your brain and body to function normally over time. Having more options and possibilities leads you to feel safer and more in control. The more you practise this, the easier it becomes. When you do this, you may see things completely differently. With this insight, your beliefs about a situation or problem change also, as you can now focus on a solution instead of the problem. In this way, you become solution-focused instead of problem-focused.

The human body is not adapted for any chronic stress that may be experienced. With chronic stress, the human body does not have time to catch up with all the changes in our modern world. Your body is adapted in the same way to survive as it was in prehistoric times. It has not advanced from there since, in physical terms. With all the rapid changes in technology, mobile phones, microwaves, electromagnetic signals from devices, and the faster pace of living in our world, it is no wonder that stress levels have risen dramatically in the human population. Also, during stress, your brainwaves become faster and can be as high as forty cycles per minute. At this level, your brain tends to operate from the logical, analytical, problem-focused left side only. So when you are stressed, you become cut off from your right-brain, where your creativity, imagination, and problem-solving abilities lie.

With chronic stress, cells in your body go into a defensive mode, as opposed to a normal healthy growth mode. Over time, in this case, the body begins to break down without the ability to repair itself, when in a chronic protective mode. This leads to a chronic fight, flight, or fright reaction, which shuts down your body's natural defences, the immune system, digestion, and brain function. The blood flow in the brain is diverted from the front thought-processing cortex to the back of the brain, which is responsible for survival mechanisms in the body. The longer the stress continues, the more it affects the systems in the body, including the function of the organs. During stress, the cells in the body receive less oxygen and water, and fewer nutrients. With chronic stress, the cells don't release waste or toxins effectively either, and they don't communicate with nearby cells, which affects general health.

There are many things you can do to avoid illness and to reverse it. The body is designed to heal itself naturally in a state of balance. If you know how to do it with your mind, you can choose how well you feel, how long you'll live, and how healthy you'll be in general. The medical approach deals with treating the symptoms, or effects, of an illness, and not the root cause. Medicine is based on controlling the energy of the body. The root cause of all illness or disease is at an unhealthy energy frequency. This lower vibration can come from the level of your thinking and emotions. When you change this unhealthy frequency to a healthy vibration, any illness or disease fades away automatically without effect or effort. Increasing your vibrational energy level can have a healing effect on your DNA. Once your body's energy source is activated, any illness or disease is addressed from the source. This brings about balance in the body, using the subconscious mind and the natural energy in the body. Balance in the body brings about homeostasis.

The medicine of the future is predicted by many to be "energy medicine", which deals with the root cause of all illness and disease. The current medical approach treats the symptom and not the causes of illness or disease. The medical approach focuses on the physicality of the human being according to Newton's laws. So, according to this approach, a + b = c in a linear fashion. So if you take a tablet, do you then you get better? Not necessarily, because the human body is not just physical and has lots of things going on in it at the same time, in a non-linear fashion. That is why tablets can have lots of side-effects; they act on more than one part of the body at the same time. By taking tablets, symptoms of illness are covered up, while the cause still remains. It's like putting a Band-Aid on a problem.

At present, the tablet treatment is an accepted form of therapy for illness in medical circles. Conventional medicine can have benefits, and some tablets can be very beneficial. However, there could be another way that does not involve taking tablets. When the root cause is dealt with directly, the symptom simply fades away automatically, never to return. More research needs to be done in the area of energy medicine. With energy medicine, mind, body, and spirit integration brings about resolution of emotional issues or blockages that show up in the body. With resolution of the body's blockages, the protective mode is shut off in the sympathetic nervous system. The protective mode of contraction then changes to one of expansion in the cells. Instead, the parasympathetic nervous system becomes activated when your body is in balance. This is what allows for growth and evolvement as your cells begin to communicate with each other once more in the community of your body.

Trauma and Post-Traumatic Stress Disorder (PTSD)

Can you remember a time you learned to be fearful, way back in childhood? Even though your conscious mind may not remember, your subconscious mind knows of this time. If you perceived a trauma while being totally unable to cope, then an ego state may have been formed with many facets as a result. This ego state, in turn, becomes a coping strategy that incorporates into your psyche, or mind, as a direct result of your psychic distress. Consequently, the qualities of an alternate ego state will often be childlike in character and will be immune to adult logic or mature reason. This dissociation cuts off one ego facet from all others in your personality. Some would refer to this as a split personality or a fracture in the personality. Sub-personality traits exhibited can include unpredictable reactions, mood swings, uncharacteristic behaviour, and uncontrollable symptoms like aggression or extreme anger. Ego-defence strategies like these in childhood serve to protect you from any psychic distress through self-deception to maintain the psychological status quo. Such a process also brings about an escape from the harsh reality and self-devaluation.

Ego states are set up subconsciously and function to relieve you from distress or to allay anxiety. This comes about by a retreat from reality in the illusion of protecting yourself. Ego states can convert to an emotional, behavioural, or psychosomatic symptom that may, in fact, serve to reinforce past trauma rather than to relieve it. Such patterns can also be reinforced by life's circumstances, where your ego state can become re-energised, which keeps it alive and active.

Any stress or trauma can lead you to be hyper-reactive in any situation that may resemble a threat. During hyper-reactivity, large doses of brain stress chemicals are secreted in response to situations that hold little or no threat but somehow are reminders of the original trauma. Hyper-reactivity to situations is caused by changes in the brain circuitry that lead to PTSD symptoms. This explains why you feel anxious, fearful, hyper-vigilant, easily upset, and ready for fight or flight if you suffer from PTSD. In this case, your body is alerted for an emergency that is not there in reality. When these brain chemicals are triggered, you are flooded with the same feelings as the original trauma caused you to experience. You start sweating, you're scared, you have chills and the shakes, or you may even have flashbacks. This startle response is overreactive when in the presence of a trigger. The effects continue, as the brain wiring doesn't allow for the startle response to settle down. The response keeps sending signals in the brain from the amygdala to the hypothalamus, which recognizes danger.

Those people who don't have PTSD can settle into a resting phase of relaxation after the initial trigger because they have 40 per cent more brain receptors to stop the overreactive brain chemicals in the brain. It is the triggering of these chemicals that flood you with the same feelings as in the original trauma. As a result of this original trauma, the emotional imprint on the brain has brought about learned fearfulness that leads to red alert, even in safe situations that normally would not be stressful. Because of this, more endorphins than usual are produced by the brain, blunting the feeling of pain. This numbing of pain can also numb feelings themselves. With PTSD, you may be unaware of how others may feel, because of not being able to feel your own feelings. For this reason, you cannot feel pleasure at times, because of a general emotional numbness. You may also feel a sense of being cut off from life or from concern about others' feelings. Dissociation from life or other people can occur with PTSD, including the ability to remember crucial minutes, hours, or even days of the traumatic event.

Brain changes can be brought on by an initial event, which may even have been a mild stressful event from a person's youth. Later in life, because of the original trauma-induced brain changes, a person can be more vulnerable to feeling stressed during ordinary events than unstressed people. This explains why, when exposed to the same catastrophe, one person goes on to develop PTSD and another does not. Your amygdala is primed to find danger, but when you are presented once again with real danger, its alarm rises to a higher pitch in one person than the other. These brain changes offer short-term advantages for dealing with real emergencies that prompt them. Under stress, it is adaptive to be highly vigilant and ready for anything. When you are impervious to pain, your body is primed for sustained physical demand, and for the moment, you are indifferent to what might be intensely disturbing events. These short-term advantages of stress, however, become lasting problems when the brain changes so that they become predispositions; when this occurs, you are like a car stuck in high gear. The amygdala and its connected brain regions take on a new gear during the moment of intense trauma. This change in excitability means all of life seems to be on the verge of becoming an emergency, where even an innocent moment is susceptible to an explosion of fear run amok. Such traumatic memories can interfere with relearning a more normal response to those traumatizing events.

In PTSD, the acquired fear can affect your mechanisms of learning and memory. In overcoming this learned fear, the neocortex, or thinking part of your brain, is critical. Fear conditioning is the process whereby something that is not in the least threatening becomes dreaded, as it becomes associated with something frightening. The key region of the brain that learns, retains, and acts on this fearful response is the circuit between the amygdala and other parts of the brain. The brain is hijacked by the amygdala because of this learned conditioning. Usually when somebody learns to be frightened by something through fear conditioning, the fear subsides with time. This seems to happen through a natural relearning as the feared object is encountered again in the absence of anything truly scary. In PTSD, spontaneous relearning of this nature fails to occur, as the amygdala hijacks the brain every time something even vaguely resembling the original trauma comes along, strengthening the fear pathway. This means that what is feared is not paired with a feeling of calm, because the amygdala does not relearn a more mild reaction.

Extinction of this fear involves an active learning process. Given the right experiences, even PTSD can be done away with. The strong emotional memories and patterns of thought and reactions that PTSD can trigger *can* change with time. This relearning takes place in the brain cortex (the thinking part of the brain, which lies at the front). The neocortex is what gives you conscious choice as a human. The original fear in the amygdala does not go away completely; rather your cortex blocks the amygdala's command to the rest of the brain to respond with fear. You let go of learned fear by re-educating the emotional or limbic brain (which lies in the middle). The good news is that brain changes in PTSD can be reversed and that you can recover from even the most dire emotional imprinting. Your emotional circuit can be re-educated. The trauma causing PTSD can heal through relearning.

Your emotional healing can happen spontaneously when the trauma is relived safely, such as in the case of children at play. This allows two pathways for healing. On the one hand, the memory of the trauma repeats in a context of low anxiety, desensitizing it and allowing a non-traumatized set of responses to become associated with it. Another way to healing is when you can imagine the trauma having another better outcome, thus giving mastery over that traumatic moment of helplessness. For children, this happens through playing out the trauma over and over again in a game. We can learn a lot from children in this way. While adults who have been through overwhelming trauma can suffer emotional numbing or blocking out any memory or feeling about the catastrophe, children's minds often handle it differently. They less often become numb to their trauma, and they use fantasy – as in imagination, play, and daydreams – to recall and rethink their ordeals. Such voluntary replays of trauma seem to head off the need for damming them up in potent memories that can later burst through as flashbacks.

For overwhelming trauma, the child needs endless repetition, replaying the trauma over and over again in a grim, monotonous ritual. One way to get at the imprinted picture frozen in the amygdala is through art. Your subconscious mind responds to visual images because your emotional brain is highly attuned to symbolic meanings and to the messages of metaphor, story, myth, and the arts. This avenue is often used in treating traumatized children, as art can open a way for talking about a moment of terror that would not be spoken of otherwise. Drawing is in itself therapeutic, and it can begin the process of mastering the trauma. Emotional relearning and recovery from trauma take place in a safe place. The three stages of attaining a sense of safety are

1. remembering the details of the trauma,
2. mourning the loss it has brought, and
3. re-establishing a normal life.

These three steps reflect how the emotional brain learns once again that life need not be regarded as an emergency about to happen. The first step is to regain a sense of safety by finding ways to calm the too fearful, too easily triggered emotional circuits enough to allow relearning. This begins with your understanding that your jumpiness, nightmares, hyper-vigilance, and panics are part of the symptoms of PTSD. The sense in which people with PTSD feel unsafe goes beyond rational fear that dangers lurk around them. As a result, their insecurity lies in the feeling that they have no control over what is happening to them, to their body, and to their emotions. This is understandable, given the hair trigger for emotional hijacking that PTSD creates by hyper-sensitizing the amygdala circuitry. Relaxation techniques provide the ability to counteract edginess and nervousness. With the induction of relaxation, a physical calm opens a window for helping the brutalized emotional circuitry rediscover that life is not a threat. This gives you back the sense of security you had before the trauma happened.

Another step in healing involves retelling and reconstructing the story of the trauma in the presence of that safety. This allows the emotional circuitry to acquire a new, more realistic understanding of and response to the traumatic memory and its triggers. With the retelling of the trauma in this way, your memory starts to be transformed, both in its emotional meaning and in its effects on your emotional brain. For people who recover from trauma without getting PTSD, the pace of this retelling is delicate; an inner clock doses them with intrusive memories that cause them to relive the trauma during weeks or months when they remember hardly anything of the horrible events. This alternation of re-immersion into the trauma and then relaxation seems to allow for a spontaneous review of the trauma and relearning of emotional responses to it. For relearning to take place, relaxation is necessary, for the two happen together. Your retelling of the traumatic event should include not only what you saw, heard, smelled and felt, but also your reaction and the dread, disgust, or nausea you experienced.

The goal is to put the entire memory into words, and this means opening up parts of the memory that may have been dissociated and so are absent from conscious recall. When putting these sensory details and feelings into words, presumably memories are brought more under control of the neocortex, or conscious part of the brain (the thinking brain). As a result, the reactions they rekindle can be rendered more understandable and thus more manageable. The emotional relearning at this point is mainly achieved through reliving the events and their emotions consciously, but this time in surroundings of safety and security, in the company of a trusted therapist. This imparts a telling lesson to the emotional circuitry – that security, rather than unremitting terror, can be experienced in tandem with the trauma memories. In this way, trauma mastery is achieved over time.

It is important to express the story of the trauma initially in the retelling while in a safe environment and then to mourn the loss that the trauma brought. These are the steps to emotional healing. The mourning of loss could be regret over a step not taken, or even just the shattering of confidence that people can be trusted. This mourning that follows while retelling such painful events serves a crucial purpose. It marks the ability to let go of the trauma itself to some degree. It means that instead of being perpetually captured by this moment in the past, you can start to look ahead, even to hope and rebuild a new life, free of the trauma's grip. It is as if the spell of the constant recycling and reliving of the trauma's terror by the emotional circuitry can finally be lifted. Every siren need not bring a flood of fear, and every second in the night need not compel a flashback to terror. Once the trauma has been overcome, there may be some after-effects or occasional recurrences of symptoms. You know you have overcome your trauma when your symptoms have been reduced to a manageable level. This is when you can bear the feelings associated with memories of the trauma. It is especially significant when you can live your life without trauma memories erupting at uncontrollable moments. Instead, you can revisit them voluntarily, as with any other memory, and put them aside, as with any other memory. Overcoming trauma means you can rebuild a new life with strong, trusting relationships and a belief system that finds meaning in a world where such injustice can happen.

It seems that once your emotional system learns something, you never let it go. Therapy teaches you to control trauma, as it teaches your neocortex how to inhibit your amygdala. The former fear instinct to act is suppressed, while your basic emotion to a previous trigger remains in a subdued form. Once emotional mastery of the trauma is achieved, you may still have some remainder of the original sensitivity or fear at the root of a troubling emotional pattern. The neocortex can put the brakes on the amygdala's impulse to rampage but cannot keep it from reacting in the first place. Thus, while you cannot decide when you have an emotional reaction, you can have more control in how long it lasts. A quicker recovery time from such outbursts may well be one mark of emotional mastery. With this mastery comes change in the way you respond when an emotional reaction is triggered. The tendency for the reaction to be triggered in the first place does not disappear entirely. What changes with mastery are the responses you give when an emotional reaction is triggered. With PTSD, the typical self-defeating responses to wishes and old fears used to become activated in your relationships with others. These reactions can include being too demanding or withdrawing in self-defence from an anticipated criticism from another person. During such encounters, you may have been flooded with upsetting feelings like hopelessness, sadness, resentment, anger, tension, fear, guilt, self-blame, and so on. With untreated PTSD, the response pattern that comes from your amygdala being triggered tends to show up in almost every important relationship, whether with brothers, sisters, parents, peers, or bosses at work.

However, with mastery of your emotions, your emotional reaction to the triggering events becomes less distressing, even calm or bemusing. Also, your overt active responses in your behaviour towards others become more effective in getting what you truly want from a relationship. The initial wish or fear does not change, and neither does initial twinge or feeling, but the response to this does. The previous hijacking of your brain by the amygdala is interrupted by your neocortex when you actively choose to become calm and peaceful instead. At first, you may notice you have only half as many negative emotional reactions, compared to when you first started therapy. You will also notice that you are twice as likely to get the positive responses you deeply desire, compared to when you first started therapy. What may not change is the particular sensitivity at the root of these needs. Now is the time to use your new healthy responses when there are alarm signals in response to cues of a feared event.

Emotional lessons, even the most deeply implanted habits of the heart learned in childhood, can be reshaped. Emotional learning is lifelong and involves the conscious and subconscious mind. Learning is facilitated by keeping note of your dreams, daydreams, and imaginings. Recording of feelings and thoughts in a journal is also advised. When you listen to relaxation audio, you know you are safe, and this calms your amygdala in breaking the old cycle. In doing so, the other parts of your brain can work to help in creating a new response, which involves a new behaviour linked to an old trigger. You may even find you are smiling to yourself when you know you have replaced the old responses with new ones. This is because you know now that you are the master of your own destiny.

The Power of Your Subconscious

By tapping directly into your subconscious mind, you can achieve much quicker resolution of conflicts and results in your life. By aligning with your own subconscious, you can work towards the attainment of personal goals in a purposeful manner. By realizing suitable goals, you can achieve recognition and value in society while interacting successfully with others in the social context. Self-realization empowers you to realize your potential and to set realistic goals for self-improvement that engender satisfaction and self-acceptance. You are already an indivisible whole. You can be your own educator, guide, and facilitator.

The process of self-discovery is a means of inspiring, empowering, and imbuing you with courage to allow for your own self-acceptance as a unique being. With self-acceptance, you know you are lovable and can interact successfully with everything around you. Your journey to self-awareness helps you to overcome inferiority and discouragement and also to correct mistaken and faulty private logic. False assumptions, perceptions, and erroneous social values can be identified, explored, and corrected to foster social interest and social contribution. By going deeper into who you really are, you gain insight over time into previous unrealistic goals. This is achieved through a process of letting go of the layers of conditioning built up over a lifetime. Productive life goals are reconstructed to allow full potential and maximum satisfaction for you on achievement of these goals. You become automatically motivated towards behavioural change, self-acceptance and the acceptance of others in the process. In overcoming any perceived inferiority, you become involved in life activities that allow for a lifestyle in harmony with your environment.

As you progress towards self-actualization, you develop a belief in your own inherent potential for growth and self-understanding. In this way, you develop a conviction that your attitudes and behaviour can be self-directed. Responsibility for your reality is fundamentally in your own hands. Tapping into the power of your subconscious fosters insight in understanding where you are, where you are coming from, and how you see things from your perspective. As a result, you become less defensive and more open, allowing for more meaningful self-exploration. You can learn to develop unconditional positive regard for yourself and others while releasing your inner self. You also develop absolute respect for the integrity of yourself and others at the same time. By tuning into the natural caring nature of your core, you facilitate your own self-acceptance.

A safe environment is where you can feel free to be yourself, without any fear of judgement or disapproval. Your safe environment first starts in your mind. Visualization of your safe place gives a message to your subconscious that you are safe in this moment. Your subconscious has a vast amount of wisdom that empowers you in finding your true self by using your internal resources to do so. When your subconscious harmonizes with your higher consciousness, this allows you to be in the flow of your life through being at cause. By giving value and respect to yourself, you learn to value yourself and, therefore, give less value to the opinions of others. You also come to realize that you don't need to be ruled by the judgements or criticisms of other people, as your own self-evaluation is what counts. Only then can you interact with others on a constructive basis.

In time, you become empowered to learn how to cope with deviations from the norm while taking up the challenge of moving towards change. You also come to realize that change is a continuous journey on which you gain more and more personal insight as you move along the way towards self-actualisation. By being neutral and objective, you can reflect on and clarify your own views. Therefore, you are allowing expression of yourself more freely. You are the only person who can make the right choices for yourself. You do not need to get carried away by others' convictions and assumptions, however sound they may appear to be. You can surround yourself with people on the same wavelength who lift you up, inspire you, and encourage you in mutually rewarding relationships. You do not need to take others' advice. Your alignment with your subconscious gives you a vehicle for freedom of speech, devoid of judgement and criticism. In a safe environment (internal and external), you are more likely to express feelings and problems, as you will be more likely to trust yourself and others. By feeling safe, you will be more open as a result. Your integration with your inner self allows you to express yourself freely.

Learning to reflect on your life helps you to identify ways when control has been relinquished during your lifetime and where events have been passively accepted as inevitable. In this way, you learn to recognize the existing opportunities and act on them. This reflection on life helps you to evaluate your existence and to search for meaning in life. Life can be looked at from a new perspective when you keep an open and curious mind about the things life has thrown at you. You are guided to take responsibility for your own life in expanding beyond previous familiar safe boundaries. In the process, you become empowered for paving the way towards your destiny. This involves getting rid of wishful thinking, and instead you have productive decision-making. You continually recreate yourself while evolving and growing, moving with a purpose towards your destiny. In facing life's challenges, you can let go of self-deception and face up to your own limitations. Rather than seeking approval from others, you need to self-affirm, which leads to a change in how you organize your life. Designing your destiny means you can reshape your future rather than being tied to the past. This means that you must live in the present with an attitude of gratitude, rather than ruminating about the past or anticipating events in the future, based on the past. Your real power lies in the now on your voyage to self-discovery! Designing your destiny encompasses your commitment to creating opportunities and forming loving relationships, as well as working and building on your achievements.

Resistance can occur during this process of self-discovery. You may want to rationalize too much about your problems intellectually rather than to trust your subconscious mind. You may prefer to chat about your problems rather than find out the cause. You may give reasons and excuses for your current state. Your focus may be on a quick fix rather than the benefits of taking the journey to your authentic self. The aim of self-discovery is to obtain a subconscious resolution for your distress, not just an intellectual understanding of it. To achieve this, you need to revisit the emotional pull of pent-up distress in connection with your recollections, before thinking of any permanent change in yourself. In resisting the movement to your core, you try to spare yourself the emotional pain. You spare yourself in this way while still deceiving yourself that by avoiding any pain, you are protecting yourself. The subconscious functions to protect you. Logic alone does not solve this problem. The root cause needs to be found and released by accessing your subconscious, which can be done in meditation or by self-hypnosis. Release of the root cause cannot be forced, as it happens only in the presence of safety and repetition, along with a relaxed mind that allows emotional healing to take place.

Transference is the process by which you transfer childlike patterns of relation onto a person you encounter, even if you don't know that person or have met him or her only briefly. You can transfer onto any significant person in your life the qualities and characteristics of any person connected with your psychological distress from your past. Any subliminal wishes or unsatisfied needs from childhood that you possess, moreover, may tend to be transferred onto this person also, when you expect him or her to fulfil such desires. It is as if you superimpose onto somebody an image of those significant others whom you have been most profoundly affected by in the past, either positively or negatively. Anger or frustration towards this person may be connected to, for example, repressed anger toward a parent, because he or she represents a figure of authority. When this happens, you are not aware of this, as it is subconscious. You may even experience resisting full independence at times because you are not comfortable with experiencing the benefits of this. The way to be comfortable with your independent experience is linked to the way you switch your thoughts in alignment with your true self. This means releasing your resentfulness, jealousy, anger, or guilt. These emotions are replicas of the original root cause of certain childhood experiences.

Motives for transference relationships reveal the nature of your psychic distress. Your transference towards a significant authority figure can also manifest in dreams and in your fantasy-world imagery. When transference is present, this prevents your true self from surfacing. Your transference is simply an illusion brought about by your own inner state. You may feel guilty about harbouring such feelings. Know that you may feel anything from love to dense feelings during the course of self-discovery. As you let go of emotional blocks, you allow peace, tranquillity, and ease to enter your life instead. In therapy, transference is a useful tool because it allows you the opportunity to offload emotional baggage in a safe environment to a stranger that you will not meet again. With effective transference, you can leave your baggage behind to be free of the past and to live life fully on your own terms. So, in this case, transference is therapeutic. Transference is what makes therapy effective in a safe environment.

Dream Interpretation

The exploration of dreams can help bring about a lot of insight also. Dreams are a rich source of bounty that can enable you to reveal what lies at the depths of your mind's distress. Dream analysis is best done under hypnosis, to give access directly to the subconscious. Freud was the first to draw attention to using dreams in therapy. He broke away from the conventional object-oriented interpretation of dream symbolism and from this gave the power to the client in interpreting his or her own dream imagery. Unconscious conflict, defensive strategies, resistance, and transference can manifest in a number of ways in dreams, which can become apparent to the keen observer. It is important to explore your dream imagery and fantasy world. Clues to your internal distress are provided by your subconscious when various images and symbolic forms seep through from the depths of your unconscious mind. By keeping a record of your dreams in a dream journal, you can interpret your dreams, and so you come to a resolution of your internal conflict. Dreams can represent a wish-fulfilment that may contain trauma or anxiety. This implies that you wish to possess an object, to correct a transgression, or to control a situation that may stem from childhood. Dream interpretation and fantasy-life (daydreaming) exploration are two means of identifying your unconscious thoughts and wishes. Dreams can help you to reveal disturbing pressures or conflicting elements. This all requires time, patience, and a safe environment for self-exploration. In recounting your dreams, you may become consciously aware of the underlying significance of what you feel during the dreams. The visual imagery of your dream can be linked to the cause of your problem, and this is usually encoded in symbolic form. In this way, you can gain insight into your motivation for a dream, wishes you seek to fulfil, and problems you have difficulty with. Give yourself the freedom to interpret the dream content and imagery in a neutral environment. Discover what the dream means to you. Only you can interpret the dream during dream analysis. Another person's opinion is irrelevant in the interpretation of your symbolic imagery. Your self-discovery process can be assisted greatly by a therapist who utilizes hypnosis(a hypno-analyst). In dream analysis using the hypnotic process, you will be asked to give a complete picture of your thoughts by the therapist.

You get to experience a relief from symptoms when you let go of old habitual patterns of behaviours, beliefs, feelings, and thoughts that do not serve you any more. This letting go of self-limiting behavioural patterns or intolerable life circumstances means you are tackling your problems by undertaking a journey towards self-betterment. It will not be at all unusual for you to discover that after one step along the road, your achievement will then highlight other unresolved issues that may also require urgent attention. In this way, you can understand the way the past has affected your present, as well as the reasons why you have been motivated in certain ways. You may come to realize how your compulsion to re-enact the past within the present is linked with deep-rooted problems that have been unresolved before.

The positive outcome is that you can discard any self-destructive behaviour which may be unconsciously at work in your mind. In this way, you can raise your self-esteem and self-worth. In the process, during the process of self-discovery, you can let go of any relationships that are fruitless. Instead, you can form new uplifting relationships that are mutually beneficial. You can now make decisions from your own point of view, without being influenced from self-imposed pressures that do not serve you. Your growing awareness of your authentic self allows you to examine, release, and let go of the emotive content of the past. This, in turn, allows you to grow and evolve on a continual basis. As you to learn to integrate your new learning and understanding about yourself, you can see former painful matters as insignificant. You can therefore assert yourself in a self-affirming manner that allows you to express your human rights freely. This in turn gives you freedom to reintegrate into society with your newfound way of being.

Release of Emotions

Feelings come up because they want to be released. When you feel like a victim, your inner voice is beating you up by your own self-defeating criticisms or self-beliefs. You always have a choice. You don't need to be a victim. You can be the hero in your life. You don't need to be rescued by anybody else, in reality. When you worry about what others think, you give your power away. You can control what you think. What others think is none of your business. In the past, you may have pushed your feelings back down and, therefore, held on to them. So in turn, they showed up in your body and your dreams. They also affected your relationships with others.

The only way around a feeling that comes up is to observe it, accept it, and go through it. Honesty takes courage. First, be honest with yourself about how you are feeling. Then be honest with other people by expressing these feelings to them. When you express your feelings, you are being true to your authentic self at your core. In this way, you feel the feelings and you speak your truth as you express who you are. Your truth sets you free. Speaking your truth sets you free. Speaking more truth keeps you free. You are in total balance with yourself when you speak your truth. When you speak your truth, you take care of yourself and others. You speak from your heart instead of your head. When you take responsibility for yourself, you avoid judging or blaming others for your feelings. Your feelings are your feelings. You can control what you feel. When you say to yourself "I am responsible for my life" enough times, that old habit of blaming and judging others falls away. When you assert your responsibility to yourself over and over in this way, then you are taking back control of your life.

By quieting your mind, you can find peace of mind and happiness also. Happiness is always present. Your happiness does not depend on another person. Happiness and peace are already inside. The ego doesn't want you to be independent of it, even if it means you are already happy. The ego wants to be right all the time in its efforts to control you. Your mind does not control you. You control your mind. Feelings come up because they want to be released. By resisting these feelings, you actually hold on to them. You have been saying no to fear in resisting it. Resistance is what gives fear energy. Imagine, on the screen of your mind, a computer. Your mind has been programmed by your thoughts. The good news is that you can reprogram your mind, which affects the feelings you have as a result. Imagine a delete key on the keyboard. By saying yes to the fear, you delete it as you see your finger pressing the delete button. Know that your fear is erased from the screen of your mind as the screen is cleared. Knowing that you are clear, now you can feel happy and more at peace. The story you've been telling yourself in the past over and over again had been strengthening it. It's only a story, not something you can touch.

Imagine the story in front of you now, evaporating like water off a stone on a hot sunny day until it's gone. Now you can create a new story for your life and keep replaying it, as you know this replaying strengthens it over and over again. Believing in it makes it so. Your thoughts create your reality and how you feel as a result. The old story you had did not serve your needs, as you now know. Let it go. Once you have done so, all is possible. The old way of thinking makes way for the new way of life that is yours now. It is only natural for you to be at balance and in peace.

Fighting for survival became our way of being in the world based on Darwin's theory of evolution, which was set in solid stone once it was conceptualized. Now current thinking is changing according to this theory. Instead of needing to fight to survive, current thinking is based on thriving in the presence of care, compassion, appreciation, and love. This goes against Darwin's theory (nature theory), which claims that humanity is genetically disposed to being a certain way based on inherited DNA and genetic coding. Nurture theorists claim that the environment plays a huge role in which genes are activated. This is because DNA responds to the environment and the electromagnetic signals in it. This includes your thoughts. A lot of research has been done that actually demonstrates how vibrational frequency affects DNA and the "uncovering" of genes that then become activated. So, in fact, how you are in your body is not necessarily pre-determined. Your thoughts also have a powerful role to play in how your body works. When your body, mind, and soul are integrated, you function as one whole being through which anything is possible. Think about it.

The deep truth of your being is balance and peace where no other human is considered a threat. This is to be the story of your new life. Instead of asking what you can get from the planet, you can now ask what you can give back to the planet. In this way, you heal naturally through your heart connection instead of your head. Your heart is the doorway to healing your mind. Your heart's magnetic field is five thousand times stronger than that of your brain. Your brain's electrical circuitry can be healed by your heart. Your heart's electrical system is similar to that of your brain, but your heart's is sixty times stronger than that of your brain. When you feel care, compassion, gratitude, and appreciation, you think from your heart centre. This then sets up a link from your heart to heal your brain with an electrical current that can be measured by science. This current measures 0.10 hertz and is the same frequency as dolphins' or whales' sounds. It is this heart–brain connection that brings about your healing.

The new science agrees with this concept. The old ways of being do not serve us. What serves us now is how we serve others with care and compassion, and also how we take care of ourselves. You can give yourself care, compassion, gratitude, and appreciation, and in this way you can then give it to others. When you do this, you actually lower your stress hormones as you raise the master hormone, DHEA. You can only feel good and healthy as a result. Instead of reacting with stress feelings and symptoms, your body instead produces life-sustaining hormones that make you feel good, peaceful, and calm. In this way, you can focus on what you want to achieve in life. This is all controlled by these heartfelt emotions. You can change the way you feel by what you think. By what you think, you can make experiences positive, no matter what happens. It all has to do with how you perceive everything. You can be more outgoing as you grow bolder, because your positive experiences continue to mould the key to building new neural circuitry in your brain. The key resides in your heart.

You can learn to be calmer even in the face of the unfamiliar. When you know you are safe in the familiar and the unfamiliar, you can move boldly towards your goals in life with focus, balance, peace, and calm. This is especially so when you choose to feel care, compassion, gratitude, and appreciation in your heart. Just by being in a state of positivity, you are naturally upbeat and easy-going. Through your experiences, you can sculpt the neural pathways in your brain for the rest of your life. You can only know what you experience. From your knowing, you can choose how you feel and also what you experience. What you think affects your feelings, and this also affects your experience of life. By changing what you think, you change your reality. By doing things the same way, everything stays the same way. According to Einstein, "the definition of insanity is doing the same thing over and over and expecting different results." Which do you choose?

Your ability to change is your social competence. When you are cooperative, you are working in collaboration with others. You benefit more from collaboration rather than by competition with others. You also get along with other people better when you are empathetic. By giving and sharing with others, while being considerate, you can develop close friendships and relationships. When you like to help other people to get what they want, they in turn want to help you get what you want. That's what cooperation is, and it is a way of giving without expecting anything in return. In doing a kind act, you actually benefit just as much as the person receiving the kindness. What you give out, you get back in another way. What you give attracts what you receive. Your cooperation with others gives you back all the help you need in life to get where you want to get with ease.

In a relaxed state, now imagine yourself free of any dense feelings while engaged in some positive activity. When you work with your subconscious mind in a deeply relaxed state, it will do whatever is necessary to free you from your pent-up emotions and deal with them in a more constructive way. You can feel competent, accepted, and approved of when you tune into that deeper part of your self. You can also develop love and respect for yourself as a person, which grows each day and every day for the rest of your days. When your conscious mind is aligned with your subconscious, your subconscious mind begins to exercise a greater and greater influence over the way you think, over the way you feel, and over the way you behave.

Over time, you can develop whole-brain thinking, in which the two hemispheres of your brain work in synchrony with each other at the same time. It's like the left analytical brain and the right intuitive brain join forces to function at the same time. This in itself gives you exponential brainpower. From a state of neutrality, with non-judgement, you can experience deep peace within yourself. By releasing any judgement and density, you allow yourself to be free of opinions and heavy emotions. Detach from frustration, fear, and disharmony. Connect with higher states of being, even if by seeing them in others. With a conscious focus on releasing pent-up emotions whenever you feel low, you habituate towards positive thoughts, plans, ideas, or activities in alignment with your subconscious mind. As a result, you become emotionally calmer, much more settled, and much less easily disturbed. As you continually focus on the vision of yourself that you like, you learn to be calm, relaxed, and confident. You are changing your life because you are developing a belief in yourself and trust in your fellow man. When you are faced with situations of feeling slighted, rejected, or a little sad, you realize you are indeed important to life. You are a child of the universe, and you have a lot to offer. In knowing this, you love and respect yourself more and more each day for the rest of your days.

Forgiveness

There are two emotions, and they are love and fear. All dense emotions fall under fear; these include anger, resentment, envy, and jealousy. Those who hold dense emotions are not allowing the state of love. Love and fear cannot coexist at the same time. When you are living in fear, you are withholding the giving and receiving of love. What you feel is your choice always. If you are carrying dense emotions, they become emotional baggage. When you acknowledge and sit with the dense emotion, you allow it to flow. Emotions or energy (E) in motion are meant to flow and not to be resisted or denied. When they are resisted, they become stuck and so are repressed in the body. This can show up in bodily symptoms, which is the body's way of letting you know there is a problem. If you do not take heed at first, the symptom or message can become stronger. Carrying dense emotions like these can lead to energy blockages in the body, depending on where the emotion becomes lodged. This energy blockage that happens in a particular part of the body affects an organ in the same area after a while when it resonates with the energy blockage. As the body part resonates at the same frequency for a time, a physical problem manifests in that nearby organ. Two different energies cannot exist in the same spot without one balancing out the other. This means that lower energies can change the frequency of a higher energy (of the organ) if they share the same space. If the dense energy is released at an early stage, it usually does not affect the material body. The functioning of the organ, whether it is the liver, the kidney, or the lungs, can be affected when there is disharmony in that area for a prolonged period of time. This eventually can affect general health.

In effect, dense emotions lodged in the body actually can do injury to the holder. Buddha likened anger to picking up a burning ember in your bare hands with the intention of throwing it at another, all the while being seared and burned by that anger. For this reason, there is no purpose in carrying or holding on to dense emotions, because they hold you back from all abundance that is yours. Energy is supposed to flow. When dense energy is stuck, that leads to an abnormal state that affects the material state of the body. In order for energy to flow, for the emotion to be energy in motion, first allow it to surface, sit with it, welcome it, and look on it neutrally, as if observing from the outside. This sounds easy, and that is because it is effortless. Resistance means you are doing something to hold on to the emotion. Letting go means doing nothing by simply allowing the flow in acceptance. Emotions are there to allow you to process experiences in order to move on. When holding on to any dense emotion, this is like introducing a virus into the computer of your mind. As in a computer, this virus affects the functioning of your mind in every area afterwards, until the virus is discovered and deleted.

In order to prevent the virus from returning, forgiveness is necessary also. There is no point in releasing a negative emotion if resentment remains. Forgiveness for others can only benefit you ultimately, as this is how you free yourself in reality. In forgiving others, you are forgiving yourself also. When you are immune to the actions, words, or thoughts of others, you are in your own zone. This is where your true power lies. In your heart-space, you are not entangled in the whims, assumptions, or opinions of others. You can focus all your energy on creating the reality you desire from the inside out, without distraction or energy drainage from the outside. The opposite of fear is love. When you live in love, you have no fear. True love has no set conditions. Therefore, when you have unconditional love for yourself and others, you are giving what you will ultimately receive. This is the law of attraction. Love is a decision. You have a choice: would you rather be in a constrictive state of fear or an expansive state of love? Forgiveness is the key that sets you free to be open to receive from the universe. An open heart has no fear and does not need a wall around it for protection. This openness allows you to send unconditional love to every single person who has ever wronged you. Realize that what has happened is actually a blessing to bring you to where you are today. Know that the way you perceived this before was an illusion. An illusion is not real. What is real is that part of you that is your authentic self.

Reflect on those who may have caused you pain in the past, either on purpose or by accident. Send them forgiveness in an effortless manner now.

Where there is no effort, there is no resistance. Resistance prevents flow. Allowing without effort is the natural state of flow. Allow your barriers to come down in the presence of openness instead. Being in the flow releases you from any energy ties that existed and kept you stuck before. In the process, you unleash yourself from any dense etheric cords that connected you with others in the past. See those who wronged you in your mind's eye, and say silently to yourself, "I forgive anyone who deliberately or accidentally caused me pain in the past by thought, speech, or action." Forgive them as best as you can. If you can imagine a cord, like an umbilical cord, being cut in one go by a pair of scissors, this means you know you have released yourself from that negative connection. You can reconnect on a different level, if you so choose, afterwards.

The process of visualization can be very powerful, as it communicates directly to your subconscious in pictures and symbols. If you still feel resentment, allow and accept it in the moment, as any density dissolves in the presence of forgiveness and unconditional love. Love has the highest energy over everything. Whatever you surround in love becomes absorbed and transformed in the energy of love. Love is a powerful force for transformation. In order to allow self-forgiveness, you can say "Anyone I have caused pain to, deliberately or accidentally, through my thought, word, or action, I ask his or her forgiveness." Allow your heart to become an open space of unconditional love and forgiveness. Let all the blocks go, and allow yourself to be forgiven. Use your name and say "I forgive you" to yourself. Become aware of the emptiness and the silent power within you that exists at all times. Now you can say to yourself with loving-kindness "May I be free to express my authentic self in joy, love, and peace. May I be at one in myself. May I be happy and free from suffering." Now you can also visualize a person, anybody you choose, and say to him or her "May you be happy and free from suffering." Do the same for all your family members. See them one at a time, surrounded by the love you send them. See them smiling back at you. See them relating to and accepting others in peace and joy. Expand this love you send out to all in your town, your county, your country, your continent, the world, and the universe, your love being all-encompassing within its space. With an open heart, you can share your love freely with all. Imagine how the world would be if every human being did this. When somebody witnesses an open heart in another, it can open his or her heart in turn, in a ripple effect. By giving others this space, you help them to free themselves in the process, and so you are freed in return. You are freed to move on wherever you choose, without limitation, because now you have liberated yourself truly.

Gratitude

By having an attitude of gratitude, you open your heart space to receiving more of the same. When you are grateful for all the good things in your life, you allow yourself to be open to receive what you give thanks for, according to the law of attraction. You are grateful for what you desire, as if you already have it. Each night, write down ten things you are grateful for before you go to sleep. Focusing on the things you are grateful for affects your state of being in terms of motivation, action, drive, and achievement towards what you desire. By being grateful, you are more likely to take action towards your goals. Gratitude heals on a physical, mental, emotional, and spiritual level in your whole being. Every cell in your body has consciousness, because your consciousness includes your body and all of what makes you, you. Expressing gratitude for your body means you appreciate and take care of it. It also means you have compassion for yourself. When you look after yourself in this way first, you can then be in your peak condition to help others. Gratitude links you and your emotions to your heart connection. It is through your heart centre that you can connect with your divine essence, which is at one with source. Gratitude raises your vibration and stabilizes your emotional body. You attract that to you which is the same vibration as you. With increased balance and integration of your body, mind, and spirit, your magnetism for manifesting increases exponentially. As Alan H. Cohen says, "The more I appreciate the blessings I have, the more blessings I find."

You are free of a trauma or problem when you can express all aspects of it without feeling emotion. This becomes possible when your emotions are released. When you suppress negative emotions, this causes similar problems in your life to reoccur in a pattern over time. They keep coming up in order to be resolved. Let go of all that happens. Instead of clenching your fists, loosen your hands. When you do this, you know you are not holding on to anything. You are telling your body that you are in control, not your mind. Is there anything you want to express and let go of now? Get into a comfortable position. Place one hand on your lap with the palm facing upwards. Now put your other hand on your heart. As you relax, you can become aware of your heart now as your hand is over it. Become aware of that part of the heart that feels care and compassion, or even gratitude and appreciation. Close your eyes. While your eyes are closed, notice that you look straight ahead behind your eyelids. This is thinking from your brain. To make your heart connection, simply point your eyes down and slightly left towards your heart, as if you are looking at it. Feels different, right? This way, you can tap into the peace and serenity of the heart more directly. If you want to see the difference, just look straight ahead again. Now, take three deep breaths, filling your stomach like a balloon on each inhalation. As you breathe in, imagine white light entering your body through the top of your head and flowing into your heart. When you breathe out, imagine the light coming from your heart into your body and forming a bubble of light up to eighty-eight feet all the way around your body. Imagine the bubble filling with light, becoming brighter with each exhalation.

After breathing in and out three times while looking at your heart, how do you feel now? That's right! By getting out of your head in this way, you have learned a new way of feeling from the heart, and should you need to remind yourself in times of stress, simply place your hand over your heart and feel the feelings of care, compassion, gratitude, and appreciation for both yourself and others. This sends the electrical signal from the heart to your brain to shut off the old stress reaction. Instead, the brain, in its natural balanced state, produces feel-good life-sustaining hormones, such as oxytocin. Enjoy the good feeling now and know that you are in control of how you feel always. Now you can question the old thinking patterns that fade away over time, as you become more adept at making new friends. As you connect more and more with your heart, you get along better with people and you engage in more social activities that you find pleasant. This is true for you. Other people's truth is true for them, and their truth is not your truth. This is because your truth lies inside your heart. Your truth brings out your natural peace, calm, and happiness, which are always there for you to experience and feel. So when you feel care, compassion, gratitude, and appreciation in your heart, you are peaceful, calm, and happy in your mind, body, and spirit.

Exercise

Sit silently in a comfortable position with your eyes closed and take three deep breaths while saying "Haaaaaa" on each exhalation. Connect with your heart centre. Think of someone you have had a disagreement with or find difficult to get along with. In your mind, send that person thoughts of appreciation. Silently tell this person all the good things you can think of about him or her. See in your mind that person smiling and replying "Thank you." Whatever the issue is, know that it is a blessing in disguise. You can become stronger from the learning and so move on to evolve and grow as you are meant to. Imagine in your mind living your tomorrows as if you are grateful to the universe for all you receive right now. Imagine feeling and expressing your appreciation for whatever arises. You are grateful for all the good things and people who are in your life now and always. Knowing this, you are at peace within yourself, and you see this reflected in how other people are calm in your presence. People like to be around you and so are drawn to you. You are attracting new relationships and people to you now from your gratitude and appreciation of life. Now your way of being is oneness with all.

PART 3:
SELF-REALIZATION

We don't realize that somewhere within us all, there does exist a supreme Self who is eternally at peace. That supreme self is our true identity: Universal and Divine. Before you realize this truth, say the Yogis, you will always be in despair.

—Elizabeth Gilbert, Author of *Eat, Pray, Love*

CHAPTER 9

BELIEVE IN YOUR SELF

If you experience great vitality, health, effective work, and smiles on the faces of those you meet, then know that your beliefs are beneficial. On the contrary, if you experience poor health, a lack of meaningful work, a lack of abundance, and a world of sorrow and evil, then you can assume that your beliefs are faulty, and so you must begin to examine them. Thoughts have an electromagnetic reality. Your beliefs form your concept of the nature of your reality. Your thoughts and beliefs generate emotion. As you think, so is your reality. Like attracts like. You create your own reality by your thoughts and beliefs. Your beliefs are powerful. Your self-beliefs attract thoughts on the same vibrational level as your beliefs about your life. Beliefs can make facts seem like a reality. When these facts are questioned and brought to the light of your awareness, you can learn to view things differently. When your beliefs are questioned as separate from facts, you can learn to view things differently. Beliefs do not make things fact, even if it seems so. Some of these beliefs can be self-limiting or self-defeating. Beliefs are like habits and are unconscious. We hold them in our unconscious mind, and because of this, beliefs can lead to automatic reactions.

What you think you are, you are. What you believe, so it is. "When you see it, you believe it", the saying goes. According to Saint Augustine, when you believe it, you see it. Your beliefs are very powerful, as they affect your perception of your world. What you believe about the world becomes a self-fulfilling prophecy. How you perceive the world affects how you behave in it. Your beliefs are your expectations of what is and what to expect. What you expect, you get. This is the law of attraction. Your beliefs about the past make it so. The past is a story that can be viewed differently through new understanding and insight. With the awareness that comes from aligning with your authentic self, you can change your perception of the past and create a new story. You can let the past go. This gives you freedom to move forward in life. Your belief about the past does not determine your future, because you can change your beliefs in the now. There is no past right now; there is only now. There is no future right now; there is only a potentiality for being in the now. Everything is now. What you believe now affects your perception of your past and your future. You can change your perception about your past and your future right now.

Your past beliefs do not determine where you go in life. When you create new self-fulfilling beliefs while acting on them in the Now, you are taking back your own power and designing your destiny. By acting on your new empowering beliefs, you are showing that you are one with your trust in them. If you want to believe in abundance, for example, know that by making some symbolic change, such as giving, in your present situation, you are open to accepting and receiving abundance itself. In this way, you are acting as if you are already abundant, because you believe you have it already. By changing your mindset in this way, you attract all the good things that abundance brings. Whatever new belief you create, this also has a neurological effect on your brain. A new belief leads to the creation of a new physical neural network in the brain, as demonstrated by science. A neural network is a collection of nerve cells in the brain that form to carry messages from one area to another. The more the belief is acted on, the more the neural network becomes reinforced. Similarly, when habits or beliefs are not reinforced, the neural network starts fading away, as do the old beliefs. There's a saying that goes "If you don't use it, you lose it." This applies to the network in your brain also. When you reinforce your ability to have and experience abundance by acting on it in the now, you are more likely to allow room for more abundance to enter your life. It's like exercising a muscle that gets stronger over time. The more time and energy you spend in exercising that muscle while using focus, the bigger and stronger it becomes. If you don't spend time, energy, or focus on that muscle, it will become smaller and weaker. The belief that it will get stronger makes the difference. Belief and action make it a reality that you have created and continue to create. You increase your abundance not by what you do, but by what you are being, feeling, and acting on with belief.

How do you know what your self-enhancing and self-limiting beliefs are? The answer lies in turning inwards to listen to your inner voice. Is it the voice of the inner critic (also called the saboteur), or is it the other voice of wisdom that just knows? A good way to become aware of your beliefs is to keep a journal of your thoughts. By making entries on a regular basis, you are writing about what you are thinking and feeling. Using your body to write means you are incorporating your learning through a physical means rather than just a mental or spiritual means. When you see on paper what you have written, on reflection, you can be more objective as the silent witness to your own thoughts, feelings, and beliefs. Because you are detached from your thoughts as you read them, you may be able to see a different perspective on things when doing so on a continual basis and even as you write it. Through journaling, your beliefs that were once subconscious begin to rise and seep into your conscious mind also. This brings about awareness and the ability to make changes in your subconscious programming. This is achieved by consciously deciding on the beliefs you want to have and by trusting and acting on them with resolve and faith.

Beliefs become incorporated into faith when you believe without needing proof. Beliefs have more power than your thoughts. That is why positive affirmations do not work just by merely saying them over and over again. Thoughts and feelings without belief do not work either. You can think and feel what it is like to have what you want. Without belief and expectation, it does not come about. Belief is the core element that brings about all manifestation in your life! It means having faith, surrendering, and trusting in the moment. There is no room for doubt where belief is concerned. Doubt holds all that you want from you. Being in a state of want means that you don't believe you are getting it. Desire itself is different from want. What you desire is for your greater good and the good of all. Desire comes from your heart and not your head. When your desire is blended with belief, your intention will be answered. Your experience of life is a reflection of the beliefs you presently hold. You can change the possibilities for your life in the future by changing your beliefs in the now. Whatever you believe in now shapes your current and future experiences in life. Whenever you feel stuck in your life, you may have two beliefs that are in conflict with each other, without you realizing this consciously. In becoming aware of your inner voice, how you speak to others, how you behave towards others, and the environment you surround yourself with, you gain some answers as to what your beliefs are at present. The good news is that you can change your beliefs consciously and subconsciously. In this way, you can choose to change your life.

Beliefs can change or become changed and do not represent the true nature of things in themselves. Your beliefs are subjective, and so what is true for one person is not true for another. In becoming aware of your self-limiting beliefs, you can choose to create beliefs that are self-empowering instead of self-defeating. It is possible to change your beliefs, because all beliefs are habits that reside in your subconscious mind. These habits lead to automatic behaviour without conscious thought – or even choice sometimes. Habits are automatic when your conscious mind is distracted or off guard while in a relaxed state. All choice resides in cognition, or conscious thought. Beliefs, once learned, become subconscious. All learning takes place in the subconscious.

So how is it possible to acquire new beliefs? First, become aware of your beliefs about yourself by monitoring what you say to yourself routinely. By listening to your own language in this way, you become aware of your own internal dialogue. You cannot change your beliefs through sheer will power alone. By willing something to be so, you exert conscious effort. Our behaviour is determined 95 per cent by the subconscious mind. Only through aligning your conscious beliefs with your subconscious mind do they become truly powerful. How is this done? How do you tap into the power of your subconscious mind? Current research points in the direction of meditation, brainwave entrainment, subliminal messages, hypnosis, or "mind movies" to get quick and effective results in changing self-beliefs. In this way, you get to create a new reality for yourself according to what you consciously want. You can co-create your reality with the universe by choice in this way. Instead of letting your subconscious programming dictate what happens in your life, you can now reprogram your mind to give you whatever you desire much quicker than you previously thought. This in itself is a paradigm shift and a major breakthrough in the field of personal development.

When you have a belief about anything, you act in line with your belief in all ways. What you believe about yourself affects how other people behave towards you also. Your beliefs bring what you expect into your reality like a self-fulfilling prophecy. Your beliefs create the reality you live in and also affect your perception of the world around you. Your perception is, in fact, influenced by your beliefs in the first place. From your beliefs and perception, your experience of your reality is created. Therefore, your reality is different to that of anybody else. You perceive and experience your reality in a way different to the way other people do, because of your beliefs. Therefore, your bubble of reality is linked with your beliefs, some of which you may not be aware of consciously. All the results you experience in your life are results of your beliefs in the first place. Your beliefs are the cause of the results in your life.

Beliefs do not automatically lead to results instantaneously. If it were so, your mind would instantly create what it thinks and believes in. You know this is not so, because there is a time lapse between what you intend with conviction (belief) and the manifestation of your intention into existence. Your beliefs create a movement or momentum towards what you co-create with the universe into your life. When you change your beliefs, you change the momentum of your life and the direction it's going in. This momentum builds up speed and strength over time, like a snowball rolling down a hill. Your beliefs determine the direction in which your momentum and energy go in life. By consciously choosing the beliefs you want to have, you can then make these your own self-beliefs that form part of your programming from within.

Belief includes trust and faith. When you have a belief, you trust and know that it is so. There is no room for doubt. When you are connected to your authentic self at your core level, you can follow your inner guidance from source. From source, you can take guided action that manifests your heart's desire. It is in this knowing that comes from belief that you create your heart's desire into your life physically. At the same time, when you connect to your authentic self, it is important to clear out those self-limiting beliefs that are not in your best interests. It is while you are connected that you can clear those self-limiting beliefs at your core. This connection can be achieved by

- using your imagination when your eyes are closed (you can visualize when listening to relaxing music, as if you're daydreaming),
- listening to meditation audio,
- listening to self-hypnosis audio,
- listening to brainwave entrainment (BWE) audio, or
- listening to subliminal message audios.

When you change your momentum in life by changing your beliefs, you shift the direction your life takes, as well as your experience of it. When you change your beliefs to change your experience, you are stopping the previous momentum that may have been leading to unhappy results. When you change these beliefs through repetition of conscious effort over time, it takes some time to adjust to the new experience of your reality. With repetition, learning can pass from the conscious mind to the subconscious, once it is accepted as possible. Learning always takes place in the subconscious. If the beliefs are changed instantly through subconscious programming, it takes less time to adjust and align with the new experience. The beliefs you have attract possibilities in line with those set beliefs. Each belief has its own probabilities, while blocking out other probabilities. So, in essence, your beliefs attract certain possibilities from the quantum field. You decide, through choice, that what you experience is in line with your belief. The old belief just falls away, because it has no energy in your life any more. As Bruce Lee said, "Use what is useful and discard that which is not." The old belief might resurface at times, until it disappears completely. It is with experiencing your belief that you know it to be so. In this way, you can use your beliefs to focus on any area in your life that you want to improve on. What was probable before can now be made real to you in your experience of life. For change like this, you need to focus on your new belief, and not on the fact that you didn't use it before.

You can't think about what you don't want to think about without thinking about it. Where your focus goes, your energy goes. Thoughts can lead to beliefs when certain thoughts become habits. Beliefs can lead to faith. Faith leads to knowing. Faith also leads to growth by trusting in the natural order of the universe. This faith knows its object before experiencing it. It is like believing in something before you get to see, hear, or feel it in reality. Faith means you know that the conditions are right for what you believe in to come into existence. Once you have faith, you can detach and let go of how it comes about. The universe itself takes care of the "how". By detaching in this way, you are letting go emotionally of what you expect to be so, according to your belief. If you stay emotionally involved with what you want, then you are not allowing according to your belief. This means that your belief will be blocked by your counter-belief of not trusting and just allowing.

When you clear your counter-beliefs, only your beliefs remain. By surrendering and trusting only, you have faith and you are ready to receive. However, this faith is not blind, because your experience of it shows how you can benefit from the changes it brings into your life. You can have better health, wealth, prosperity, and abundance through the understanding that faith transforms you. Faith in your higher power brings into being those abilities and characteristics of your hero self. Previously these abilities remained dormant and unused until the light of belief shone on them. Your belief charges and activates those dormant forces within and without. This is how the law of attraction works. You can attract only that which you have and are already in the now, even if it is in the form of belief.

The law of attraction does not merely work by what you intend with emotion for yourself. This is why positive affirmations, setting goals, and focusing on what you want did not get you the results you wanted up till now. When you expect what you want, then the law of attraction will work according to your beliefs and unwavering faith. While repetition and practise of a new habit eventually places that habit into the subconscious, this can take a long time. This form of learning takes many, many repetitions for it to go into the subconscious, where it then affects behaviour in an automatic fashion, like autopilot. The quicker route to learning a new habit or self-belief is through the subconscious directly, either by hypnosis or meditation. All hypnosis is self-hypnosis.

If you do not believe you are worthy or deserve your dream, then this is what will happen, no matter how much you want it. This is why some people fail when they are just about to succeed. Their subconscious belief of not succeeding gets in the way of them succeeding. Because of this, the saboteur blocks their success in line with their belief. In the book *The Secret*, this point is not explained, and for this reason a false sense of hope is given that anybody can have whatever they want just by asking the universe for it. The law of attraction does not work in this way. It works through your subconscious and your beliefs stored therein. This is why your journey to self-discovery brings to the surface who you think you are and what you believe. Who do you think you are? What do you believe about yourself? When you get to know yourself, this leads to self-awareness. Self-awareness leads you to your authentic self. Your authentic self is where your true power lies. By tuning into your own power, you learn to master what you create in your life – even your own reality. Your beliefs attract to you everything on the same wavelength easily and effortlessly. So be mindful of your thoughts, emotions, and beliefs, because they affect everything around you on the outside. You are a magnet for what you think and believe. Think about it. When you change your thoughts, emotions, and beliefs, you change your potential and possibilities. By expanding your beliefs about yourself and your world, you expand yourself and your life in reality.

The Power of Belief

What you focus on grows. Believe in abundance for yourself and others. As this belief grows amongst people in general, abundance becomes possible for all. Through new insights, ideas, and discoveries, abundance is continually being brought into being. Your environment affects your consciousness in terms of what you perceive as abundance. By getting rid of old stuff that you don't need and replacing it with new things, this sends a message to your subconscious that abundance is in supply. By keeping symbols and signs of abundance in your environment, you impress upon your subconscious the feeling of abundance. In this way, you create conditions of abundance.

When you notice abundance around you, this may cause a shift towards creating more of the same. By focusing on all the things that demonstrate abundance in your life, you are focusing on the reality of abundance that is possible. With this comes the belief that allows you to create more abundance and prosperity into material form automatically. By living according to the belief that you are already abundant, you create the conditions of abundance in turn. Believing you are abundant means you expect the best for yourself because you know you're worth it.

Your beliefs create your reality without limitation. If you believe you must make sacrifices or work hard, then this will be your reality. You are here on earth to experience bliss, peace, and happiness, not to have struggle and pain. You do not need to give up your life for other people. Your life is your own and belongs to you completely. This is not selfish. If you allow yourself to be controlled by other people because of your beliefs, then you are giving your power to them. In this way, they become the master of your life. You know you can be your own master when you tune into your authentic self. When you do, you realize that you always had the control and power at your core. You realize that you were led astray (from your authentic self) by your programming coming from your beliefs, memories, and experiences. These gave rise to your perception of life to be the illusion you thought it was at the time. When you remove the veil of disbelief in yourself, you can see how your empowering beliefs are truly a part of your essential nature. When you love and accept yourself unconditionally, you follow your heart without hesitation. You accept all that is, and no matter how it seems, you know it is all connected with your higher purpose. The best question to ask yourself then is, what can I learn from this? The answer that leads you evermore forward will come in time.

You can set yourself free from your struggles and pain in life by expressing your authentic self. Your journey to authenticity equips you with self-knowledge and self-awareness. This allows you to take a stand in your own life for you. Your time has come. Speaking your truth empowers you from within. You deserve to live the life of your dreams. Expressing your authentic self gives you the freedom to co-create your life with the universe according to what you desire. By expressing yourself and your beliefs with courage, you can remain true to yourself at your core. When you are being honest with yourself and the world around you, you avoid conflict. Instead, you forge a path for yourself with limitless opportunities, abundance, and prosperity. When you believe it, you see it. Believe in yourself and the rest follows.

As you think in terms of prosperity and abundance, your vibration increases accordingly. Because of this vibrational change, you become a magnet for like-minded people who are also prosperous when you see others being successful. Realize how they are showing you how abundance is possible for everybody. Believe that others' success means you can be successful too. If everyone around you is succeeding, you are surrounded by the vibration of success. When you are surrounded by successful people, this leads to the growth of more success in your life. Your mindset for abundance and success allows you to see these things wherever you go. Your belief in success and abundance leads to the expectation of success and abundance in your life. When you appreciate others' success and abundance, you acknowledge the abundance and success that exists for you too. If you compete with or feel threatened by others' success, then your state of mind in turn blocks success and abundance flowing to you. When you wish success for others, you attract it for yourself also. When you believe that the universe is abundant in its nature, your belief and expectation attract what you are thinking about in terms of our concepts and understanding of the world. You are what you think and what you believe. Your reality is created by what you believe in.

You know now that you form reality through your beliefs, and this includes your physical body. Your molecules and atoms in your body are shaped by your thoughts and beliefs, which have a knock-on effect on your emotions. Your emotions affect the glands in your body. Your emotions can affect how your glands secrete hormones, which in turn affect the function of your organs. Your general health is determined by how well your organs function in your body. In *The Biology of Belief*, Bruce Lipton claims that your DNA is affected by your beliefs and that your DNA expression is not static and determined, as scientists believed up till now. Therefore, your beliefs can affect the genetic expression of your DNA. This also means if your beliefs change, then so can your DNA expression. Your DNA expression can be transformed and transmuted according to your beliefs. In this way, you can change your body by changing your beliefs. The implications for this are limitless. What untapped powers have you not learned to believe in yet? What do you believe is possible for you? Believe in it, and it is so. It may not manifest straight away, but if you truly do believe, then the universe will rearrange and weave events to tie in with bringing that into existence. It cannot be any other way. This is the nature of the universe, for what can be possible can always be in reality.

Your health is regulated by your conscious thoughts. Focusing on illness can make you ill. When you believe that you become ill because of viruses, infections, or accidents, then you seek help from the outside in the form of a doctor and hospital. Because of the power of your belief in this medical approach of treating your ailment, you should get some relief. When you do not realize that your thoughts are connected to your illness, you continue to experience it, and new symptoms may appear. Once you begin to make the connection that there is a link between your thoughts and the illness, your beliefs are in the process of change. At first, you may continue to seek relief according to your old beliefs. This is because you do not fully realize the power of your own thoughts and the beneficial effect of you changing them. This knowing may stretch your insight at first, until you experience the link between feelings of joy and happiness and their effects on your physical body. Your body knows what is good for it. It has its own intelligence, which can be demonstrated through muscle testing. When you go to a doctor, your symptoms are treated, but the cause is not, necessarily. Even if you believe the doctor can help you, the cause of your illness still remains. This is because only you can transform the root cause once it comes into awareness. By releasing the root through awareness and understanding, you get the lesson your body was trying to tell you.

Your body is a temple through which your subconscious communicates to you. This communication can take the form of illness if there is an emotional imbalance in your life. This imbalance may come from a self-defeating belief. When this belief comes into conscious awareness and is processed and released, then the illness itself disappears. The illness serves no purpose after that because the lesson has been learned. Once integration of the new awareness has taken place within your consciousness, you can let go of the old self-limiting belief. It does not belong to your way of being any more, and so you are free. In its place, you will have replaced it with a new insight or empowering belief. This is how true healing comes from within. You truly have the ability to heal yourself and your life. This is your birthright. When you know how to access your knowing, miracles can happen. When you realize that in (your) reality miracles are natural, you know this because they are a part of your natural world. When you believe in miracles, you are open to accepting and receiving these into your life. Life then becomes magical, exciting, and extraordinary. This is where your true power lies through belief.

Your true power comes from within, in connecting with your authentic self. Your authentic self is the truth of who you really are. As you move towards your authentic self, so your beliefs become aligned with your own truth. What is not needed is discarded, and what is useful remains. As your beliefs change, so does your experience of life. Your authenticity opens up a world of magic and possibility. The world really is your oyster, and you are the pearl at its core. You are the centre of your world, because you shape your reality through your beliefs from the inside. Your world is not created from outside of you, as it may appear to your senses. The only limits in life are the ones you set for yourself. Your creative energy is what makes your world as it appears. Your creativity is a gift from above. What do you choose to create? Start from the end in bringing it into being. When it belongs to you in your belief, you have it already. It exists already at another level. All you need to do is take action in merging with it, and it is so.

When you merge with your reality, you experience directly what it has to offer. If you close off from your reality, you can lose out on the opportunities that you do not see, and so you live a smaller life. Your resistance is the mind's way of keeping you safe and protected – or, in other words, small and separate. You always have a choice. Belief can lead to decisive action. This is possible when you have unconditional positive regard for yourself. Your unconditional love for yourself allows you to trust your own direction, according to your authentic self. This is the solid foundation for your very being of who you really are. At your core, you are pure love. You do not need anything extra from the outside. Those that do not know their authentic self sometimes lose their way or become misdirected from their true path. This is because they look to the outside for direction from others.

The possibility for reconnection to your authentic self exists at all times, which coincides with reconnecting to your calling in life. Become aware of and listen to your beliefs. What is your life experience like today? When you know what your experience is, you know what your beliefs are about yourself and the world. If there is conflict in your life, then what feels right? Your feeling will always give you your answer. Whatever makes you uncomfortable is something to be worked on. What makes you feel good is linked to your authentic self. You can always use your free will to move closer to your authentic self by consciously choosing those beliefs that feel empowering. In this way, you are tapping into your own power and essence. You truly are a powerful being. When you are aligned with your authentic self, you are remembering who you really are. Your self-beliefs allow you to embrace, love, and accept yourself when you connect with your true essence. With this connection, you can now unleash the power you really have into the external world from within. You attract that by which you are attracted, and so miracles become natural. You marvel at the web of life and how everything is connected. Your belief in connection makes it so, and because of this, you attract miracles by your connection to your real self. Life takes on its own ease and grace, while being effortless in turn.

When you create a new empowering belief in the now, you can alter the effects of the past in terms of cellular memory, genetic coding, and neural networks that are created. Your perception of yourself is a product of your experiences and beliefs in totality. This also includes your present experiences and beliefs, which can override previous ones. By creating beliefs like "I am healthy" and "I am well", you become active in creating this self-fulfilling prophecy. Beliefs are something you know to be the case. Merely saying affirmations without feeling and believing in them is not enough. You can re-pattern the programs set up in the past from now, in the present. Now is where your true power lies. Effectively, you can change the neurological make-up of your brain and body through your beliefs right now.

It is well known now through research that your thoughts, feelings, and beliefs affect the physical make-up of your body on an ongoing basis. For every belief you have, there is a matching neural network of cells in the brain that grows bigger the more the belief is used or processed. Imagine the brain being like a mass of muscles. When a certain area is exercised through repeated use, that area of the brain gets bigger. This does not happen just from physical activity alone, but through imagining that action also in the mind's eye. Because your beliefs affect your perception of the world, they also affect how you behave and what you focus on in your life. Over time, what you focus on can become automatic as you become habituated to the belief when it becomes a habit. Habits are not just physical actions; they can be beliefs also. Beliefs determine your reality and how you perceive it. By changing your beliefs, you change your reality. While you may not be able to change your past, you can change your perception of it, as well as your beliefs about it right now. There is no point in looking to the past to try to make sense of it. Trying to analyse and find an answer in the past means you are looking backwards and so are not present. Being present in the present is where you find your true power. What you believe right now determines your future in the now.

For the future you want, what beliefs do you need to have right now? If you haven't got those beliefs at present, then what do you need to do to own each belief? You can learn from those who have already achieved what you want. Listen for their words of inspiration and what resonates with you. When you have living proof of what you want to achieve, you come to know that this is possible for you too. Taking action with conviction towards your dream can also create the empowering beliefs you need in making it so. At the same time, action and beliefs can change your perception of the past and, therefore, your reaction to it. What may have seemed like a struggle before can now be viewed as a blessing allowing you to become the person you are now. Your belief in the past struggle has now been replaced with another belief that everything is in divine order. With this belief, you know that there is a purpose for everything that happens. Now you can see through the eyes of love instead of the eyes of fear, and so you are free. Your belief makes it so. Surely, then, you would like to have beliefs that move you forward in your life towards your heart's desire. When you let go of beliefs that hold you back by ruminating over the past, you make room for taking responsibility in your life right now. This is because you are no longer a victim in your own eyes. Now you get to decide who you are, where your life is going, and what you want out of life. This is where your true power lies, and that is in the now. How do you accept a new belief?

Sometimes your subconscious beliefs can be self-defeating. For example, when you are sick, your illness can be created by a secondary gain. A secondary gain is, in this case, a belief that you benefit from the illness either directly or indirectly. While you may not like the sickness, at the same time, you are not consciously aware that you have created it to serve some purpose. Your subconscious is there to protect you, and like a five-year-old, it follows your commands literally, even though its logic may be not what you expect. While the subconscious has access to vast wisdom in the universal realm, it follows your commands literally to achieve what you want. For this reason, to avoid confusion, it's best to keep affirmations simple and in the present tense. The same applies to beliefs. By affirming over and over again "I am healthy" while in a deeply relaxed state, you can reverse the effects of illness or disease over time as the affirmation becomes ingrained in your brain and subconscious as a belief. The original sickness may have come from a belief that it serves a purpose of providing you with a constructive gain. This form of limiting belief can come from your perception of being unworthy, unlovable, and undeserving. This attitude of powerlessness means that you believe you can be made to feel better only by what you receive on the outside.

By giving yourself what you need on the inside first, in the form of empowering beliefs like "I am worthy", "I love myself", and "I deserve health", you can reverse the effects of sickness while also preventing it in the first place. By finding the root cause of the sickness, you determine why it came about in the first place. If it is caused by a trauma, this root cause can be repressed from the conscious mind. One way to access this repression is through the "talking therapy" of psychotherapy, which is more effective when combined with hypnosis. Once it is fully realized, the repression can be released and let go of. Once this repression is cleared, an empowering belief can be chosen consciously and substituted via the subconscious to replace it. Whenever a habit is changed or released, if it is not replaced consciously with another empowering habit, then the subconscious will replace it with another habit that may not be so empowering. The subconscious does this to protect you. It will readily accept the belief you feed it when that belief goes directly into the subconscious mind. Positive affirmations have no effect without belief. Once in the subconscious, that new belief prevents the illness from coming back. It is now part of your internal programming. If the root cause of your own sickness or illness does not become conscious, the subconscious mind can substitute one set of symptoms for another to achieve the same secondary gain.

When a person is (subconsciously) convinced that an illness meets his or her needs, the illness remains. We all have the power to heal ourselves in the present. Healing of any kind is a process that starts with a belief. By using your mind as a tool to overcome your self-limiting beliefs, you are tapping into your innate power that all humans have. You have far more power than you can imagine. Once you expand your consciousness, your beliefs and your experience also expand. This is what gives you more choice in life. The more empowering beliefs you have, the more choice you have. The more choice you have in life, the more opportunities you have. Your current beliefs determine the opportunities you see around you. Your readiness for action is determined by your programming and beliefs. The good news is that you can always adapt your readiness for action according to what you want through your beliefs. Belief is everything. Your beliefs determine what you attract to yourself. So, in order to attract what you want, you simply align your beliefs to what you desire. When you do this, you do not need to chase what you want. When your beliefs match what you want, there is no struggle. Everything is effortless and easy in achieving your heart's desire. If you believe you must struggle to achieve it, then this will be true for you also.

Similarly, if you feel lonely, this comes from a belief that you are alone. To counteract this, you can create a feeling of being surrounded by friends. Beliefs lead to feelings. You can feel only what is true for you, even in the imagination. So if you imagine that you have companionship all around you, while feeling this to be so, this can have a neurological effect on the re-patterning of your brain. This re-patterning becomes automatic after about three weeks, when the brain circuitry has grown considerably. Your old feeling of loneliness, which may have been triggered by certain surroundings, has now become reconditioned to one of companionship, as a result of retraining your brain. Your feeling about a situation brings it into being by creating the conditions for its manifestation in due course.

Your beliefs and feelings are inextricably linked. You believe what you feel, and you feel what you believe. The amazing thing is that you can imagine what you feel and believe also. The brain experiences in real time (now) what the mind sees, even if it is seen during visualization when the eyes are closed. Current science has shown this to be so through brain-scan studies. The same areas of the brain light up whether you see something for real or imagine it in your mind's eye. This demonstrates that certain brain networks fire only during visualization, depending on what is being imagined. Thus, the brain sees it now as if it is happening now. The brain believes it to be so and sets up a new pattern of cells that are receptive to this new possibility. In turn, these neural networks can create that possibility when they are reinforced. This process of neural network building becomes automatic through any new belief that is formed for what is possible.

For this reason, the imagination is much more powerful than the conscious mind. The imagination communicates directly with the subconscious through symbols and imagery. The conscious mind has a critical factor that blocks conscious thoughts from entering the subconscious. Sometimes, though, subconscious thoughts and beliefs can seep through to the conscious mind. These come in the form of feelings, dream imagery, slips of the tongue, gut feelings, creative expressions (as in art), knowing, or even daydreams. This is how the subconscious hints at certain things. It is not direct, as with the conscious mind. That is why the imagination is needed when forming new beliefs.

So, to change your perception of reality in any way, it is necessary to reprogram your subconscious in that regard by creating a specific belief. It is possible to program this new belief into your subconscious through your natural power of self-hypnosis or meditation. The more your intention is repeated, the more it becomes a habit, thus leading to a belief. You can also program your subconscious through subliminal messages, which are not heard by the conscious mind and so go straight into the subconscious mind. The conscious mind cannot stop the messages from going into the subconscious if they can't be heard consciously. With repetition, the message becomes a belief in your subconscious mind. The messages your mind receives from your thoughts and the outside world can influence the beliefs that are formed in your subconscious over time. For this reason, be aware of what you tell yourself and what you feed your mind with from the outside. What you expose your mind to hearing and receiving can shape your views, perceptions, and beliefs about the world. This includes the people you spend the most of your time with. It is said that you earn the average wage of the five people you spend time with the most. Also, the last thirty books you read can have an influence on your values and beliefs. Social hypnosis exists in the messages surrounding you in society. Advertising is a powerful medium that hypnotizes people into being consumers with a desire to fulfil needs and wants in order to be whole and complete.

When you know already that you are whole and complete, you do not need to search for anything extra to be fulfilled and happy. When you know and believe that you have everything you need already, then you are at peace and happiness is yours already. This is your natural state. Peace, joy, and happiness are your natural state of being. When you believe that your life is abundant, then this is how you live your life. Being and living your life according to your beliefs makes it so. Your beliefs can come about from what you tell yourself in a repeated fashion. So, in essence, all your beliefs have come from a natural self-hypnosis or what you have been telling yourself about the nature of reality during your life. When you use the technique of hypnosis consciously, you are merely speeding up this power of belief creation. You can be influenced by other people if you perceive them as authorities or experts. In this case, you can allow yourself to be influenced by others. In turn, you can influence others without being consciously aware of it. In this way, people can hypnotize each other consistently. In hypnosis, your awareness becomes more intensified, as does your hearing.

In a suggestible state, your concentration is focused on the input you receive, especially if you are confused or shocked. In confusion or shock, your brainwaves have slowed to such a degree that your subconscious mind is open to receiving any suggestions that are made. The conscious mind, which normally acts as a sentry for the subconscious mind, lets down its barriers and allows messages to go straight through to the subconscious during hypnosis, usually because you are deeply relaxed. Messages received by the subconscious are automatically acted upon without conscious thought. During hypnosis, habitual reactions are suspended in this intensified state of focus in the present moment. Shock or confusion from unexpected events can lead to a form of hypnosis that leaves you vulnerable to directly accepting suggestions into the subconscious. This is why therapists are called to the scene of traumas, such as train crashes – to insert new empowering beliefs for the victims before post-traumatic stress disorder (PTSD) can take root.

For the same reason, when you are watching any images on a television, your brainwaves tend to go from beta into alpha waves. This means you are in a daydream state when watching television. When your brainwaves are slower than beta waves, you are in a trance and are therefore more open to suggestions. So if watching the news means you are viewing a lot of shocking, negative images, then in reality you are hypnotizing yourself. You would also be hypnotizing yourself if watching positive images, though. When you are aware of this, you can counteract your shock or confusion with self-affirming intentions or affirmations. Also, you can turn off the news. If you're not aware, then what is the message you are programming your mind to believe? Think about it.

The same applies to the movies you watch in the cinema. I prefer to watch comedies, because they make me laugh. My reason for this is that I know and believe laughter boosts the immune system, as shown by research. Also, I believe that watching comedy reinforces my belief that everything has a funny side to it, no matter how ridiculous it may seem. A third reason I choose to watch comedies is that I believe that humour is a great coping mechanism for most situations. When you can see the funny side to life, you've just got to laugh. That way you don't take yourself or others too seriously and you learn not to take things personally. It's not about you. What other people do is a reflection on them and their thought processes. Be mindful of what you allow your mind to be open to. Your mind is a tool. You control your mind. You mould your mind to bring out the best in you.

Your beliefs are how your mind is set – your mindset. Belief is everything. What you believe, you are. As you think, so are you.

Your brain processes the information you filter through into your experience, while deleting, distorting, or generalizing the rest. In this way, you can see how every person's experience of reality can vary, even those who are sitting in the same room while looking at the same object. You have a unique experience of your own reality, according to your mindset. Your experience of life actually shapes your mindset as well as your brain. You have the power to change your beliefs and, therefore, your experience of life. In fact, you have more power than you may realize. Everything is not as it seems. By changing your beliefs and, therefore, your expectations, you automatically change your experience of reality, because this changes your filters in turn. When you clear old self-defeating beliefs while creating new empowering beliefs, you allow more of what you want into your experience of life. By shifting your feelings, thoughts, and self-identity into a higher level of being, you automatically shift your experience of reality to a higher vibration. Your beliefs are this powerful!

You can consciously change your beliefs by first becoming aware of those that do not serve you any more. This can be achieved by looking inside, becoming aware, and getting to know who you are at your core, where your authentic self lies. When you connect with your authentic self, you are raising your self-awareness, as well as your ability to create the changes you want in your life. If you don't have insight into yourself, you won't know which changes you want to make. If you are looking outside all the time, then you don't get to see what's on the inside. You save yourself a lot of time of looking and searching for what you want by realigning and harmonizing with your true self on the inside in the first place. There is no need for searching, trying, failing, or struggling any more. When you are connected with your authentic self, you are moving forward in your life with balance and harmony from within. Your life experience now harmonizes with the joy, peace, and effortless being of your authentic self. In the same way, life happens through you because you are one with it. The closer your connection with your authentic self, the greater your ability for creating your best life yet. Your power to create comes from your empowerment within.

You cannot connect with your authentic self without help from the environment and everything that's in it. This is how you get to experience your self through your body. You create your environment from the inside out. This environment includes your body and your brain. Your body lies outside your consciousness. It is affected by your thoughts, beliefs, and feelings in terms of what chemicals it produces. The epigenetic principle introduced by Bruce Lipton is linked with the "biology of belief." Your body is not determined by your genetic make-up or blueprint at birth, as was previously thought by scientists. According to Bruce Lipton, your beliefs affect your genes on an ongoing basis. That means that your cells in your body change according to your thoughts and beliefs. It is your thoughts and beliefs that affect whatever gene is activated. Lipton states that from his research, he has found that the human gene is actually affected by its own environment, as is the human cell. This environment includes the human body that surrounds the cell, which in turn surrounds the genes therein. According to epigenetics, the receptor proteins on the surface of the cell membrane act in the same way as sensory perception in the body. The effector proteins on the inside of the cell membrane monitor the environment inside the cell. When the receptor proteins send messages from the environment to the effector proteins and vice versa, toxins are allowed to be released from the cell and nutrients are allowed to be taken in.

The receptor cells are influenced not only by physical particles, Lipton says. They are also influenced by electromagnetic signals and frequencies in the environment. This includes your thoughts. So your body is not just influenced by your physical environment. It can also be influenced by what you cannot see, hear, feel, touch, or smell. In the quantum universe, everything carries a vibration or frequency of resonation. Every thought carries a vibration. Every sound carries a vibration or frequency also. What you think or listen to can have powerful effects on the state of your physical being. This principle makes sense when you think from the position of the observer-expectancy effect in quantum physics. What you look for determines what you see, according to experiments done in the area of quantum physics, and this includes your beliefs. The results you expect before doing the experiment actually affect the outcome, even when your expectations change beforehand.

Your cells react and respond to your thoughts in general, based on your beliefs. Scientists have now discovered that every cell in your body has cellular memory that is shaped from previous experiences. This includes every thought and experience you have ever had. Organisms have now been found to have this kind of cellular memory based on experience. The interesting thing is that this cellular memory does not need your brain for memory to be possible. What does this mean? It means that your memory is stored in all the cells of your body. Also, your genes do not determine the make-up of your body, but your consciousness does. All your experiences in life are stored in your subconscious, which is linked with the universal consciousness. Your consciousness affects everything outside of itself, and that includes the body. Your authentic self lies deep within your consciousness, under many layers of beliefs and conditioning.

Once you let go of these layers through awareness and self-understanding, you become one with your authentic self. This is where your true power lies, from where you can bring major changes to your life in an easy and effortless fashion, without any self-limiting beliefs getting in the way. Your body and brain are merely tools for you to use in achieving your purpose in life. Your true power lies in realizing that you are not your body. You are not your mind. Your mind is not controlled by your brain. In fact, you control your body – how it works, how it is shaped – using your intention and belief, even if it is subconscious. Belief is what makes it happen. It is when you are in alignment with your authentic self that your beliefs will make this so. Your belief is something you own, not something told to you or described to you. You acquire your beliefs through experience. When you experience what is possible, you continually move to new heights of possibility

How do you undo the programming of limiting beliefs that lead to limited behaviour? Your limiting beliefs can prevent you from moving forward towards your heart's desire. You may be consciously aware that when you procrastinate, you are not getting anywhere. At the same time, you may not be aware of your subconscious beliefs behind this lack of action. There is no point in forcing your conscious view if it is in conflict with your subconscious belief. Limiting beliefs are an illusion of who you truly are in reality.

When you can let go of the false conditioning, you let go of the grid that you lived your life in at that moment. By replacing your limiting beliefs of "I am not worthy", for example, with "I am worthy", you express the true nature of your being, which counteracts any prior perceived lack or limit in your reality. When you know you are worthy, you begin to see proof of this in your newly perceived surroundings that are superimposed on your old view of reality. The previous picture of your life-view changes to reveal that you are indeed surrounded by abundance in everything that surrounds and is in you. It is all connected, as your inner worth connects you to all that is worthy of you on the outside. You have abundance because you are abundant. You know this when your conscious and subconscious mind are in agreement as one. When you want to manifest or create into your life, synchronize your brain as one through meditation or hypnosis. This synchronization creates the best conditions for your conscious and subconscious mind to work as one. In this way, you connect the intention of who you are with the energy of who you truly are. When you do this, your energy becomes balanced as your authentic self emerges forth into your being. By creating balance, stability, and unification within yourself, you become the best temple for your authentic self to live in. As you are, so are you. As you have become one with yourself, so your authentic self has become one with you.

Belief creates your reality. You create through the power of your belief. You create your beliefs in order to recreate. With your beliefs, you co-create with the universe. You create with who you are. Who you are creates what you manifest. When you know who you are, you know what is for your highest and greatest good. When you know who you are, you have more internal power to create from your source. Your connection to your authentic self allows you to instantly manifest according to your beliefs. Expect and believe. Believe and expect and it is so. All is in divine order. Believe in yourself. When you accept who you are in reality, this means saying yes to yourself and your own life. Self-acceptance means you can express your truth. Accept who you are and allow all that you want to flow through you. Believing in your self means you do not have to say yes to people, events, or anything that bothers you. It also means taking your feelings into account before accepting anything into your life.

When you express your authentic self, this brings about perfect health for you. You are flowing in your essence of life. You let go of what does not serve you, and you utilize what is useful. Expressing your authentic self blends your body, mind, and spiritual aspects of being as one whole. You are an integrated being when you combine these three aspects of yourself as one. Acceptance of this means you are affirming your very being. You know you are a spiritual being having a human experience when you speak from your heart and not your head. By freely expressing yourself, you can say no when it suits you. In truth, you can express your desires and also be open about your feelings. By accepting your authentic self, you can express and own your true essence when you bring it forth. In knowing who you are and how you are, you continue to grow and evolve from this solid foundation. Aligning with your authentic self brings the knowledge of the power that lies within, of your spirit within flesh that experiences the physical aspects of your reality. Through self-discovery, your beliefs become enlightened in the truth of who you really are. When you are aligned with your authentic self, your beliefs become conscious. Conscious awareness means you have control over what happens in your consciousness at the same time. In this way, you have aligned your conscious and subconscious mind as one.

Exercise

All learning takes place at the subconscious level, and this includes the acquiring of new beliefs. Your beliefs are stored in the subconscious also. So access to the subconscious is required when changing beliefs. This can be achieved through natural self-hypnosis or meditation on a daily basis. Find a quiet place to relax, and make sure you won't be disturbed. Close your eyes and repeat your chosen belief as an affirmation for about five to ten minutes consistently, while visualizing what you see, feel, hear, taste, and smell. I find it best to follow a guided audio either on meditation or hypnosis. For me, listening to the voice of a guided visualization is easier to follow than just visualizing in your own mind. A guided visualization allows you to easily slip into a deeply relaxed state while your conscious mind is at rest. During the process, you use your imagination to visualize your intention as if it exists now in the present. See what people you are surrounded with while seeing your outcome. You can say the belief (e.g., "I am healthy" or "I am abundant") out loud or in your head. Through repetition, you are activating neurological re-patterning in the brain.

Your brain is a tool from where your perceptions are projected onto the world. The world, in turn, mirrors back to you what you project onto it. The more you reinforce this pattern of thinking, the more results you will get, according to your line of thinking. Even when you start receiving that which you intend, continue with this practise to keep the "muscle" strong. When you finish this exercise, let it go and get on with your daily living. Just trust that all is well. This is what is meant by surrendering when you accept without questioning what is. By surrendering, you allow. By ruminating, you hold yourself back. You are moving forward when you take action right now, without looking back. You are looking forward from the present moment when you create new empowering beliefs in the now. Take one step today, no matter how small, towards changing your beliefs for the better. That way you know you are committed.

CHAPTER 10

YOUR POWER IN THE NOW

Your Power Is in the Now

Even though time does not exist as you know it, within your body you perceive your life as a series of passing moments through your five senses, and this gives rise to your experiences. There is no past or future in reality. There is only now. The story you identified with up till now comes from your past, which does not exist any more. The story you told yourself about who you are and where you come from was linked with your past. You can let go of the old story and create a new one for yourself right now. You do not need to believe what others told you in the past. It is now time to step out from a place of your own truth, where your story now is a construct of the true representation of your essential being. By changing your story in this way, you change your beliefs, attitudes, values, perceptions, and even memories themselves. Through understanding at this level, you can review your memories and see them in a different light than before.

Everything happens for a reason. Your authentic self, in reality, defines who you are at your core. This never changes, no matter what your circumstances seem to be like. Your perception of events is influenced by your beliefs. Your beliefs, in turn, are influenced by your thoughts on where you come from, where you are, and where you're going. Your thoughts on where you come from and where you're going are in turn influenced by where you are in the now. There is only now. With insight, you can learn how your own way of thinking has caused you suffering. Buddha describes enlightenment as "the end of suffering". Through being your own deepest self, your true nature can be known when your mind is still in the now and knowing your essence of "I am." Ego thinking defines the self as separate in a world of competition. Identification of the self with ego leads to suffering in the form of judgements, concepts, comparisons, labels, and words. Ego identification blocks your real self from everything and everybody around you, from the illusion of separateness in the physical world. In reality, all is one, but many people forget this, as it does not feel real for them in their experience.

The mind is given to you; you are not given to the mind. Neither are you your mind. The illusions of life lie in the misuse of the mind and what it stands for. The illusion lies in unconsciously thinking you are your mind. Your real self, however, lies outside your mind, outside your thinking, from where you can observe in a state of awareness. Your real self is aware that thinking itself is only a small aspect of consciousness. It is also aware that there is a higher level of consciousness beyond thought, in a realm of infinite intelligence. The ego mind is conditioned to think in a way where it dwells on the past and worries about the future without being present in the present. Therefore, the present is veiled by an association with past events and an unhealthy frame of mind that focuses on density, which causes suffering.

By watching the thinker (ego mind), you see how repeated patterns show up in your inner dialogue. Do not resist what you hear, for that will bring more of the same. You, the observer, are listening to the voice of your mind from beyond the mind. "I am" is separate from the mind. The more you observe and listen, the more you begin to recognize thoughts as separate from your presence. This is when they lose their hold over you. You are separate from your thoughts and can let them go. This leaves space for no-thought or no-thinking as a gap between your thoughts. In the gap, you feel oneness and being. Being present can be clouded by your mind and its thoughts. The more you feel your real presence, the more you become aware of inner peace, joy, and stability, which pale in significance to thoughts, emotions, your body, and the outside world. For this reason, it is important to dis-identify from your mind. As the gaps of no-mind increase, your inner consciousness grows stronger while your sense of self is redefined as separate from thoughts and the mind. The mind is a tool for getting tasks done, and that's all. The mind takes over when you become fixated on thinking in a negative mindset. Now is all that is in reality. Being present in the moment means you are present in your self, where you can interact directly with the world, unhindered by the ego.

Thoughts need consciousness, whereas consciousness does not need thought. Higher consciousness means rising above thought while still using the mind in a more focused way when needed. Inner stillness leads to creativity. Self-defeating thoughts affect your emotions and the biochemistry of your body. People who carry dense emotions give off vibes to other people who pick up on them subliminally. This can trigger the same latent emotions in those picking up the vibes. When you recognize your emotion in your body, you can observe it without becoming identified with it. Your presence frees you from becoming controlled by your emotions. Focus on your energy within, and feel the emotion. The ego mind does not know the solution to negative emotions. The more it pays attention to negativity, the more it adds to the problem. What you focus on grows.

What you observe, you can let go of by feeling that emotion and understanding the law of its opposites that exist on the outside. Pleasure versus pain is an example. Pleasure is obtained from something outside of you that is not permanent; therefore, pleasure is not permanent. Joy, on the other hand, arises from within. It has no opposite and, just like peace and love, is not subject to the illusion of duality on the outside. Love, peace, and joy emanate from within, in the higher consciousness of being. In your real self, there are no opposites and, therefore, no emotions, but a way of being. Everything is as it is in the now. After being dis-identified from the ego mind, you no longer have the need to be right. Your sense of self is no longer associated with the need to be right, which is ego-dominated. Whether right or wrong, your sense of self remains unchanged and uninfluenced in its natural state of love, peace, and joy. There is no need to any longer defend the illusion that existed in identifying with your ego mind. You can, therefore, state clearly your thoughts and feelings to others at ease, without identifying with them and also without fear.

Time exists outside of now. Time is outside of your real self. Time coexists with the ego mind as an illusion to living in the past through memory and living in the future through worry or anticipation. The past does not define who you are, and the future can never exist or be in its own right. Live in the now by living in the moment. The timeless now allows you presence of being. When you observe and watch your mind, you are no longer trapped in it. Be mindful of your thoughts and reactions without trying to analyse what you observe.

When you are mindful of your thoughts, you are also mindful of the words you use to express yourself. "First, there was the Word, and the word was made flesh" is a well-known saying that comes from the Bible. Words have the power to create. Any word that is expressed must have belief to bring it into being. The words you use are powerful in themselves. The more you connect with your authentic self in the moment, the more you begin to notice a change in the way you use your words. You become more conscious of your words because you realize the power of words to create. Everything in existence starts with a word, an idea, or an intention. Words carry vibration and energy according to the intention. All that is needed to bring a word into being is belief in the intention now, in the moment. Your subconscious is aware and hears every word that you say internally and externally. When you know this, you choose your words with care.

Your words in the now make up your thoughts in the now that lead to your beliefs in the now. From your beliefs, you create your reality. You can change how you think any time you decide. Such is the power of your intention in the now. By changing the vibration of your words at this moment in time, you in turn change your life. By raising the vibration of your word, you raise the vibration of your reality also, in a physical sense. Your word determines what and who you surround yourself with. Your self-expression in the now carries its own vibration as it draws to you everything on the same energetic level, at the same time. Your presence to who you are right now determines the quality of your life. This comes from the quality of your thoughts and the words you use right now. Suffering is caused by thinking in a way that is not in alignment with your authentic self. By keeping in alignment with your authentic self, you can unlearn what you've learned up till now. You become aware and awake straight away when you wander off track. It is with awareness in the moment that your conscious choice comes in, according to your free will. When you change your mind, you change your life. When you hold on to familiarity, you become stuck. Procrastination is a way of holding on to familiarity, and it can come from fear of success. Have faith and courage in yourself. Faith is belief with that extra touch. When you believe in something right now, you know it to be so before seeing it. Having faith means you will do whatever it takes to achieve what you believe in. Faith moves you out of procrastination towards activating your potential. The saying "charity begins at home" also applies to your self. When you have faith, hope and charity in and for yourself, you can move mountains! It all starts with you now.

Living in the now is all that is. It is the key to the now of the future. Understand and let go of the past; don't worry about the future by trusting in the now. Being fully present in your body grounds you in the moment when there is turmoil going on around you. It is possible to be at peace within, even while amidst chaos on the outside. You can also realize that by not taking things personally, you can observe events objectively and conserve your energy for constructive purposes in helping yourself and others at the same time. In doing so, you are moving towards your ultimate goal. You can be courageous to speak your truth and express who you really are, while knowing that you are okay the way you truly are. By practising reflection on your learning experiences, you can become aware of and build up new habits that will propel you forward towards your life purpose.

You control your time. You control your space. Time and space do not actually exist in reality. They are concepts in your mind that come from your experience of life through your five senses. What is can only be in the now. The past is gone, and the future is not yet created in actuality. The future is created in potentiality only in the now. Your moment of power is now. What you do now determines the path you choose to go down. Focus on what you want now, and concentrate your attention on it. Your attention is the energy of your thoughts, while your intention is the compass that guides your thoughts in the right direction. Whatever you intend, pay attention to it now. Make this a habit, because then it becomes automatic in programming the subconscious part of your mind. Whatever is automatic is always present in the moment. In other words, it is always present now, even if it is not obvious. Your thinking habits create your reality, because that is where your attention and intention are present. The more you practise a habit, the more you come to believe it, even if it is not true. Your prolonged attention, intention, and belief about something bring its manifestation into being.

Feel your emotions and be aware of your reactions now, without making any personal problems for your self. Wanting and needing are expressions of lack which keep you in a state of lack. Would you rather want or need something, instead of having or being it already? This letting go of old ways of thinking is a process that you evolve into, and this gets easier with time. After a while, it becomes your norm and you have less to hold you back from tuning into your authentic self. In the process, you become aware of the silent observing presence beyond the mind. You can use your mind as a tool to refer to the past or the future for practical purposes, after which you immediately return to awareness of the present moment. The past and its lessons are relevant to applying them in the now. Planning and working towards achieving goals are also relevant in the now. Clock time can also be used, without incorporating time itself as part of the self. Be aware of the difference. The ego mind is concerned with doing as a means of achieving pleasure or fulfilment in the future, or trying to get somewhere other than where you are now. How you see your future comes from your perception of it in the now. Your presence in the now shapes your future in the now. Do not resist what happened in the past by not resisting what is now. Allow everything to be in the "is-ness" of things, not the "engaged-ness" of things. Listen without judging; hear the silence in the gaps; feel your breathing; see lights, colours, and shapes; and use touch to feel and acknowledge an object's being. In the process, you leave behind the dream of insane abstractions or distractions and wake up to the reality of the present unburdened and free.

According to Parmenides, what is, is, without the possibility of change or movement. According to him, reality is not what it appears to be. For Parmenides, what is, was never created. If it was created, then it was created from something or nothing. As something already exists and nothing can come from nothing, what is, therefore exists forever and cannot be created.

Because your authentic self always exists, it is eternally present and never changes. What is, cannot come into being outside of now. It exists always. What is, is timeless. Through your physical senses, you perceive all things to change with time. Your authentic self is changeless and timeless and cannot be perceived through your five senses. The concept of timelessness is conveyed by Parmenides when he says "for me, where I am to begin from is the same, for to there I will come back again." Also, the fact that "what is" is not generated or destroyed, and therefore forever "present" shows that it is undivided. The same can be said about your authentic self; it is forever present, undivided, and changeless.

According to Parmenides, the way of opinion describes the appearance of things according to humans. It is your sensory perception that gives rise to the plurality of appearances, giving rise to an illusion of reality. Reality itself is unchanging, in the moment, whole and timeless. As you move closer to your authentic self, your perception of your self becomes more real. It is in your growth and evolvement that you get to tap into your power within. Your authentic self always is at your core. Through your senses, you experience change and motion. This gives rise to your concepts of space and time. Without change, there cannot be movement. Without movement, there cannot be change. As you move towards your authentic self, you change your way of being. By moving evermore inward, you become more aligned with your real self. When you change in this way, you become transformed as your authentic self emerges and is expressed to the outside world. When you can learn to discern the universal truth of reality from the particular experiences of your five senses, you have learned that looking in gives you truth, while looking out gives appearances. What exists outside of you in time and space exists in your sensory sense of your perceptions of the world. "What is" cannot change; otherwise it would not be true. Similarly, your authentic self does not change, because it is true. It is uncreated, complete, timeless, spaceless, unchanging, and whole in its being.

It is possible to become detached from your mind and its distractions. In becoming detached, you can be more objective about your life and your own personal agenda in it. You are already creative, resourceful, and whole. It's not about resources, necessarily, but your resourcefulness. It is very important for you to know where you are now and where is here. It is also important for you to be aware of all aspects of your world view in general and not just to focus on any one thing only. This holistic approach to viewing your wholeness may be a new way of thinking for you. It may be difficult to get your mind around initially. With practise, it gets easier and becomes a way of life with less suffering. This state of presence allows you to be still and yet highly alert while free of thought.

When you are listening to others, you are not listening with just your mind, but with your whole body. As you listen in this way, you are feeling the inner energy field of your inner body. This kind of listening prevents you from thinking and also enables you to hold a still space inside. To stay present means inhabiting your body fully by having some of your attention on your inner field of energy in the body. In this way, you feel your body from within, so to speak – no mind and total presence. Focusing on your breathing can help you to ground yourself in your body. With presence, you reside in your essence or your authentic self. Being without effort is pure consciousness itself. Be the watcher of your mind. Withdrawing consciousness from forms leads you to pure consciousness beyond form. Being is your deepest self. Being can be felt as "I am" beyond name and form. "I am that I am" is the name of God given to Moses. To abide in being is the truth that Jesus says will make you free from the illusion that you are nothing more than your physical body and mind. This means freedom from fear of sin and guilt, according to the ego mind. The inner body is the key to crossing from your form identity to your authentic self, your true nature. Let the breath take you into your body. When you are conscious without thought, you can use your mind creatively. The easiest way of entering this state of no-thought is through your body. This can be achieved through meditation, creative visualisation, or hypnosis, all of which slow down the brainwaves.

Consciousness is pure energy with its own vibration. Every thought has a vibration that emits a frequency. Therefore, your cells respond to frequency. Do you know what your next frequency of thought is going to be? While the answer may be no, you can always remain mindful of your thoughts in the present. In being present to yourself, you are maintaining control from the inside, and so you feel safe. Feeling safe has a lot to do with how your brain functions naturally. Being mindful means you are observing yourself in each moment that passes. This includes your own thoughts and how you express yourself. A safe environment is one you create in the now from the safe space you create on the inside. When you do this, you can sharpen the tool of your brain to work more efficiently with the feel-good hormones and neurotransmitters circulating around it. You can sharpen your brainpower through meditation, BWE, or hypnosis when your brainwaves slow down, leaving you more receptive to positive suggestion. Also, with SBM, your brain automatically changes its neural pathways as new habits of thinking and new beliefs are formed while you carry out your daily routines.

You can change your thoughts and beliefs through all of these methods, through the power of suggestion. Now that you know how this works, you can harness your own innate power that you always have potential for. As your thoughts and beliefs change, so does the physical structure of your brain and how it works. The previous pathways laid down become worn away as new empowering ones are laid down through repetition and practise. What you ignore in the now falls away. What you focus on now grows stronger. What are you focusing on right now in your life? Become aware, see it and know who you are now. It is in the knowing that you become more of who you really are now. Your inner power lies in following your own guidance from within at all times. You do not need to conform to other people's expectations of you. You do not need to conform to society either. Your own true power comes from remaining in alignment with your authentic self always. Do what makes you feel good, for that is what your guidance tells you. When something feels good, it is good for you.

You always have choice in the now. You can let go of that which does not serve you. Look for the lesson in everything you learn. Ask yourself, "What is the lesson here for me now?" or "How can I learn from this?" Once you know the lesson is learned, you can let it go. You know it doesn't need to repeat itself any more. Your experiences in life lead you forward towards your destiny. What destiny have you decided on for yourself in this moment? Your destiny is now. It is not in the future, though it may appear that it is. Whatever you decide on now is what you are now. Who do you see yourself as being? From this place of knowing your destiny, you know that you already have it outside of time and space in your mind. Now when you move forward, you are just moving into what you already are in your destiny. Trust that you have that which is your intention or something better. The universe knows what is best for you. As the universe has no limits, it has infinite possibility for you. Owing to limited thinking of conditioning, sometimes you may not intend enough for yourself to live your life authentically. Surrender to the universe, and trust that you will be provided with everything to live the life of your dreams. Everything is in divine order. It will show up when you are ready. Create harmony and peace within. Create the right conditions for what you want to show up in your life. You cannot become something that you are not already. You can only merge with that which you already are. Realize how powerful you truly are in your being. Your true power is benevolent and looks for the good of all always. It can be used only for good. Knowing this is how you tap into the power of your being. Knowing that is how you tap into the power of now.

You are always worthy of receiving that which is for your highest good. You are, in fact, worth more than you realize. You deserve the best life has to offer you. You do not need to struggle to get it, as you may have been taught. A life of struggle is an illusion. Know the value of who you really are. You are truly cherished and loved at all times, even if you don't know it. Can you imagine what kind of world we would live in if everybody felt loved and cherished? You are right where you are meant to be at this present moment. There is no such thing as punishment or feeling punished for not doing enough. Why beat up on yourself by feeling guilty or ashamed for your perceived worth? You have nothing to feel bad about. You have everything to feel good about regarding who you really are. Recognize who you are and remember what that means. Once you remember, you will never forget that who you are means that you can be who you are. When you "remember" your authentic self, you increase the possibilities for your life enormously. That's what makes the difference.

Now that you know the power of your true worth, you are prepared to use it in a way that is worthy of you. That's because you now know the value of who you really are. That way you avoid any drama, stress, and struggle in life. Hold steadfast in your knowing of who you are, no matter what others say. What they think does not affect who you already are. It does not change who you already are now either. You do not give your power to other people in this way, because you know that your inner power comes from knowing who you are now. This knowing comes from you alone, not anybody else. When you are aligned with your authentic self, the universe conspires for your ultimate good. Know this to be so, and so it is. You do not need to seek anything to make yourself better than you already are. Know that you are perfect as you are. You have infinite potential. You are your own master. You are your own perfect self right now.

Focus on your inner energy field and be aware of stillness. When you start thinking again, your thinking will be renewed and fresh. In this way, you think with your whole body. Real listening does not rely on thinking. It does not depend on listening to another person's words and mind. It involves feeling the being of the other person through being able to feel your own being. In this way, you are one with all that is. When you are present, you are one with the light of pure consciousness that emanates from the source. You and the light are one in your very essence. All suffering is ego-created and is due to resistance. Accept what is. Offer no resistance to what is. Allow the present moment to be, and accept the impermanent nature of all things and conditions. With this acceptance comes peace. Be the change that you want to see in others. In this way, you can serve others through peace, with peace, and in peace. When you reach a complete level of faith in your power of intention and creation with the universe, your knowing in the now manifests your heart's desire more quickly than before.

The universe gives you what you ask for when you are in alignment with your authentic self at your soul level. You begin this process of creation with the end in sight by using your imagination to create a picture of what you are asking for. Belief is everything, because it creates expectancy. When you expect something to happen with a belief and a knowing of complete faith, manifestation occurs instantly. This complete faith can be achieved by meditating, praying, or chanting. While this complete faith is accessible to everybody, some people need to undergo some process of preparation so as to embrace the concept. When enough faith is used, the universal realm supplies what is asked for in a way that transcends time, as if it already exists in an instant. "The holy instant is the interval in which the mind is still enough to hear an answer that is not entailed within the question asked. It offers something new and different from the question. How could it be answered if it but repeats itself?" (Schucman and Thetford 2008: 13). When you open the door of your mind through relaxation, going within and letting go, you allow the answer to sink in.

When you are at one with yourself in any moment, you can only be happy in the peace and inner calm that is you. This is the holy instant. Your peace of mind is what makes you feel content and at one with all in your life. When you are at one with your self, you are at one with all that is. You accept yourself fully because you can feel your full connection with your authentic self. You are now open to receiving all the abundance and prosperity you always deserved in your life. You can now see past the illusions of life that reveal the riches it holds in reality. You can see the spark of light in everything that exists, living and nonliving.

Everything that exists holds an energy signature that vibrates at a certain level. When you can view everything from a vibration level, you know this is because you view yourself as a vibrational being. What you see comes from your expectation of what you see. In this way, you open doors that were previously closed to your mind. When your level of perception rises, so does your experience of the world. In this way, you view the energetic being of everything. You also begin to see that level of being from your understanding of how things are in themselves. This knowing gives you more access to seek further knowledge of the mysteries of life. In gaining more and more knowledge, you are also evolving and growing at the same time, for you become what you know to be so.

Always remember who you really are. Embrace, love, and accept who you are. Always know that the ego's way of keeping you safe and protected is to keep you small and separate. What feels expansive for you is good for you. Remembering who you really are unleashes the power you really have with ease and grace. When you unleash your real power, everything in life becomes a miracle. Miracles become a natural event for attracting to you that which you are. You are the miracle that brings about transformation in your life. You can attract abundance to you from your very being within, in any moment of now. Know that you are a magnificent being. You are perfect and whole right now.

Self-Awareness

When you are developing self-awareness, you learn to listen to your language at a deeper level, whether it is internal or external. You are listening not just to the words but also to what is not said and the gaps between words. In communicating effectively, you learn to tune into the energy, emotion, and tone of voice used by you and others. You look for the best in yourself and others, even when this is not apparent to them. You can look on yourself and others with unconditional positive regard. Because of this you learn to view yourself and others objectively, without assumptions, opinions, or judgements. With self-awareness, you listen for what is behind others' words and their stories. In ascertaining where you are in your own process, you can listen for your values, purpose, and vision. You can also listen for signs of resistance, excuses, going backwards, or the saboteur in your language. Being mindful of the levels of your process, balance, and fulfilment simultaneously, you can be aware of where you are in relation to all of these. By knowing when you have reached the limits of your own self-boundaries, this allows you to question accordingly. If you are not being true to yourself, you may have hesitation or a forced manner of speaking that doesn't ring true to the context of what is being said by you. Listening with awareness involves using all the senses and your intuition. Deep awareness allows you to decide or choose your next step with ease. By listening beyond words for energy and emotion that are spoken or not spoken about, you can choose your direction and focus in life. With awareness, you know whether you are moving towards or away from balance or resistance in relation to where you are now, and whether you are on track with your goal. With awareness and courage, you can learn to speak your truth as one with your authentic self. This you can do without the need or the pressure to be right.

There is no right or wrong when it comes to speaking your truth. It can be beneficial for others to hear your truth, as this may wake them up from the illusion they are living in. When speaking your truth, you can articulate your observations without judgement while giving others room for different interpretations. You can also clarify a point where necessary in the form of questions. Clarifying involves listening, questioning, and reframing in terms of perspectives so that you can focus on what you want with greater clarity. In clarification, your answers lead to the next question. In getting fresh perspectives when looking at the big picture, you can see your life from a different vantage point. In this way, you can rise above any tasks you perceive to be daunting in getting there. Using the big picture can provide context for situations that would otherwise seem to be problems in themselves. By comparing a situation with the big picture of your life, you learn that all meaning is context related and not situation related. Become aware of the metaphors you use in order to expand on and learn from them. A metaphor is a symbol, picture, or story that has meaning for you, and can thus provide a lot of information for further exploration. Recognize your internal strengths and character that may have been overlooked by you before. Acknowledge to yourself values honoured by you in taking an action.

Your inner truth sets you free. What does this mean? It means that when you know what your own truth is, you can freely express it from within. The process of coming to know your own truth is a process and a journey inwards. It means learning on a continual basis about yourself and what you really feel inside. This needs to take place from time to time in a quiet place where you can reflect on your beliefs, values, attitudes, thoughts, and life experiences. This kind of contemplation is not an analysis but rather an observation. When you observe your beliefs, values, attitudes, thoughts, and life experiences in this way, it is as if you are removed from such things. It is like the *I* observing the *me*. It is like a contemplative meditation, undisturbed by the outside world, in which you can listen to your inner knowing at your source. It means stilling your mind so that you may hear the inner voice of your authentic self. When you allow and trust your inner voice of guidance, this type of contemplation gets easier and easier over time. In this way, your intuition develops also. It does not matter what others say or think. They may not agree with your inner voice, because your truth is not their truth. Your truth is for you only. It is the key to your freedom in life. In realizing the self of who you truly are at your core, you come to know that your truth feels right for you.

People will always try to tell you their truth and bend your way of thinking to agree with theirs. You don't need to agree with other people to be accepted by them. It is up to them to respect your truth even if they don't understand it. Once you accept yourself, that is enough. Stand by your truth always, for it is there to guide you along the path to your destiny. Have courage and persevere. It is worth the effort. If you accept others' truth as your own, then you live your life according to what they want. Your own truth will be recognized by your feelings about it. Your feelings communicate from that deepest part of yourself, your authentic self. Your own truth may be tested at times. Be strong and persist, no matter what others say, even if they resist you. Be aware that this is why they are fulfilling their role – to make you realize what your truth is and how much it means to you. For this reason, you can be grateful for their service to you in this regard.

Communicating with Others

Using all your senses gives you perception of the world that has subjective meaning for you. This is your model of the world. Everybody's model will be different, as we are all unique. Gain insight into your own model through listening to your own language, especially the predicates used, according to your visual, auditory, kinaesthetic (touch) or audio-digital (inner talk) representations. Notice your physiology (how you hold your body), your tone of voice, and the words you use also. How much eye contact do you use with others? Eye contact is important, as it shows you are interested and confident. Too little eye contact may denote disinterest or distraction, whereas too much eye contact may come across as intense and staring. Listening with intuition allows you to get hunches and sense vibes from others. When you listen to others with respect, rapport, and objectivity, your neutrality gives them the space to speak their truth also. Intuition is invaluable when communicating with others. It allows you to listen at a depth beyond words, with a knowing that is always present. Intuition can be described as a hunch, a gut feeling, or the knowledge that something is true without hard proof. The way you communicate is how you represent to the world your interpretation of it. The world will always reflect this back to you on the same wavelength, like a mirror. The mirror doesn't lie, even though you may not like what you see in it sometimes. Whatever you see is a reflection of what is on the inside of yourself. When you become aware of this, you allow for self-reflection and self-discovery to take place. In reality, the only reality is what is inside you. There is no outside, as your senses would have you believe.

What you give, you receive. When you give to others, this can take the form of love, care, a gesture, an act of kindness, forgiveness, or a physical thing. Once you are giving, you are creating a circulation of energy that flows right back to you in kind. Truly giving is not about how much you give, but rather the feeling of abundance and joy that you feel in giving to others. When others appreciate what you give, this can also lead to good feelings and well-being within you. Giving and receiving freely creates a flow of abundance. When you allow others to give to you, they become empowered. Their empowerment comes from your appreciation and being able to use the gift they give. It is just as important to receive as it is to give. When you are open to receiving more, you become open to giving more.

Use your imagination to visualize success for other people in their prosperity and abundance. As you do so, you increase your magnetism for prosperity and abundance also. If you try to help people with financial problems, for example, by giving them money, you are enabling their neediness and not allowing them to tap into their own inner resources and power within. While it is good to help people, it is better to help people to help themselves. This is how people become empowered, sometimes with a little guidance from another. With a gentle nudge, they find their own answer from within and so learn to become self-reliant, while not being influenced from the outside. Every moment is an opportunity for greatness in yourself and other people. You can be your own change agent right now by setting your life on the course of your dreams. As you change your life, so you can change other people's. It is the lessons you learn about yourself that enable you to help other people from your own experience in every moment of your life, and that includes where you are right now.

Asserting Your Real Self Now

Being assertive is a skill that can be learned. When you can look people in the eye, you are being assertive. You communicate 55 per cent with the way you hold or move your body during communication. Your tone of voice communicates 38 per cent of the message, while the words themselves carry only 7 per cent of the meaning in a conversation. Assertiveness means you can look after yourself without being selfish. You can say no to other people's demands and requests because you have a right to value your own needs. What other people think is all about them, as they are they and you are you. You look after your own priorities because you come first. You accept others, but not necessarily their behaviour. You have a right to follow your own intuition for your well-being and health. Einstein said, "The only real valuable thing is intuition." You enjoy the moment, as you deserve it, because you're worth it. You have a right to say "I don't know" without having to worry about what other people think, and you can also say you'll think about it and weigh it up. You can be comfortable in your own skin by just being yourself. You deserve dignity and respect so you can be happy within yourself. Your wants and needs are legitimate, and you deserve to ask for these. You have a right to protect your health, sanity, responsibilities, and boundaries by refusing inappropriate demands from others. Your feelings are legitimate and deserve expression as much as anyone else's. You are constantly learning, and you have the right to change your mind, and so you are allowed to make mistakes. Einstein said, "A person who never made a mistake, never tried anything new."

There is no such thing as mistakes; there is only feedback to learn from. Because your own values and standards are the signposts to your ideal life, you deserve to say no on the grounds of safety, morality, peace of mind, and boundaries. Your priorities are the only keys to your future, as you take responsibility for your life, decisions, goals, and future. You are responsible only for your own behaviour, actions, feelings, and problems. You deserve the truth from others, as accurate information helps you in adapting to your current reality. You have the right to feel hurt and to constructively communicate this, because you love yourself as you are, unconditionally. You are allowed to acknowledge anxiety-provoking situations and their effects on you, as well as to develop ways of letting go of the doubts, fears, worries, and limitations. You are not required to justify or explain your behaviour. Your decisions can be based on your feelings as well as your rational thoughts. Your basic human right is time and space for yourself to recharge and reconnect so you find peace of mind and order, because you love yourself. You also have the right to humour and laughter as you express your inner child from time to time. You can feel good about the betterment of yourself and the avoidance of unhealthy situations or activities. You have the right to be free from bullying and abuse, and to have others respect you. People as humans are social beings, and you deserve to have your social needs met as much as anybody else does.

People may want you to stay the same, but the nature of life is change. People may resist your desire to change, but the pursuit of happiness as you see fit is your human right, and each human pursues it in his or her own unique way. You are respected by others to the degree that you respect both yourself and them. Your needs and wants are uniquely yours and come from your unconscious mind. When you are impeccable with your word, you say only what you mean, because you avoid using the word to speak against yourself or to gossip about others. This is so when you use the power of your word in the direction of faith and love. Nothing others do is because of you, so you don't need to take anything personally. When you realize this, you become immune to the opinions and actions of others. With courage, you can ask questions and express what you really want as you communicate with others as clearly as you can to avoid misunderstandings, sadness, or drama. Instead, you can completely transform your life because you know you always do your best, and so you avoid self-judgement, self-abuse, and regret.

Fifteen Steps to Freedom

The exodus from Egypt over 3000 years ago passed on an inspiring true story of release from slavery to freedom to live life on one's own terms. First an arduous journey was undertaken from Egypt across the desert by a freed people, under the leadership of Moses. The people did not know where they were going but trusted fully in their leader. They took the journey one step at a time. This led them to the promised land of Israel, where they settled and prospered. This story of release from tyranny to personal freedom of a nation has inspired our world ever since. It is said that when the first American government was being formed, the Exodus formed an important part of the principles being laid down for freedom for all Americans. This story shows that it is possible for any of us to be free, no matter what our circumstances. You just need to trust and take the journey out of what was the norm. You can take the steps to your own personal freedom. In doing so, you give others permission to free themselves also. You too can free yourself from being a slave to your emotions and instead become the master of your life. The following fifteen steps are taken from the symbolic rituals at the Seder meal of Passover, which has been celebrated in the same way ever since the Exodus by Jews to symbolise their freedom from slavery.

1. You need to realize and become aware of the need for freedom from whatever is captivating or holding you back. This means you need to give yourself space and set an intention for yourself and what you want.

2. You need to change your mindset about what is considered acceptable and what is unacceptable in your life. This means having the courage to step outside of your boundaries in taking a look at yourself objectively. Only by looking at yourself objectively can you become self-aware and develop self-understanding. This is necessary before you can change what you know you need to change in your mindset. Changing your mindset means washing it off, or releasing and letting go of judgement or blame.

3. By meditating on something like your hand, you become conscious of it and can see it in a different way. Look at it closely. It is a physical entity and a tool for the soul. Meditating on your hand gives you the insight that it is a channel or an instrument of spirituality that allows you to reach out to help someone in serving the spirit.

4. The breaking of the bread of humility (matzo) is a symbol of modesty, like breaking the hold of any tentacles that trap you. You can stop anything that is trapping you; for example, you can break a bad habit.

5. This step involves telling the story. Telling the story, whatever it is, is therapeutic in breaking the silence. It allows for dialogue. How

many of us have suffered in silence? Silence does not express its needs or wants. Telling your story is an ultimate declaration and testimony of freedom. You have a right to challenge. You have a right to your dignity. You can allow yourself a time to communicate, a time to express.

6. This is the second time to "wash your hands". At this stage, you are entering a new level of space and are in transition. You are in the process of shedding the layers that held you back before.

7. This is the time for blessing and eating the bread of humility (matzo). In the Bible, it is said that "the meek shall inherit the earth". If you don't have humility, you don't transcend yourself. You need humility to have the ability to free yourself. Humility means you are not tied to anything or anybody. While others may view this as a sign of weakness, it is, in fact, a strength.

8. This is a time for developing compassion for yourself and others. Having compassion means having unconditional love. Compassion is when love meets suffering, either for yourself or for others. Have compassion for yourself first. Only then can you be free to have compassion for others in turn.

9. Having compassion for yourself and others allows you to develop empathy. Empathy is like knowing what it's like to walk in another person's shoes. You can see things from the other person's perspective or point of view. This keeps you free so you don't get caught up in outside situations or people. You can be objective about the situation or person and so remain removed.

10. This step is symbolised by combining the bitter herbs of compassion and empathy on the bread of humility. In being able to identify with the pain of others, and not just yourself, you are able to reach out to them. Being empathetic towards another person's needs gives you what you need first. What you give, you receive, according to the

law of attraction and the law of quantum physics. That which you give, you are. That which you are, you receive.

11. At this stage, you may be tested to see if you can eat the meal properly. Life throws challenges at us sometimes. By using your skill of humility, compassion, and empathy, you can overcome these challenges much easier. You can look at challenges as opportunities to learn and grow. In the process, you get a better sense of what to do in the future. You will be ready for any further challenges by using what you have learned.

12. This is where the conscious and the subconscious are addressed. This happens at the conclusion of the meal. By aligning the conscious mind with the subconscious mind, you gain control in your life from within. You create all that is in your life. You are free to be, do, have, or create whatever you desire in your life.

13. This step involves saying grace after the meal is eaten. It is important to appreciate and be grateful for everything in your life. This brings more of the same. Being thankful means you allow more of the same into your life. You can be thankful before you receive. That brings it to you in the now. When you are thankful, you expect it to happen. You attract what you are already. This is how the law of attraction works.

14. Now you are ready to receive a transcendent energy that raises your vibrations. This comes from your source, which lies in your authentic self. Because your energy is raised, so is your experience of life. This transcendent energy could be an aha moment, a knowing, a spiritual experience, or a sudden flash of insight with no logical explanation. Maslow referred to this as having a "peak" experience. As your energy vibration rises, so can these peak experiences.

15. Now you are free to live life and to express who you really are with complete freedom. Your life is your own. You are free of your emotions, as you can let them go. They no longer have any hold over

you. You have a right to question. Asking questions is healthy. You have the dignity to ask questions. Questioning gets you out of the trap of old habits, in which you automatically behaved in a certain way. This journey towards freedom involves nurturing and connecting with your authentic self, which resides within your heart. Now your heart can let your mind be free. Thought and emotion are connected at the point where you can program your own reality. By embracing and believing in yourself in this way, you activate your seed of creative energy from a place of unconditional love. Knowing this truth is what sets you free.

See challenges as opportunities to grow and evolve in this moment. Ask your self, "What can I learn from this?" Know that everything is as it should be. You attract the energy flow that you send out. You receive what you give. Be in the flow of your authentic self in allowing it to propel you towards your purpose. In life, lessons are sent repeatedly in the form of challenges until you learn to recognise them as such, as a means to grow and evolve. New challenges then become your experience in expanding your horizons. You can benefit from all experiences in life, good and bad. Without good, there would not be bad. Without light, there is no darkness. This duality of experience is how things appear to be. In reality they exist as one unit in everything. There is no duality, but unity. You are unified with everything and everybody around you. With challenges comes strength of character and wisdom from experience. Joy, peace, inspiration, and optimism are your rewards in leading a fulfilling life in the flow of your authentic self, always learning, always growing. Everything that is continues to grow, expand, and evolve. Expansion, growth, and evolvement is the natural flow of nature, the universal energy, and the cosmos. You can bring it all into the here and now!

Exercise: Visualization

Now, by exercising your decision-making muscles, you can proceed along the pathless path to a peaceful future full of wisdom, acceptance, understanding, and love. Get yourself into a comfortable position and place your hands on your lap with palms facing upwards. Close your eyes and look down towards your heart. Take a deep breath in through all the pores of your body, as if you're taking in energy. Now, as you breathe out, let go of tension, stress, and anxiety as you breathe out any excess energy. Imagine that you put this excess energy into a bubble while transforming it into energy of love and compassion. This is the energy you send out into the world, and this is what will return to you in turn.

You know you've let go when you feel relaxed. When you are changing for the better, you feel more relaxed and at peace every day. You can have the courage to let go, as you feel safe. When you let go, you feel safe, at peace, and more relaxed. You notice that you can let things that used to bother you pass as you walk away confidently and calmly. You're at ease feeling happiness, a sense of peace, and order. You realize now that the simple things are important, as are the major things, and it's okay to go after those things and accept them. You deserve to receive what you go after, as you accept yourself completely right now. In this space of clarity, ask and it is given. Trust in yourself to complete a plan or a project. Success builds upon success. You have the potential to have anything you set your mind to, so long as you believe in yourself in the moment. Your power is now. You do not need anything from the outside to achieve your heart's desire. In this moment, you have everything you need already. The power of you that is now is more than enough. Say to yourself three times, "I am enough, I have enough, and I know enough." Know that you do not need to do any more; just be true to your self. That way you are harmonized with everything that is, including your authentic self.

CHAPTER 11

YOUR DIVINE ESSENCE

When you come to realize that co-creation of reality is linked with your spiritual development, this helps you to make sense of your life on a larger scale. You can see the big picture of why everything needed to happen the way it did to bring you to where you are now with everything you've learned. As you move away from ego towards your authentic self at your soul level, you are attracted to the idea of co-creation. This is not an end in itself on your path to conscious evolution of your authentic self. It is another step on the continuum towards your divine essence as you focus on your higher self or higher consciousness. In the process, your ability to manifest your heart's desire becomes more instantaneous. The reason for your existence on earth is to master your perceived limitations. This comes about through conscious evolution into a higher consciousness and vibration of being.

Impossible is nothing. Your level of consciousness can set the boundaries for what may seem impossible to you. By empowering yourself from within, you raise your consciousness and so expand your previous boundaries of what is possible. By shifting your consciousness onto a higher level, you expand on the possibilities in your life also. When you realize that you are indeed limitless, you start to live from this knowing. You know you can overcome those previous limitations that held you back before for so long. By waking up to your authentic self and living your life with authenticity, you come to accept your new level of empowerment with grace and ease. When the veil is lifted, you come to realize that you are indeed a wise being of divine light at your core. When you tune into your authentic self, you begin to see that the only limitations in your life are those that you have control over. These limitations, created by you, last only as long as you accept them. By standing strong in your own truth with courage, you deny their power over you. When you express your own truth, these limitations disappear like steam off a hot stone on a warm, sunny day.

Even though your divine essence is your essential nature, your personality allows you to experience particular aspects of earthly life. It is your ego that gives you freedom of thought. If you had no ego, you would not be individual. Your individuality that comes from ego enables you to have choice. Tuning into your divine essence means you do not have to reject or resist ego. It just means you handle ego in a different way, as it is a part of you. You can accept your ego while letting it know that you are in charge. When you are in tune with your divine essence, you are more detached from ego's influence. Instead, you have spiritual control in your life, which differs from control based on fear, lack, or want. Your spiritual core serves as your control centre. In this way, you are centred in your divinity, and this is what gives you strength from within. Your previous searching for control on the outside came from ego and the illusion of the outside world. In your divine essence, you are already whole. Your ego is a vehicle by which you can express the spark of your divine essence on earth. Ego is an important part of the person that you are. When you can express yourself freely, without being hindered by the ego, you are free.

As a human being, you are already whole in body, mind, and spirit. If you have conflict within, then there are parts inside you that need to be integrated once more. This includes your ego. When you are all-inclusive, you accept yourself fully, even your ego. When you are whole in your being, you are whole in your thinking, as your essential nature shines through with ease and grace. This puts you in the flow of life, where everything you want comes easily to you. You are here to experience life as your own unique person. From this experience and learning, you can express your divine spiritual nature. By living your purpose, you are fulfilling your destiny. When you self-actualize, you know who you really are. From this knowing, you can express the truth of your divinity. You can see the divinity in life and other people surrounding you. You are at one with the universe and the earth.

When you realize this, your life becomes sacred and everything you do is a prayer. You experience a better way of living from your heart, and this guides you onward towards your destiny. You know you are on the right path, and you feel safe at all times.

By living from your divine essence, you realize how magnificent you really are at your core. You expect better for yourself and commit to doing whatever it takes. There is no fear in doing; there is only a sense of purpose. It is your purpose to succeed, have abundance, and be in service to others by expressing your authentic self. What you can contribute comes from growth in your own life. Your awareness makes possible what you believe is possible. Believe and it is so! Act and it is done. Know and it is known. Be and it is. Your divine essence allows you to believe, act, know, and be who you truly are. When you express all that you are, you become a change maker for the world. When others see your expression of divinity, it inspires them to bring forth their own divinity. Can you imagine what it would be like to live in a world where everybody expressed his or her divine essence?

It is important to connect with your divine essence on a daily basis, even for fifteen minutes, by meditating. This is what keeps you in touch with your authentic self, which is where your true empowerment comes from. When you are disconnected from your source, your reality appears like an illusion presented from the outside that may seem real to you. With this illusion comes the feeling that there is something missing and that there must be more to life. You may find yourself asking questions like "Why am I here?" "What can I give to the world?" or "How can one person make a difference?" When you are connected with your authentic self, you automatically have your answers. You know what your purpose and calling in your life are. You know what you are here to do. You acknowledge the gift of who you are and what you can contribute to the world in helping others. You also realize your power as one person – one voice that can shift mass consciousness to a higher level of being. This shift of mass consciousness beyond the critical level goes beyond the tipping point, leading to a new paradigm, a new way of being.

As your authenticity emerges, so does your message. The more "in-powered" you become, the more you can express your inner voice with power. When your inner voice becomes expressed, you reveal the real you that has the ability to transform the world. Your authentic expression creates that shift in other people when they resonate with your energy. Your connection and faith in source make this all possible. When the critical level of mass consciousness is reached, humanity can shift from one level of reality to another in the twinkle of an eye. Your own experience of reality in its appearance is affected by mass consciousness also, as is the big picture of how things appear. While your consciousness determines your own destiny within the big picture of mass consciousness, you can also affect mass consciousness through raising your own vibration in the field. In this way, you are one with humanity and humanity is one with you. While you appear to be separate, you share the quantum field with mass consciousness. Your single expression of who you are is a single representation of the whole. Just as your DNA is your individual expression when compared to the DNA of other people, so is your expression of who you really are. In expressing who you really are, you become integrated into the whole, which is lifted by your vibration as a result. You become and are at one with all that is. You see the spirit in everything, as you realize there is more to reality than appearances.

As the veil of illusion is lifted, you see with clarity the truth of who you really are. This comes from knowing your self first. You are a divine spark of God in reality. God is omnipotent and omnipresent. That means he/she is in you. Your expression of your authentic self is your expression of that God aspect that resides within your core being. Your core is where your true genius and all-knowing emanate from. Everybody has access to this same power from within. Your consciousness in itself has the power to affect change in others, just by being in your presence. Your own consciousness is affected by your thoughts and feelings. By connecting with your authentic self, you automatically increase your consciousness and your ability to bring about change in the world. You are divine essence at your core, and this is who you really are. Your divine essence is your authentic self.

Your authentic self is your source of inner empowerment. You are a powerful being at your core. When you express your authentic self freely, you express from a place of infinite intelligence, God, or universal wisdom, whichever you want to call it. You manifest the power of God from within, from your individual aspect of divine essence. The more you understand the nature of reality and the creative power of thought, the more knowing you have about how the universe operates. Once you learn that you co-create reality, you can begin to learn how to manipulate and handle your own consciousness for your own good and the good of others. This makes you a leader and a guide for others as you continue to learn and expand your vision and understanding. In order to evolve, there needs to be change, flow, and movement. Conscious evolution means change, flow, and movement of consciousness.

It can be easy sometimes to forget your divine essence as a result of struggle, pain, and feeling stuck in your life when there seems to be no movement. Know that everything is in divine order. There is no such thing as good or bad in itself. This is how duality of thinking leads us to perceive the world. It is the way we have been trained to think up till now. Everything is one, as it is now. There is no separation into good or bad. Everything that happens, happens for a reason, for your ultimate good and the good of all. When you learn to think and perceive the world as one whole in mind, body, and spirit, your experience of the world will change accordingly, to include more of what you perceive now. Co-creation works best when there is change, flow, and movement consciously. When you are in the flow, you have momentum spiritually, because you are more connected to your heart, which is the source of the universe. Flow, change, and movement are part of the universal realm, and any consciousness that flows and changes resonates with this realm also. The more you are open to flow, change, and movement, the more you can co-create with the universe.

According to Aristotle, the only object worthy of divine thought is that which is divine, eternal, and unchanging. This can be found only in divine nature itself – that is, God. For Aristotle, the soul must be united to the body to be a human being, and therefore, it must obtain its knowledge through its instrument, the body. Hence, your knowledge is based on your sensory perception. Saint Thomas Aquinas believed that your happiness is achieved by seeking truth and direct knowledge of God through the intellect, which influences your understanding of what is good. Your body and soul united are essential for those experiences to be interpreted and understood as a concept within your mind. According to Aquinas, your intellect is a power of your human soul. Your rational soul is what distinguishes you from animals. "All human beings desire to know," says Aristotle. For Aquinas, what is actually understood intellectually is the intellect, or power of the soul, actualized.

Your understanding becomes a likeness of the thing that is understood as you move closer towards your divine essence. According to Aquinas, the human soul needs a higher intellect by which it can be guided in reaching understanding. Your higher consciousness is what guides you in accessing your divine essence. Your higher consciousness is linked with the soul part of your being human. Your intellect cannot understand the infinite in actuality, but only in potentiality. Your intellect will always have the potentiality for understanding more. The true light of God enlightens you as a universal cause, from which your human soul derives a particular power. Aquinas said, "We must proceed as humans from the universal truth to the singular truth." Only God knows all things at the same time, as he sees all in one, which is to say, in his essence.

By the seal of the divine light in you, all things are made known to you. The intellectual light within you is a likeness to the uncreated light of God. All knowledge is achieved by assimilation of the known thing (divine essence) to the knower – that is, you. Your divine essence leads to your knowledge of this through understanding. You cannot know what the word "God" means without knowing the essence of God. Through your concepts and ideas, you can understand the difference between the whole (universal) and a part (individual). Because your nature is to understand, your nature is linked to understanding. This comes about through self-reflection. Everybody reasons and understands at different levels. Aquinas said that "intellectually cognized good moves will." In this way, you become master of your own acts through your understanding of your divine essence. Your understanding, in this way, influences your will to act according to your divine essence.

Aquinas believed that things are received according to the mode of the receiver. This means that when your ability to understand more expands, this makes it possible for you to know more. Your self-understanding comes from your self-awareness. Therefore, by connecting with your divine essence, you become enlightened and you understand more. Universal truths are not necessarily known instantly. These truths are understood as a result of sensing the many particulars in which they are present. By seeing divine essence in particular aspects of your earthly life, you begin to gain understanding of its ultimate truth. The more you understand your divinity, the more you open the door to actually experiencing divinity directly. You cannot experience that which you do not understand; otherwise, you would not know what it is. When you believe in your divinity through understanding what it is, then you know how to access it in the silence. The more you connect with your divinity, the easier it becomes. In this way, your intellect understands progressively through particular experiences.

Your understanding of your divine essence occurs at different levels, while sometimes it can be known instantly. God, by his own essence, knows himself. The more you get to know your divine essence, the closer you get to know God inside you. All understanding in the human soul takes place by some likeness of that object known within the soul. You can only understand that which you recognize and know already. Your level of understanding comes from what you know already. It is always possible to know more and, therefore, to understand more. God can be seen by certain images, but not by the likeness of his own nature. What is understood is perfectly known. To know God is to have His knowledge and essence. You have this spark of God within your divine essence, just like all human beings. God is the cause of things by his knowledge. It can be known that God exists without understanding him fully. Because humans' actual knowledge of everything is finite, similarly, actual knowledge of God is impossible, for God is the ultimate being and is infinite. If you think of God as being outside you, then you are detached from him. God is within you, and your divine essence is your connection to him. By seeking knowledge, you are seeking God, who is good, and doing what He wills. God is your first cause, and all that follows naturally is your desire to find and understand the source of your cause. Why else would God, your primary cause, have endowed you as a human with sensory perception and a rational soul? Divine revelation makes known certain truths which human reasoning on its own could never discover. By tuning into your divinity within, you become insightful in your awareness, knowledge, and "in-spiration."

Your heart's desire is your true calling that is divinely inspired. Your divinity and your soul purpose are intimately connected, because your desire is what brings you fulfilment. With fulfilment comes enlightenment of your true essence. Once, when an Indian mountain guide asked me the question "Do you seek enlightenment?" I answered yes. All he said in response was "That is not the way!" I now understand what he meant. As long as you are looking for something, you will never find it. When you know you have it, you do not have to seek it any longer, because it lies in the palm of your hand. In the same way, when you acknowledge your divine essence, you allow its light to shine through you from your source. Your desire does not come from ego, but from your authentic self. In denying your own desire, you are holding yourself back from true enlightenment. In fulfilling your desire, at the same time, you become en-"lightened" from within. Your desire, in whatever form, comes from your yearning to be in alignment with your authentic self, which is at one with your divine essence. This desire is not materialistic, even though it may have material form. It is in moving towards this desire that you are moving towards your own spiritual fulfilment, ultimately.

The ego itself is not to be rejected but is to be incorporated on a more ex-panded level within your being, where your individual expression is seen as part of the whole universe. Your divine spark is made up of the same light as that of the universe. The light is within you, and you are in it. The light is you, and you are the light! In the same way, your divine essence lies within, just as your essence lies in your divinity. They are one and the same. When you are identifying with your divine essence, you are connected to all that is within and without, because you are at one with the universe and the universe is one with you. When you are fulfilled by your desire, you know what it is to have peace, joy, and freedom. You are the creator of your own life.

Your own innate blueprint is your individual code that is stored in your DNA. Even your DNA is connected with your divine essence, while it is not a part of it. When you tune into your divinity, your connection posi-tively impacts the body, stemming from your thoughts and way of being. Your thought patterns can also act as keys that can unlock the sacred codes of your DNA. As the frequency of your thoughts and emotions rises in vibration, so does your way of being on a physical level. Your vibration, when raised, can activate your DNA even further in ways you have not experienced up to now. As your DNA activates, it can mutate into higher levels of being. Now it is known that your DNA is influenced by electromagnetic fields, and this includes thoughts.

Expressing your divine essence is the key to your DNA activation. You resonate at a higher frequency in vibration when you are attuned with your divine self. At this higher vibration, your experience changes as you can see more of all that is. Now you understand at a deeper level how the universe operates and how you can manifest all the abundance, joy, and happiness you desire. This is your birthright. You are a magnificent being, much more so than you realize. You really have the power to manifest your true desire in physical form, for this is your mission in realizing the vision of your desire. The higher your vibration, the easier it is for you to manifest what you desire into your life. Your divinity is at one with your authentic self, and only by going inward can you bring out what you truly want in life to fulfil you soul purpose. The key is to go through your authentic self, where you can become at one with your divine essence. Your authentic self is the doorway to your divine essence. Keep your spirit high by radiating love (unconditional) and light. Keep your thoughts enlightened and in line with your own truth instead of outside appearances. No matter what is taking place on the outside, remain calm, collected, and serene with access to your own true power in this way. You can see through the calm waters of a pond with clarity only when there are no ripples. You can see with clarity when you remain steadfast in your divine essence. This allows you grace and ease through life as you continue to express your truth and so be at one with your authentic self.

At birth, this knowledge of your essential nature is forgotten. It can be recollected during life through your bodily experiences of your senses interacting with the environment. Even though you may think you are a human being that has a few occasional spiritual experiences, you are actually spirit having a human experience. Your essence is the core of who you are in your heart. This divine essence is your birthright. It is where your power emanates from, and it is linked to the field of quantum possibilities. This is your authentic self. You are much more than you think you are. You have more power inside than you may realize. Through the conditioning of human life, you have forgotten who you really are. Remembering is a journey in itself that results in the layers of conditioning being removed. At the centre is your divinity. Once you become aware of this aspect of You, know that you have more power in co-creating what you want in your life.

When your thoughts and feelings are aligned with the universal laws, you become a magnet for what you want to attract into your life. It's important to be kind towards all living creatures and life on earth. The environment is part of nature. You are part of nature and should treat it with kindness as you would yourself. The universe responds to that which you send out to it. You attract more of the same. That's the law of attraction. What you wish for others comes back to you in turn. See everybody as being successful. Send others loving thoughts, no matter what they have said or done to you. This takes strength of character, but it is in forgiving them for their weaknesses that you release yourself from any negative ties with them. You forgive them for your own good. The thoughts you send out resonate with what you attract back to you. Your knowing comes from the core of who you really are; your divine essence. Send love and light to all those who have caused you pain in the past, for they need it. When others talk about lack and not having enough, you can change their focus by pointing out what they do have, as well as the successes in their life. See them as being prosperous and abundant. Wish the best for them. Have compassion for their suffering. Shine your light on them in order to let them shine their own light also. Use your imagination to send them positive pictures of love. All of this will be returned to you magnetically by the vibrations you send out.

Help others to appreciate and be grateful for what they do have. Having appreciation, care, love, and compassion heals the heart–brain connection in you and others. When you help to bring out that in others, you are helping them to heal from within. The path to freedom lies in aligning with your authentic self. Your authentic self lies within your heart space of unconditional Love. When you love everything and everybody around you unconditionally, you are totally free. Love is a higher energy than fear. Fear is transmuted to love in the presence of loving energy. Be a manifestation of love to experience the harmony that exists in nature by cooperating rather than competing with other people. Divine love is the will of God that is everywhere. It's in everyone. It brings forth divine creation from the non-physical into concrete expression. Contemplate loving-kindness in your thoughts, words, and actions with those around you, friends and family. Loving-kindness expands beyond this circle like a ripple effect to your community and the universe ultimately. Deliberately send love to those who have harmed you in the past. In giving love, you become love itself, allowing its expression. By thinking, feeling, and acting with loving-kindness, you tune into and appreciate love in all that is around you. You emanate from that which is unconditional love, and you are an expression of this in the material world. By becoming aware of this, you can choose to be love in every word, thought, and deed.

Humanity has passed through the age of information, and we have now entered the age of spirituality. For this reason, it is important for you to express who you truly are in the totality of your being. By this I mean not just in your mind and body, but in spirit as well. This means expressing the energy of your authentic self by letting your soul speak through you. When you align with your authentic self, your perspective on life shifts in the process. By staying in tune with your authentic self, you live life according to the authenticity of your soul, even while your personality is intact at the same time. When your authentic self shines forth on your personality, your ego becomes useful in its function of individual awareness (instead of being master of the personality, where it can cause chaos). As the influence of your authentic self becomes stronger, you find yourself increasingly expressing the highest aspect of your higher consciousness at your soul level. Everything you need to know is at the level of your highest self, and as you express your authentic self, so you express the energy and wisdom of your higher self. You are a channel for a higher energy. Each of us has something to contribute that's unique. We are on a mission, and we are vessels to use our strengths, our talents, and our unique opportunities in order to reveal a deeper spiritual dimension in everything we do. In a sense, our mission is to spiritualize the material world we live in, in everything we do.

In your daily interactions, there are divine sparks to be revealed in light of your divine essence. This recognition changes the way you live your life. Your responsibility to yourself is, in fact, your ability to respond to wherever you are, whoever is present. There are no random events. Wherever you go and whatever you do, there's a spark there for you to bond with, for you to connect with. Even a small act of kindness changes the world in some way. We don't always see this, as we tend to look at the world with narrow vision ourselves. By looking at what's going on in the world around you, in a deeper sense, you get to see that there's a bigger picture emerging. If you don't respect or have spirit in what you do, then you're missing an important dimension of experience. Integration of mind, body and your divine essence is the doorway to this dimensional experience. Spirit on its own does not bring about actualization in a physical sense in which it impacts the world. Your body is what grounds you. By tuning into your authentic self, which is your divine essence, you integrate your physical experience with spirit. Your purpose and mission in whatever you do is to bring spirit to this earth plane in whatever manifestation you can. In this way, you raise the planetary vibration as a whole, as well as the vibration of those who live on it. The collective consciousness is affected by your consciousness. You play a part as a whole and as a part of the whole. Your divine essence is the way, the truth, and the light. You have a choice. What do you choose?

By cultivating your connection with your authentic self, you are tapping into the power that lies deep within at the core of your being. When you are aligned with source, you have access to all possibilities in the universal field. Therefore, the more connected you are with your authentic self, the more you can use your internal power to help others. The universe has its own intelligence. If your intentions are sincere, then nothing will stop this power coming through you in transforming others by your message – nothing, that is, except your free will. When you express your truth, this comes all the way from the core of your being. The depth of your expression depends on the depth of your connection to your authentic self. You can bring forth only that which you are already. In expressing your truth, you bring forth the depth of your being into the world. It is this expression of your divine essence that can bring about transformation in people and the world. This power lies within at your source. Your divine essence is the spiritual aspect of your being. By expressing the spiritual side of your being, you can change the world. You have that much power within you. This is not ego thinking, but thinking from your divine essence. When you believe this, you know it. All it takes is faith in your self. Through your knowing, whatever you intend, wish for, or desire with intensity will manifest much quicker because of your expression of and connection with your divine essence. Your connection with your authentic self makes you a powerful magnet for all that you want to attract in whatever form. The universe conspires in your favour when you are in service to others. Expression of your divine essence can be picked up by other people as vibes. Your vibrations are higher when you are true to yourself.

When you have access to your divine essence, you know it because of the experiences you have. You have no doubt about what you know. When you know, you just know. Knowing comes from experience and feeling something to be so. Every single person on the planet has access to his or her authentic self and can experience divine essence. The journey starts with clearing your energetic or emotional blockages first. Then focus on your language and think pure thoughts. Your thoughts are more powerful than you think. Wish all people well, and see the good things in them. That is what is meant by "treat every neighbour as you would like to be treated." Also, "love thy enemy" is another example. If you love your enemy, then all you hold is love inside. You remain unaffected within your being as a result. If you hold on to dense feelings, these can hold you back from your true essence. When you have love and well-wishes for all people, no matter if they have wronged you, then you attract love and well-wishes back to yourself. You are responsible for your own inner being. By learning to express your divinity from within, you awaken that part of yourself you didn't get to experience before. You may find words coming out of your mouth automatically, without conscious thought; and when you listen to the words as you say them, you can hear the wisdom therein. You feel in the flow as the words just keep coming, and you feel great because you know you are spreading your message to help others. When your words come directly from source energy, you light the way forward for waking other people up to their own divinity.

See the divine in every person. When you see divinity in others with con-viction, you focus your attention and energy on their spiritual nature and potential for growth, no matter what their circumstances. All situations are transitory. Nothing is permanent in the physical world. That's the illusion. What is cannot ever be anything else. It just is. Your divine essence is. How things appear to be is not the same as they are in themselves. It's the same for people. How people appear on the surface may not be a true reflection of their divine essence. Mother Teresa used to say she could see Jesus in the face of beggars. In this way, she saw their divine essence, because she was looking at them from her own authentic self. She could recognize that which she was herself. It is by knowing your own divine essence that you can see this in others at their core. By expressing your divinity, you can draw the same out in others. In this way, you spread love and compassion throughout the world, like a ripple effect. The holy relationship is the one where people communicate with mutual love and compassion for each other. There is no room for doubt, anger, jealousy, or resentment in the holy relationship. You may be thinking this sounds very idealistic. The way of competition, struggle, and striving to survive belongs to the old way of the world. The new way of being that brings prosperity and peace comes from treating all others with unconditional love and compassion. The world is shifting from one to the other at present. Which side would you like to be on? Or are you sitting on the fence?

How we think now can affect the mass consciousness of humanity. What do you choose to think and believe? Your belief makes it so for you! When enough humans think along the same lines, the wavelength created can cause a paradigm shift. What do you need to focus on to create the shift you want? What do you need to pay less attention to so that it falls away from your world and way of being? Something can only be energized by the attention you pay it. What world do you want to create? You can use your divine essence in this regard. By expressing your divinity, you may feel vul-nerable, but you are actually showing your true strength when you do this. You have no fear or ego pride for how others may react. It's worth the risk of saving others from their illusion of themselves. Even if you are rebuked, you know you are doing the right thing. It's not like you are preaching from the pulpit. You can speak to people at their level, and after a few moments, they know they are safe with you. That's when they feel free to open up, and then you learn how you can help them.

People want to trust you essentially. Your connection to your authentic self will give you the right words to say at the right time. Just allow it to flow. Everybody has free will, and for this reason, let others find their way in their own way. If they ask for help, offer help. It is good to help others, but it is not good to enable them to feel helpless. It is even better to empower others from within so that they can find their own solutions. If you look at every problem as if you see the solution, then that is what you will find. It is the same with people. The solution always lies within. It is in expressing your divine essence that you inspire others to look inside and realize that there is another way of being. This glimpse into reality opens the door for others to learn and connect with their own divine essence. They learn from your example, and so it spreads from one person to many. The momentum builds as the wave spreads, lifting up the hearts and souls of all who come into contact with this divine essence of yours. There is a saying that one person directly or indirectly affects ten thousand other people while on this earth. Your expression of your divine essence can actually cause a global shift in mass consciousness, believe it or not! The closer you align with your authentic self, the more impact you have on a global scale.

We are all one. While we appear as individual expressions, our spark of divinity is integrated into the whole divine intelligence of the universe already. When you access your own divinity, you shine forth your essence onto this earth, for it is much needed in these times. Can you imagine what kind of world we would live in if this were so with everybody? We are at the tipping point of a new paradigm, or way of being. The old way does not serve humanity any more. It is only with collaboration, cooperation, and sharing that we can build a world we love to be in. Your divine essence is your key to accessing your power within. As within, so without. From your divine essence, you can see everything in a different light, and what may have seemed like problems before are revealed for the blessings they really are in bringing you to where you are now. If you had not experienced challenges or obstacles, you wouldn't have the understanding and insight currently available to you. If your life had been different, so would you, on the surface. In this way, you can become grateful for all experiences in life, even though you may have found some difficult at times.

You accept all that happened. You know that your past life does not define you or your future. You have the power to create any future you desire, and this comes from your knowing. You know it is best to release all blocks, because that is the only way that you can move forward in life. You know it is best to let go of all perceived wrongdoings and mistreatment of you in the past by others. This letting go frees you up to fill your life with wonderful things and wonderful people instead. You know you are not alone when connected with your divine essence. You also know that there is more to life than appearances seem to dictate. The real truth lies deep within everything on the physical plane, yet the truth is not of this plane. How you are in the world depends on what you identify your self with. You can think of yourself as in the world but not of it. When you become identified with your own divinity more and more, you may also get to experience what might seem out of this world. This adds to your experience of life in its fullness. You get to see a whole other side to the meaning of life and your being here right now. You realize the privilege of experiencing earthly life while in a human body; for in reality, you are spirit having an earthly experience in human form.

People always have choice. Those that do not choose the path of truth may be living in fear that holds them back from being the best expression of their own truth. They know that they are not fulfilled, but they may not know why. Do not judge them. Have compassion and see their divinity within. Say in your own mind, "I can see you." This means you can see past appearances, beyond the veil of illusion, where the truth of their being lies deep. When you greet their divinity and when you talk with their divinity, their divine essence hears you and wants to respond. In this way, you lift them up from the darkness of who they thought they were, allowing them to realize their own greatness. You have greatness within, and you are a magnificent being in reality. Spend time with people who recognize your magnificence, and avoid those that treat you otherwise. You have such capacity for greatness beyond your imagination! There are so many untapped abilities that lie inside you right now. What does it take to activate them? Well, by moving inwards consistently, you will eventually reach a place where you know there is room for so much more. You will know what I mean when you get there. Just trust that your divine essence does indeed lie within, and when you access it, you will know.

This does not happen straight away, as the journey itself is a process of removing the layers of illusion as you continue to move evermore inward. As you move closer each time when meditating, your experience of who you really are deepens bit by bit. You are essentially moving towards your inner light, which gets brighter each time you move towards it. As you move towards the light, you are merging with your own divine essence at your core. At the same time, your divine essence comes forth into your physical being also. This is what happens when you integrate with your divinity. Over time, you can bring your light out into the world from within. It just happens automatically when you speak your truth. Your truth carries a higher vibration of authenticity that lifts you up.

Your truth is that part of you that is vocalized through your throat. The expression of who you truly are is your divine expression. When you can see the effect of your illuminated word on those around you, know this energy is coming through you and not from you. You may notice this with your family and close friends at first, because these people think they know you best. When they see you expressing yourself in a light different to what they are used to, you might get a few funny looks at first, or a few funny comments, but take no notice. Be patient. Then, when you meet with their steady gaze, you know you have their attention not because you are trying to get their attention, but because you are expressing your divine essence without thinking about it. This is when your divine essence becomes a part of your daily living on this earth because it has emerged from within like a seed that has grown and come to fruition above ground. Now all others can see it, admire its beauty, and know that it is possible for them to grow their own seed as well. You haven't changed in reality.

You have just become more of your authentic self, and now everybody can see it. What was once lost is now found. What was once forgotten is now remembered. What was once hidden is now visible. This is when you become transparent in your being. The veil is removed, and others can see into your soul through your eyes. Your connection with your authentic self means you have more ability to connect with other people than ever before. There is nothing between you and others, as you are one with them. Your ability to connect with others comes from your connection with your authentic self. Your presence can also bring about transformation in others – what some may call miracles. If miracles are believed to be impossible, then they are impossible, according to your subconscious. If miracles are considered a natural course of everyday life by you, then there is nothing supernatural about them. By incorporating miracles into your experience of reality, you allow for this potential to exist as a natural event. Your thoughts and beliefs are this powerful.

Jesus spoke of how any person lesser than him could perform greater works than he ever did. This is exactly what he meant when he said this. You have this power to transform your life, other people's lives, and the world itself. When are you going to step into your own power? What does it take to get past any fear you may have of breaking convention or of shaking up the status quo? Humans are creatures of habit because habit makes them feel safe. Whatever makes you feel whole and expanded is good for you, so stay with it. Whatever makes you feel small and separate, avoid it. Feed your soul in the quantum soup of potentiality, where anything is possible. It's good to break out of the safe zone from time to time so that you can learn to expand and grow as you show your authentic self more and more to the world. For this you need courage and determination, while also holding the vision of what you want to achieve. Once you are connected with your divine essence, you will be shown the way, as you will then be able to spot whatever opportunities are presented to you by means of your sharp discernment and intuition. As you connect inwards with your divine essence, your intuition, or gut feeling, also increases, and this is another tool you can use when making any choices or decisions in life about the next step to take.

Move forward knowing that you are not alone; that you are indeed loved, supported, and encouraged by the universe. Even if you do not know the next step to take on your journey, just trust and remain open to allow insights, hunches, gut feelings, or synchronicity to reveal themselves. Keep asking questions, for that is what an open mind does. A closed mind thinks it has all the answers and does not search for the truth in everything. A closed mind leads to a closed view of the world. An open mind leads to a world of self-discovery, exploration, and adventure to reveal the hidden treasure that is your divine essence within. You cannot reveal your authentic self to the world until you first discover it for yourself. Therefore, self-discovery leads you to a more meaningful journey in life as you discover new things about how the world is in its own essence. You discover that your own essential nature is an essential part of nature itself. Even nature has its own spiritual aspect and is not just physical, as it appears. Everything that exists has infinite intelligence and energy in its very being. What does this mean? It means that we are all connected as one in the gap. What is this gap that is referred to by the great sages of our time?

- The gap is that space between the nucleus and the electron in the atom. (Atoms make up everything in physical existence.)
- The gap is the quantum field of possibility.
- The gap is your source, which connects you to all that is in the universe.
- The gap is your divine essence, which connects you to the divine essence of others in the energy field.
- The gap is where you go to when you meditate.
- The gap is where you go to when you slow your brainwaves down through hypnosis or brainwave entrainment.
- The gap is where you access your superconscious mind, from where you download inspirations, insights, discoveries, and divine guidance from your highest self.
- The gap is your centre of revitalisation and refreshment, where your body, mind, and soul come into balance.
- The gap is where healing takes place.
- The gap is where you find infinite love, peace, joy, and happiness always.

The gap is all this and much more. It is the dwelling place of your infinite intelligence and divinity. When you align with your authentic self, you bring your divinity into your physical experience. Your authentic self is that God aspect of your being. You are a spark of the "sun" of God. You are one with it. Therefore, you can be in the world and not of it. Who you really are at your core is your divine self. When you express your authentic self, you express your divinity into this world. This world needs those aspects of your divinity to heal and spread love throughout the planet. Even you can make a difference in raising the vibration of the planet. When you raise your vibration as an individual, this affects the planet as a whole. You are a part of the universe, and the universe is in you also. When a critical mass, for example 1 per cent, is reached in the number of people who awaken, this can be enough to shift mass consciousness on a global scale.

In expressing your divinity, you are also expressing your Christ consciousness. Every single person has that God spark within them. In the bible, it states that when the Jews were about to stone Jesus for blasphemy (for claiming he was God's son), Jesus said, "Is it not been written in your law. I have said you are Gods." (John 10: 34, New International Version). Jesus also says in the bible that "Very truly I tell you, whoever believes in me will do the works I have been doing, and they will do even greater things than these, because I am going to the Father." (John 14:12, New International Version). Believe in your own true power within and what you can achieve when you tap into your divine essence. Allow yourself to receive the light. It is now time to shine your divine light into the world. As you do, you are shining forth your true essence of who you are, that part of you that is ever-present and all-knowing. When you shine that integral part of your being, you are bringing coherence into the world. Your connection with your divine essence helps the planet to connect as one whole as well. What once was dark and dense becomes light when your light shines forth. The consciousness of your divine essence connects with consciousness as a whole. As your divine essence merges with the whole, so the mass consciousness of the planet raises its vibration also. Relax in the light of the divine, which connects you to all that is. Bathe in the unconditional love that washes away all unease and unrest. This shower of light fills you with ease, rest, and unconditional love at your core. The closer you go to your essence, the more at home you feel inside yourself. Love fills your being with your intention or feeling of love. If you visualize sunlight shining all the way through you, it gives you a light, warm, loving feeling within yourself. When you feel love, it is easier for you to connect with your divine essence. In becoming love, you align with your natural essence effortlessly.

As you expand in the process, you realize that you can now hold more light than ever before. Your vessel can now contain more love and light. Love and light make up the true essence of your being. Love and light transform, heal, and expand. Your divine essence is that part of your real nature. The deeper you go within, the higher you go. Your divine self is at one with your authentic self. Being present allows your connection with your self. The more you connect with your highest self, the more your present reality changes. While you remain constant within your divine essence, the world you live in takes on a higher level of being. Your connection with your divine essence can be transformational for those around you. When you are in your higher state, they pick up on your vibes as they soak up the rays.

Your divine light is hidden to the naked eye. It is concealed from the physical realm. That physical part of you which is your body has access to this divine light by using your internal vision. You can draw this light forth into the world from a place of pure connection within. Benevolence and loving-kindness are how you relate to other people. You recognize their divinity within. You begin to develop holy relationships with others as you build a community and circle of love around you. Your example of building a community is picked up on by others, who then begin to develop their own communities. Eventually, as communities around the world expand and merge, they meet and join to form one whole as a whole. The earth becomes one once more, and she becomes one with all who live on her. As we connect with each other, so we recognize our oneness in each other. Whatever unites and connects comes from love. Love is all-inclusive both within and without your divine essence. Your divine essence is what brings forth unification, connection, and oneness on our planet earth. Yes, even you can do this. When all that flows is from all that you are, it leads to all that is. All is one and the same.

As your awareness of your own divine self increases, you find yourself applying spirituality to your everyday life more and more. When you change your perception of people, occurrences, and events, your life takes on a whole new meaning. It is by tuning into your higher consciousness that you become more aware of your natural self. By shifting your former perceptions, you have surrendered your illusions. These former illusions previously kept you attached to lower consciousness. This lower consciousness formerly kept you stuck in the world of appearances, where your heart was saddened by what you believed to be true for you. This lower state of being prevented you from receiving good things before, because your connection with your authentic self was diminished. You were more influenced as a result by what was going on in the outside world, and so you became distracted as a result.

Now that you have let go of your monkey mind, you can know information directly from your heart source. With your heart connection, you can now allow yourself to be in service to others, based on your guidance from within. Your higher consciousness connects you to the power from your heart centre. Now you get to experience all the wonder and awe that exists in your life. You feel your innate happiness, peace, and bliss as a result. As you tap into your higher consciousness, your vibration rises. As your vibration rises to a higher frequency, you resonate more with the vibration of your divine essence. As you do so, everything begins to change in your being and in the outside world. This is because of your self-realization. The connection between you and your divine essence has become free-flowing as the two have become one. Trust your own intuition. Remember the name that God called himself when he spoke to Moses: "I Am That I Am." You are already that which you seek. Let your inner feeling be your guide about what is right for you.

Feel what does not serve you any more. Let go of what does not serve you. When you let go in this way, you stop giving energy to who and what you are not. You can disconnect yourself from dense and heavy things and people. You know how that heavy feeling feels. Heavy and light cannot be in the same place at the same time, just like love and fear. By disconnecting in this way, you are not being unkind. In fact, you are allowing those situations that may have held you back in the past to no longer have any control over you. Now you can give your attention and energy to what does serve you. In this way, you are affirming who you really are. In this way, you get to experience inner peace at a level that you may not have felt for a while. With your present state of peace and calm, you experience the strength of who you are. You can now rise above situations that may have entangled you before. Even when you are surrounded by what appears to be chaos, you can stand in the eye of the storm in your own space. All you feel is peace and calm. As you maintain your state, others around you may stop running around and take a look at you in disbelief. They may wonder as you shine your inner light and luminosity at them. They see the calm in your face and want to know how to be the same. Your being is an example of what is possible for them too, no matter what the circumstances.

Whatever happens, know that it is for your higher good, even though you may not know what the lesson is straight away. You can ask yourself "What is the lesson here for me to learn?" You know you can rise above it, because you deserve to be better than what happens to you. You are much more than what happens to you. Life is all about experience, relationships, and how much love you allow yourself to give and receive. How you experience your life comes from your perception of it. You always have free will in this regard. How you perceive something is that reality for you, based on your beliefs. You always have choice in how you get to experience your life based on your experiences. Your connection with your divine self affects your experiences in life. By letting go of your former illusions, you begin to uncover who you really are.

Letting go is a process, like the polishing of a diamond to bring out its inner luminosity. Your divine essence is your inner diamond that sparkles with a dazzling white light. It holds its sparkle once it is uncovered for all to see. It is in opening your heart that you allow others to see the beauty within. With an open heart, your ability to give and receive love increases exponentially. Now your relationships become more meaningful as you surround yourself with like-minded people. You have let go of those relationships that do not honour who you are. People are not their behaviour. While you love a person, you do not have to like his or her behaviour. From the place of your divine essence, you hold compassion in your heart for them. By feeling compassion, you automatically want what is best for everybody. You can empathize with what they are feeling, while not becoming entangled with them. You know that they are caught up in their appearances and judgements of the world. You also know that they are suffering because of this. Their suffering does not need to be your suffering. You do not need to take on the suffering of others like a martyr, because that will only weaken you as you lose energy. For this reason, you can love the person with compassion while letting go of receiving the behaviour. You don't deserve that, and your inner guidance tells you this is true.

You are disconnected from the effects of others' behaviour, and you are available if they want to receive your help. You can help only those who want to receive your help. You cannot force your advice or opinions on others, because they have their free will also. You can respect their freedom to make their own choices when you know this. You do not need to fit in with other people's expectations of who they think you are. Focus on how you feel, no matter what anybody says. Your self-realization of your authentic self at the level of your divine essence means that you attract to you those people at the same level as you. You attract people who are like you and who like you. You do not need to go looking for them. They will be drawn to your higher energy vibration. When in service to others, give without expectation. You are not giving in order to receive when you are being in service. Being in service means fulfilling your soul purpose in alignment with your authentic self.

Your divine essence is that part of you which always is. It always has been, and it always will be. There is no time that your divine essence has not existed, whether before, during, or after your present life experience. It is your infinite essence and comes from that deepest part of you at your source. As you connect more with your authentic self, you learn to identify more with your divine essence. When your identity becomes one with your divine self, you view the world from this perspective. This is who you are in truth. How you see your self changes over time, and what that means to you changes as you connect with your divine essence. The more you reconnect with who you really are, the more benevolence and loving-kindness become your way of being. As Jesus said in the Bible, "Know ye not that ye are the temple of God, and that the spirit of God dwelleth in you?" (Corinthians 3:16-17, King James Version). Your divine essence is that God part of yourself that always is. In this way, you are one with god. You are the only authority in your life. You are divinely protected by the light of your being. When you know and believe this to be so, you open yourself to the spiritual world. Your self-empowerment maintains integrity and inner strength and so raises your energy field.

The Sanskrit mantra "Aham Brahmasmi" means "The core of my being is the ultimate reality, the root and ground of the universe, the source of all that exists." When you are aligned with cosmic law, your actions achieve maximal benefit with minimal effort. Everything you desire is within you. When you are aligned with universal intelligence, you become attuned to your heart's desire. This is when your actions and desires become supported by cosmic intelligence. As a result, your actions are blissfully free from attachment to outcome. To reinforce this, you can say to yourself while meditating "I use my conscious intentions to manifest my dreams." When praying, you can give thanks right now for what you want. That way you are saying that you know it is on its way. At the same time, you hold gratitude in your heart while holding the intention for what you desire. Gratitude opens your heart for receiving more of the same. Your state of being is one of expectation and gratefulness when holding your heart's desire in your mind. Really, you are holding it in your heart, because your mind's thoughts are kept out of the picture. In reality, you are keeping out of your own way by feeling gratitude when praying or meditating.

Exercise

To connect with your divine essence, you can maintain a daily practise of prayer and meditation. As you may have a busy schedule, you can choose the same time each day to meditate or pray in the morning and the evening. When you are praying, you are not asking; rather, you are thanking as if you already have what you want. You can aim to have regular communication with the universe on a daily basis. This reinforces your connection with your source within. At first, this may be done for fifteen to twenty minutes, until you get into a routine. Your prayer becomes an intention that you set when you want to feel what you are grateful for. On a daily basis, your prayer becomes your communication to your higher being, who is always listening. Your prayer can be something like the following:

Morning

Thank you, God, for allowing me to receive my _____ [heart's desire] when the time is right. Everything is in divine order and divine timing. I am open to receiving with gratitude and appreciation. Thank you for teaching and working with me today. I am grateful for the possibilities that are presented to me daily.

Evening

Thank you so much for all that I've learned. I am grateful for the opportunities I received this day. Thank you for being there for me. I know that I am moving closer to my heart's desire daily. I really appreciate what you've done for me.

CHAPTER 12

LOVE, HAPPINESS, AND FULFILMENT ARE YOURS ALWAYS

Happiness is a state of being. You don't need to do anything to be happy. There is a misperception sometimes about what happiness means. The illusion is that you must seek on the outside for what it is that makes you happy on the inside. Happiness comes from within and does not require any doing. You can be happy now without effort or struggle just by tapping into happiness in this moment. It has been said that it takes only eight muscles to smile and that it takes thirty-two to frown. When you smile, your face relaxes. As you smile, you send messages to your brain to produce feel-good hormones that wash over the organs in your body. When you frown, your face tenses. By looking up and smiling, you automatically raise your spirit. "Keep your chin up", the saying goes. You will find it is very difficult to think of an unhappy thought if you tilt your chin up and smile as you look upwards. As you do so, you will see this for yourself.

Your mind does not control you or your state of being. You control your mind when you learn to be still in your body and your thoughts. It is through the relaxation of your thoughts in allowing what is that you can be happy now. When you allow what is, you receive. By relaxing and accepting all that is, you avoid resistance, struggle, and suffering. Everything that happens is in divine order. Happiness is a state of trust allowing acceptance of all that is in the now. After all, we are human beings and not human "doings". Your thoughts can get in the way sometimes. Your state of mind affects your state of reality and how you perceive the world. Happiness, joy, and peace lie at the core of your authentic self always. It is natural for you to be happy. This is your natural state. It is not natural for you to be living in a state of fear. The more you get to know your true self, the more you move to the core of your being, past all the layers of conditioning. The more the layers start being peeled off, through self awareness, the more you tune into your inner bliss. Your inner bliss is where you are at one with yourself. When you reach your core, you can interact with everything directly on the outside, in the moment. There are no distractions, negative thoughts, limiting beliefs, or layers of conditioning to get past. You can see directly and are aware of exactly what is going on. Your senses are sharper, as is your awareness. You are at one with yourself and the world. There is no right or wrong. There is just is.

Happiness and fulfilment already exist unconditionally when you can tune into that part of you that remains untouched by external events. By awakening to the conditioning from your past experiences and the illusion you have been living under, you can see everything as it really is, directly. Your presence in the now means you have disconnected from the past. Also, when you are present to your self right now, you are not worrying about the future either. Peace of mind can be achieved through mindfulness, which is a skill in itself that can be developed over time. Mindfulness keeps you in the present moment, where you true power lies. Your true power comes from within and not without (outside). Being mindful means focusing your attention on what is in the moment. You are in the moment when you are being mindful. You are in the zone. You contemplate what is. There is no past or future in your mind when you are being mindful. There is only now. Mindfulness includes quieting the mind to experience full presence in the present moment. It is a state of unconditional well-being, peace, and happiness. This state can be accessed through meditation, which takes practise and gets easier over time. Mindfulness and meditation involve using your body to access your inner bliss. Focusing on your breath while meditating is very important. This keeps you focused on your inner being and avoids distraction from the outside.

Another way to achieve mindfulness is through self-hypnosis. All hypnosis is self-hypnosis. Hypnosis works through allowing in suggestions made when the brainwaves have been slowed down to an alpha- or theta-wave state. The suggestions made are for your ultimate good. Mindfulness can also be achieved through brainwave entrainment, in which the brainwaves are slowed down by listening to special vibrational music. Brainwave entrainment means you are training your brain to have direct access to your natural state of happiness and fulfilment. In the process, your brain becomes a fine-tuned tool that has access to the information from the universe like never before. It can now tune into frequencies that bring about awareness and insights not accessible to you before. Subliminal messages allow in positive suggestions directly to the subconscious, without the need for trance. This happens even when you are in the beta state.

With training, your brain becomes an open vessel ready to receive. It's like it has been spring cleaned of the clutter within it. Any previous traumas that have been imprinted on the neural network of your brain are washed away. This happens when your brain cells become bathed in the feel-good hormones and neuropeptides. As you begin to lose old habits that did not serve you, they begin to fade away. Instead, you can learn to create empowering new habits for yourself that become sharper with more use. What remains in your brain then is a finely tuned program for success in life. This reprogramming also allows your organs to operate efficiently in your body, so now you have more energy, clarity, and zest for life. When you are in balance and harmony with yourself, your body functions more efficiently. This oneness within yourself leads to a healthy body functioning in peak condition.

It is only natural for you to be happy. What makes you fulfilled in life comes from carrying out your purpose. Your purpose is driven by your love and passion for what you do, and this is a reward in itself. In understanding yourself with deep insight, only then can you really understand other people in order to be able to help them objectively. It is important for you to be able to deal with your own emotional problems first, so that you are detached from other people's in the best possible way. You need to be grounded in yourself before dealing with the outside appearances of the world. In order to accept and give others unconditional positive regard, you need to be in a place where you accept and give yourself unconditional positive regard first. Then you can look for and see the potential in others that is waiting to be realized. This means you can help them, as a guide, to tap into their own resources in solving their problems in their own best possible way, suiting their needs as determined by their own subconscious. So you need to work on yourself before you can be in service to them.

Self-work is never done. There's always room for improvement in peeling off the layers of old conditioning in bringing forth your authentic self once more. As your authentic self emerges, so does your own expression of your own authenticity. When you are being authentic, you are being true to yourself, and this is what sets you free. You are free to be your self, and so you are free to interact with others in a mutually beneficial way. As you do, you surround yourself with similar people who uplift your life, as you do theirs. In the process, you have created a warm, loving hub around you that supports and nourishes your soul.

Happiness is not something you need to pursue. It is not the end goal in itself. You do not need to do anything in order to be happy. Some people think their achievements in life will make them happy. While achievements can bring about personal fulfilment, this is not the same as your natural happiness that is without conditions in life. Your happiness just is. When you are connected with your authentic self, you are aligned with your own inner happiness. While you do not need to have anything material in order to be happy, there is nothing wrong with having luxury and nice things in your life. It is good to surround yourself with nice things. It is only natural for you to be abundant also. When you are following your path, abundance naturally flows to you. How you are being is what brings out your natural happiness. Being true to yourself and expressing your truth means you are being authentic. You do not need to prove anything to anybody else or even to yourself. You know you are enough just the way you are. You do not need to do anything other than be who you really are right now. So many people look for happiness on the outside in order to be happy on the inside. This is an illusion, because it is what you have been taught. The illusion is that you must fill your space with things from the outside. This creates a craving to continually fill that space with the same things from the outside in order to feel good on the inside. Thus, instant gratification is mistaken for happiness. Instant gratification is only temporary and does not last. Natural happiness is an internal state, and happy conditions follow on the outside from that state. Your life on the outside follows from your state of being on the inside. It is not the other way around, as you have been taught.

Your physical possessions do not equal your happiness. Some people measure their level of success by how much they have on the outside. Yet they cannot understand why they are not happy on the inside. While they have everything they could possibly ever want, it is not enough for them. There seems to be something missing, but they don't know what it is. That missing part in their being is linked to the needs of the soul. The seat of the soul is the heart. The heart has its needs also on an emotional level. These needs are attention, acknowledgment, affection, and acceptance. The heart's natural state is one of unconditional love. When you are in a state of unconditional love, you can give and receive love without conditions attached. You accept people for who they are, even their shortcomings. You recognize, without judging, that every human is on his or her own journey in life with his or her own lessons to learn. Your happiness is directly linked with your ability to give and receive love. Your happiness is also linked to your ability to connect with others, develop relationships, and maintain relationships that are mutually beneficial. Once you are tuned into your authentic self, you are in your zone of power, from where everything else flows. Your authentic self is the set point on your internal compass dial. In aligning with your authentic self, you become your own life compass in this way. You learn to follow your own direction from the inside and not from the outside. Your internal guidance points the way forward in the magnetic field of thought as you pick up inspirations and ideas from source. Your heart shows you that your gut feeling is good, and so you know which direction to take in the "quantum field" of life. Your magnetic energy is at one with the field, and you can see the way forward with ease and grace.

You can become your own authority, teacher, guru, and even master. You do not need to follow others to get your own answers. You can now learn to master those aspects of yourself that were an illusion before, only because you forgot who you really are. Let go of the illusion and embrace the magnificent being that you are. You are right now your own master. You do not need to look to others for your answers any more. You never did in reality. The more you get to know your self, the more sure you are of your own decisions and what direction you are to take in life. As you do so, your feelings become intensified into a knowing in this way. Your heart will always lead you in the right direction to what comes from happiness. Happiness leads to a life full of bliss surrounded by the beauty that you already hold within you. This is the life you are meant to live. It is your divine birthright. You deserve this, and you always did. No more struggles and no more pain. Your past conditioning has become undone to reveal the sparkling, shiny essence that is your divinity. As you allow more and more of your true nature to shine forth, just watch for the changes happening in your life now. As you do, you hear yourself speaking more and more in a powerful way. You will also see others respond to you more favourably than ever before. Your life will transform automatically in ways you cannot imagine and you will be amazed. It is all so effortless and easy. Life will definitely take a turn for the better, and all because you are being you!

Your power to transform your life comes from within. Aligning with your true self is all it takes. When you align with your authentic self, you allow your inner being to expand and grow. When you expand, you allow more of the light that raises your vibration to enter. With your higher vibration you find yourself living life at a higher level. What before may have seemed important no longer is. Your priorities in life have changed also to become more aligned with who you truly are. You have shifted in your being, and so your outside world has also shifted. Other people may notice the change and try to "put you back in your box". Remain firm while being gentle with them. You know who you really are, even if they don't. Eventually they will get used to seeing you in a new light. In this way, you become a shining beacon for others when they see the great results in your life and they become curious. While you cannot give them their answers, carrying out your purpose can help them to find their own truth for themselves.

You can be happy now, when you choose to be. You now know that happiness does not come from the outside. You can use your mind and your body in connecting with your innate happiness on the inside. There are three things that can affect your state of mind on the surface level, as illustrated in the following diagram:

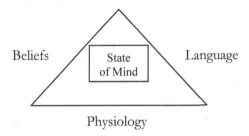

Your belief that you can be happy and fulfilled determines your perception and behaviour in the world to that end. The language of your own inner talk affects your thought processes and even beliefs. Become aware of what words you are saying to yourself and the kind of language you are using internally. When you become aware of your inner critic, or saboteur, you can learn to handle this part of yourself in the best way. Awareness of it comes first. Your Inner critic, or saboteur, is a part of your ego that tries to protect you by overprotecting you. You do not need to be protected from anything in reality. If you believe you do, then you also believe that your happiness depends on your need to be protected. Needing to feel protected means you are in fear of something. Happiness is a state of mind that is free from any conditions. When you are happy, your love that emanates from within to the outer world is all that you experience. Fear and love do not exist in your state of mind at the same time. Happiness is also a state of love.

Ego operates from fear, and it is fear that holds you back from the many possibilities that always exist. If you live your life too carefully, then you may lose out on some opportunities that present themselves to you. When you listen to your ego, you do not step through doors that open. On the other hand, your ego can loosen its grip over you when you pay it no heed. Instead of resisting it, you accept it while paying no attention to what it is saying. You are not your ego. The ego is just a part of you, and if you resist it, you will enforce it. The less attention you pay to your ego's words, the better. Instead, you can say to your inner critic, "Thank you, I can handle this myself." If you are not sure if your ego is talking to you, you could ask yourself "Is this for my highest good?" or "Does this serve me?" As you come to discern your ego from your real self, you learn to pay more attention to the real you. Paying attention in the right direction paves the way forward for you as you forge new habits and ways of thinking for yourself. Eventually your inner critic's words fade away, as do their effects on blocking your happiness.

When you feel free is when you are open to the flow of the universe and all that it contains. Let go of your fear and the need to be protected. You are enough. You have enough in your being, and remember that love conquers all. With love, you are happy and everybody wins. Win-win is for you and for others. The more you can let go of fear, the more you are open to the peace that is within you. When your mind is at peace, you are at rest. With your mind at rest, you receive that which is flowing to you without any blocks. You have direct access to your guidance from within. You are more connected to your heart centre when you are in a peaceful state. You have learned to detach from what you think and instead connect to your own inner feeling. By removing yourself from your ego mind, you feel lighter in your being. You know now that you are much more than you ever thought you were. The reality of you is ever present, no matter what happens. Knowing this, you can always let go of that which does not serve you. You no longer focus on what previously appeared as problems in your life. Your focus is elsewhere now.

Yes, your focus is now. Now is your moment of power. Now is your moment of happiness. For every moment of now that exists, you have the possibility for happiness, peace, and joy in your life. You get to make the choice in every moment. Whenever you feel less than happy, understand why. You know you are less than happy when your vibration drops below the level of happiness. What happens in your life when this occurs? What meaning do you give to this? How can you change the meaning you ascribe to this situation so that you know the problem no longer exists? What judgement and blame do you need to let go of? How can you take responsibility for how you feel in this situation, should it ever occur again? In questioning yourself in this way, you are learning to let go of old habits of the ego mind. As you do so, you move closer to your happiness that always exists in every moment.

When you learn to silently observe what you are thinking about, you gain insight and awareness into what you are telling yourself. With this awareness, you can focus your mind on your happiness that already exists within. The language you use in terms of words – thought or spoken words – can restrict or give you access to your happiness that already is. Your subconscious, which is a part of your mind, hears your spoken words at all times. It records every event in your life, as well as what you think and say. Your words are very powerful. Each word that you use carries its own vibration both within you and by what you express out into the world. When you let go of judgement and blame, you also let go of the self-imposed blocks to your own happiness. You can let go of your blocks when you realize that they come from the perceptions of your ego mind. By getting a different perspective on life, you can change your own perception. In the process, you move from perceiving through your tinted spectacles to a clear vision of what is actually around you. When you can see with clarity, you no longer need the spectacles of illusion. With clarity of mind, you know that happiness can always be achieved in every moment.

It is easier to be happy than you think. If you think it is complicated, then what is the problem your mind perceives? When you let go of your perception, by seeing things differently, the problem disappears. There is no problem, and there never was. Your perception made it so. When you tap into your innate happiness, your words, language, belief, and physiology reflect your pleasant state of mind also. Physiology is the way you stand or sit, how you move your body, your gestures, and also your facial expressions. Your physiology, or how you hold your body, affects your state of mind. What do you do when you are happy? Relax and smile, of course. According to Dr. David Hamilton PhD, when you smile, you immediately put into effect beneficial hormones being produced inside your body. When you hold an upright posture, you are more likely to feel good. You feel good as you stand tall in the world and you hold your head high. So, whenever you want to feel powerful, assume that position that makes you feel powerful, and hey presto! It really does work. If you slouch and hunch over while looking down, how do you think you will feel? Exactly; I don't need to tell you. Always be aware of how you hold your body, as it does affect your state of mind.

What you focus on grows. The more you focus on your happiness, the more it grows. You can nourish and cultivate you own state of happiness on a daily basis. Remind yourself daily of at least one thing to be happy for. In this way, you are showing gratitude for the beauty that surrounds you in your world. Being grateful opens up your heart chakra, or energy centre. When you open up your heart centre in this way, you are opening yourself up to receive more goodness into your life. With an open heart, you are available to give and receive more. The beauty you witness on the outside comes from that which is on the inside already. When you see beauty, you are beauty already. When you see happiness, you are happy already. When you see love, you are love already. When you see peace, joy, and bliss, you are those as well. As you focus, so you are. You do not need to chase happiness. How can you chase something which you already are?

Even if you don't think or feel you are happy, this is because your focus is elsewhere. Once you point your focus back in the direction of happiness, it will show its happy face once again from inside. It is much easier to let go of something like a pen than to hold on to it, don't you agree? In relaxing your grip, you let go. In clenching your fist, you hold on. When you relax your grip on any blocks you may have previously had, you will find yourself relaxing into your natural state of being; that is happiness. By letting go, you are surrendering your need to control any outcome, and so you become detached from it. As you do, you remove any set conditions from your life and so your state of mind is unaffected. If your life has conditions and everything does not go according to plan, how do you know this is not for your highest good? Your natural happiness is not dependent on any conditions on the outside. Letting go means you are letting go of the conditions also. In letting go, you are surrendering in trust. You trust because of your inner knowing. It is in your knowing that you can by truly happy, because you know this is how you really are. When you know, all the abundance which is your birthright flows right in your direction. Are you ready to receive it? Can you see the open door?

Your happiness is also not dependent on other people. Nobody can give to you or take from you anything which affects your natural state of happiness. This happiness you have is who you are at your core. You are better than anything that happens to you. Therefore, you can separate your real self from what happens to you. Your authentic self is unaffected always by anything that happens to you. When your sense of self is aligned with your authentic self, you can be happy no matter what. You can also be at peace within yourself at the same time. You have your own answers. Nobody else can give you your answers. As you connect with your authentic self, allow the answers to flow to you. When you ask a question, you will always get an answer, but sometimes you have to wait. Just trust, be peaceful, and allow. Then get on with your daily life while knowing that it is on its way. Rise above appearances and what happens to you. You know you are above all that in reality. As you see things from a higher perspective, you are not caught up in what happens in the land of appearances. While you are in the world of appearances, you are not of it. Your ability to see with clarity means you can see your own truth in everything that happens. The truth of who you are never changes. That is why appearances cannot change the truth of who you are. Your happiness is your own connection to your truth. It is your connection to your authentic self. When your truth shines forth, others want to know their own truth too. They want to be happy like you, and they want to know how to be happy too. That is because they don't know happiness is there all along within themselves.

Other people's problems do not need to become your problems, for if they did, how could you help them? You can have empathy for others' problems without getting caught up in them. If you want to help others and be in service to them, you can be detached while helping them to find their own answers. Your answers are not their answers. Your advice and opinions may not be the best thing for them in their life at that moment. They will always find their answers if they ask the right questions. Remember, it is only natural for you and everybody else to be happy. Trust that this is so. In letting go and allowing for yourself, you do the same for others also. At the same time, you do not need to agree with others' behaviour. Who they really are and their behaviour are two different things. When you can see others for who they really are, you can see past their behaviours. You know that they are just looking to be happy, no matter what they do. They don't know any better than what they *know*, right?

Happiness is what everybody wants, right? This does not mean that the end justifies the means. Looking for happiness in material possessions is not the answer. The only way to true happiness is by going within. True happiness does not come from the outside and what the world has to offer. Your inner state of happiness is what sets up the happy conditions in your life on the outside. Think of the Dalai Lama, for instance. I don't think I've ever seen his face without a smile on it. When he talks, he also tends to laugh or giggle while giving the most profound wisdom you can imagine. For me, he is a perfect example of living in happiness and love. Who can you think of that reminds you of a happy person? Is it somebody in your life, or is it somebody in the world arena? What qualities does this person have? What is he or she like? What beliefs does this person have? What is his or her world view? How can you learn to tune into your own natural happiness from what you know about this person? You may just get a few answers. When you model your life on successful people, your life becomes successful. When you model your life on what makes people feel happy, you also learn how to feel your own happiness. When you do, you realize it was there all along, as you become more and more aligned with your authentic self.

When you are in alignment with your inner happiness, you are open to receiving more. Your happiness allows you to expand as you grow and evolve, and as you grow, you are fulfilled. The paradox is that you are always happy and fulfilled in reality. When you allow this possibility for yourself, you allow your true expression of who you are to emerge from within. You are naturally joyful, at peace, compassionate, happy, and fulfilled at your core, no matter what may be going on at the surface level. The surface level is where you interact with the illusion of appearances. These appearances may seemingly conflict with your state of happiness, but it is possible to be happy and at peace amidst chaos. That is possible when you have a trained mind and a connection with your authentic self. Your alignment with your authentic self allows you to use your inner resources that already exist. This is where your true power lies. As you become empowered from within, you become less affected by outside events when you are balanced with your authentic self. You do not react to provocations, because your direction comes from your reason within. For this reason, you do not react to situations; you respond to them instead. It does not matter what others say about you, because you do not dwell on their words. Your attention is directed on what is important in your life. Your focus is on your purpose, mission, and vision. Your own concept of who you know you are is more important to you than what anybody else thinks about you. It is this steady grounding in yourself that gives you a solid footing in life. Your position is always strong in this way. Your strength increases from within as you identify with your authentic self more and more. As you evolve and grow, your authentic self merges with yourself more and more from within. You can sense this happening over time, as it is a process. You have more peace and calm in your life now, as you are emotionally removed from the goings on in life on the outside. In this way, you are emotionally free.

While you do not react to situations, you can still assert your authentic self with power. You empower yourself from within by remaining steady, strong, serene, and sassy no matter what is going on around you. Your love, happiness, and fulfilment resonate at a higher vibration. When you align yourself with that higher vibration, in terms of beliefs, language, physiology, thoughts, and actions, you resonate with the same frequency as your innate love, happiness, and fulfilment. You are meant to thrive on earth and not just to survive. When you are one with your happiness, your mind, body, and soul are thriving. You are tuned in with your spiritual essence. Your body benefits from all the feel-good hormones flowing around the various organs. You have a glow about you. You have a zest for life, and you feel highly energized "in the flow". Everything seems easy and effortless. You see the good in everything. You also see the God in everything. Now you can see through eyes of love instead of fear. Abundance surrounds you and the beauty of nature is highlighted even more for you when you are happy.

Being happy is like being in love; you could call it being in love with yourself. This self-love is unconditional and just *is*. You can show genuine love for others only when it is already on the inside for yourself. How can you give to others what you do not give to yourself? You can only give that which you know. It's the same for happiness. You can only create happy conditions from a place of being happy already. Love grows love. Happiness within yourself grows happy conditions for yourself and others. This comes about when others resonate with your happiness. By shining your light, you give permission for others to shine theirs too. In this way, love, happiness, and fulfilment can spread throughout the world. One person can make a difference. You can make a difference. One person can release a ripple of energy that spreads throughout the entire universe. As each person sends his or her ripple of love, happiness, and fulfilment out into the universe, imagine the harmonic wave that is created when all the ripples meet. Imagine the power of mass consciousness converging in this wave, while compounding the effect of its energy. This harmonization of vibration creates a tidal wave of love that sweeps over every living being on earth.

It can start right now. All it takes is a decision. Love is a decision. Living in love is all it takes to be happy and fulfilled, and this means being love. When you wish the best for others, see past their shortcomings, and see who they can be at their best, you are living in love. Living in love means you can bless those who have wronged you, while shining your light of understanding on their being. This light and love will return to you in kind. Abiding in love means you are evolving the universal mind. You are evolving your own consciousness, and as you are a part of the whole, you are evolving planetary consciousness also. We are all connected on an energetic level in the quantum field. We share the same divine spark within. It is what lights us up both individually and as a collective whole at the same time.

As you expand your consciousness, your ability to allow your spark to grow increases also. Living from a higher level of consciousness means you have more direct access to your happiness. At this level, you are living in love, from love, and with love. Living in love means you have let go of anger, fear, blame, or judgement of yourself or others. This is because you are at one with all that is. Everything has a reason for being the way it is, and you accept that it is a part of the "great big plan". There is no resistance to the goodness or "Godness" that prevails over everything. Everything and everyone has a purpose. Everything has a reason for being, even though this may not be apparent on the surface in the reality of appearances. How things are in themselves gives a different version of reality. When you are aligned with your authentic self, you are more open to connecting the dots of how things are in themselves. This gives you a different perspective on the nature of reality – one that you may not have thought of before, because now you can see outside the box. Your insights make sense as you see everything in a new light in each passing moment.

Plato's Views on Happiness

Plato was a Greek philosopher whose insights in his book *The Republic* very much relate to the world we live in today. According to Plato, happiness for a community as a whole depends on each individual fulfilling his or her function (purpose) in life. Plato claims that fulfilling your function puts you in harmony with others' virtues (values) when they are fulfilling their functions also. These virtues for Plato include wisdom, courage, and self-control. When your virtues are in balance with each other, they allow for justice and morality in you. When everybody fulfils his or her function, similarly, justice and morality in the community prevail also. According to Plato, only philosophers know real goodness, and they make the best rulers because their nature has been nurtured to consider the welfare of the state (whole), without expecting rewards. For Plato, the philosopher-ruler (reason) can identify with the good of the community (whole), the same as with the good of himself. The philosopher-ruler (reason) who has knowledge of goodness must fulfil his function in this ideal "polis" (city) if happiness is to be achieved through morality and justice. Similarly, reason must rule within you if you are to be happy, because only then can you know what justice and morality are. This means, essentially, that you must follow your own intuition for what is right for you. Only philosophers know real goodness. Plato aims to portray a community upon which to model your own life in assimilating yourself to God, who is supremely good, moral, and just. Plato sees philosophers as needing to transcend from their metaphysical perfect world in the ivory towers, to get involved in human affairs in the material world. Plato acknowledges that the philosopher-ruler has knowledge through the enlightenment of his mind's eye, which perceives reality when he leaves the "cave" (material world).

According to Plato, the ordinary man is a prisoner of his illusions and opinions while inside the cave, because of the shadows cast on the wall from the fire inside. The prisoner is bound by his illusory belief in the reality of these shadows as being the reality of all things. It is only by withdrawing from the "cave" of the material world that you can experience things as they really are in the sunlight (source). Only on leaving the cave can the freed prisoner reflect on natural objects (in nature) that are illuminated by the sun. In this way, he can see them as particular instances of the presence of universals (truths), until eventually he can look at the sun itself. It is only by lifting your mind's eye from your opinions and illusions and fixing it on the particular instances of love, happiness, and fulfilment that you begin to get a glimpse of the inherent universal truth of each one. According to Plato, there comes a stage where you can look higher, and so you can see the sun, or source, which illuminates all. Only the philosopher-ruler (reason) is capable of this, and so his wisdom is not apparent to the ordinary man, who cannot leave the "cave", being bound to it by his illusions and opinions.

For Plato, the harmony of the community (and the individual) depends on the different parts performing their functions only. If everyone contributes what he or she is supposed to, then all are cooperating with each other. In this way, Plato says, people can be at harmony within themselves and with each other, by using reason to achieve morality in the "psyche" (mind). Reason fulfils itself by obtaining knowledge. According to Plato, proper education and training realizes the philosopher-ruler's nature to achieve its full potential, without which it would be forgotten. Therefore, it is important to continue learning throughout life, as this allows you to grow and evolve.

Also, Plato says that by being moral and helping others, you can achieve happiness. Plato describes the cave that represents the material world, and he says it is possible to leave the cave in order to see the truth of all that is. The philosopher-ruler (reason) returns to the "cave" (material world) to share knowledge for the benefit of mankind, in order to enlighten and unchain him, so that he (mankind) can look from the imperfection of physical objects in the cave to the perfection of goodness itself, by means of reason. In this way, Plato is referring to you expressing your authentic self to the world, in bringing forth your wisdom for the benefit of humanity. For Plato, morality is achieved by obeying the voice of reason (intuition) within yourself, which rules how you behave towards others. According to Plato, where humans give in to desire for excess, conflict and unhappiness can prevail. If higher reason rules within, then true goodness can by understood by you.

This understanding allows you to be in control of yourself. Plato says that immorality occurs when one part of the soul disrupts the whole by giving in to lower desires. For this reason, Plato believes it is very important for you to monitor impressions (what you impress on your mind) from the material world, as the wrong kind can influence you from the pathway to morality. Through wisdom, your reason promotes courage and self-discipline in you. Your happiness comes as a result of your harmony with yourself and others that unites you with them. Reality is known by your intuition using reason. By fulfilling your human intuition, happiness is achieved. Self-fulfilment is achieved through reason that leads to happiness. Reason guides you to lift your mind's eye to a source of all light so you can see the good itself. From this source, you can put order in your own life, as well as that of the "polis" (community).

Plato also talks about you leaving behind a legacy, for which you will be honoured in the "cave", as well as leaving "successors" that will carry on your work. In the meantime, you continue to enjoy the benefits of justice and morality in the afterlife. Plato believes that you are eternally happy by being just and moral in leading a "good" life, which is made possible by knowledge. Plato's "polis" (community) represents a unified, stable, and orderly system which is an ideal to the pattern and rule of fulfilled human life, under the rule of reason. It is a paradigm which humanity can aim for in assimilating ourselves to God. Plato's polis serves as a community that has achieved morality, justice, and happiness. Social morality involves everybody, including the philosopher-ruler, fulfilling the function of all, which in turn promotes unity within the community. The true philosopher-ruler has no desire to rule, but adheres to what is expected of him without gratification or rewards.

Plato's community serves as an analogy for the individual who achieves happiness by being moral. You are the ruler of your own destiny and happiness. You should ignore false illusions and distracting impressions received during life, as these could influence the rule of intelligence and passion within you. Trust that your reason (intuition) has the right qualities to oversee, protect, and promote your happiness. Morality is achieved when you are united and in harmony with yourself. With this unity comes happiness. Plato says that people have the free will within their minds to be either miserable under the "tyrannical ruler" or happy under the "philosopher-ruler". He is also saying that you need to listen and be guided by your inner voice of reason, which knows best how you can achieve happiness.

By going within, you can be at peace with who you really are. In any situation, be in the moment at all times from your connection with your authentic self. That way you avoid becoming distracted by outside events before you get to respond. When you go within, you are at peace first. You feel calm in this space, from which you communicate to the world. You can be the change that you want to see in others in this way. Be the peacefulness you wish to bring to a situation. Be the change you want to make in your life. It is up to other people to make their own changes. Be the happiness you want to see around you. Reflect who you are onto the world from your face. Let your deeds reflect your divine essence in everything you do. Show your source how grateful you are for being able to spread your love and light into the world. Spread your calming effect by remaining rooted in your very being. That way you are not knocked off balance by anything that happens, no matter how crazy it appears. You are not trying to change anybody else in this way, even though this is what happens. By remaining true to your innate nature, you have the ability to bring about enormous change around you in effect. Maintain your connection to your authentic self and the divinity that is you. Never forget that you are a divine being. You are spirit in reality having a human experience. Your body is the vessel that transports your spirit in this reality as you see it. Always check in with how you are feeling about your life in the moment. Your gut feeling always guides you in the right direction.

When you are happy, you tend to spend time around happy people who are on the same wavelength. The saying "Birds of a feather flock together" really is true. When you are living with authenticity, you tend to let go of those relationships that do not serve you and connect with like-minded individuals instead. The group of people you surround yourself with is important, as this gives you the safe and sacred space to just be and express yourself. When you express from the place of your authentic self, you are already free. Your freedom comes from within. Your message is received and accepted with joy from those who resonate with you. You inspire each other and so become uplifted by others living from their authentic selves also. As your connection on an individual and collective level becomes stronger, so does your impact on those living from a lower consciousness and level of vibration. By unleashing your authentic self in this way, you free yourself and the world at large. In giving yourself freedom, you allow the world to be free also. In giving yourself happiness, you allow the world to be happy also. In giving yourself fulfilment, you allow the world to fulfil its true nature also. You are in the universe, and the universe is in you. How you are on the inside affects the world at large. Just imagine what kind of world we could live in if every human being lived from the space of his or her authentic self. How would things be different? How would things be the same? For me, this world is already here in potentiality, truly! All it takes is a decision. I envision a world of peace and unity where collaboration and cooperation are the norm amongst humankind. Competition and separation no longer exist, as humanity realizes that we are all connected and are one, in reality. We are all equal, and there is nothing to separate us.

In this world of oneness, humans operate from their heart centre and not their head. The heart centre is the seat of the soul. Love, joy, compassion, care, and gratitude are the emotions by which we live our lives. The new way is for the greatest and highest good of all. This is the new earth. In this world, we take care of everybody. The hungry are fed, and the poor are clothed and sheltered. The wealth and resources of the planet are shared. Sharing becomes the new motto for our way of being. There is no need for struggle and pain any longer, and so it doesn't exist. Healing modalities are integrated on a more natural level as we become more empowered in maintaining our own health. Natural biodegradable resources are utilized and developed for the good of the planet and its people also. For this reason, there will be no more pollution of the ground, sea, or air. Even growing food will take on a more spiritual nature that yields bigger crops, thus eliminating the need for toxic fertilizers. Nature will be nurtured by mankind, who takes only what he needs, instead of needing to just take all the time. Nature will be respected for its own sake and appreciated for its own natural beauty. The true gift of nature will be realized for what it can really offer us on an energetic level. Deforestation will cease, as will the pollution of the rivers and the oceans from industry.

From research already carried out, seeds have been shown to grow bigger and quicker when thoughts or intentions of healing love are sent to them. Masaru Emoto has also done studies on water crystals that form when he freezes water. Each water crystal forms like a six-sided snowflake, every single one being completely unique. When feelings, words, pictures, or music of love is projected at the water beforehand, it forms into the most beautiful crystals. Masaru told me himself that the most beautiful crystals he has seen are from the words "love" and "thanks". We as humans are made up of 80 per cent water. The water in our body is also affected by our environment. This environment includes our thoughts and physical surroundings around the cells in our body and outside our body. It is important to take care of your body, for it is the vessel of your authentic self. A healthy body can tune into your true nature more directly. A healthy body is harmonized with itself. Love brings about health within your body. Love truly has the power to heal in every facet of your life. This extensive truth behind the healing power of love has been hidden from us up until now, but now the truth is out! It is there if you know where to find it, but first you must first find your authentic self. Everything else flows from there when you follow your internal guidance.

When you hold joy in your heart, you increase your prosperity. The more you feel joy in expressing your energy, the more magnetic your energy becomes. Whatever you do with joy brings more of the same from the universal flow that always is. Every time you feel happy in what you do, you attract conditions of happiness to you. If you doubt or do not believe in increasing your joy or happiness, you block yourself off from the flow of the universe in this regard. Resentment, anger, and frustration also block you from the flow. To realign with the universal flow of abundance, you can become centred once more in your heart by stilling your mind and imagining that every creature and all of creation is blessed unconditionally. Set an intention that all beings may be happy, healthy, joyful, and fulfilled. When you are in service to others, this brings you joy and fulfilment when you are carrying out your life purpose.

What is your life worth? What value do you place on the service you provide? It is important to value your service and to receive what you think it is worth. In this way, you are receiving financial value for what you are giving out in the form of energy. When you value yourself, you know you are worth it. Because of this, you feel good about providing the service, as its value is reciprocated. If you received less than the value of your service, you would feel short-changed. This could lead to feelings of resentment and frustration, which would then block you from the flow. When you feel good about what you give, you keep yourself open to the flow. This increases your ability to give more in turn and to receive more. When you give with joy, you know you can receive with joy also. When you love yourself, you expect the best for yourself. This includes being and feeling valued. Always set your price for your service at what you think is truly worthy of you. When you do this, you are showing congruence within your being. Your actions are in alignment with your beliefs. Your subconscious knows this to be so, and you feel fulfilled as a result.

Truly living your values in life gives you fulfilment. Realize, then, that suppressing or compromising values is what makes you incongruent with your real self, leading to unhappiness. Trust in your gut feeling. Trust in your intuition. Trust in your self. Accept who you are, how you are, and what "I am" means in your essence. Your energy comes from within, from your source in the energy field, from the universe or God. What is within can protect you from what is without. Every trial is a lesson to be learned, to be built on in making your self a better person. No fear, just love. There is only love. What is positive is. What is negative can never be. Love conquers all! By accepting unconditionally all that is, you tap into your limitless reservoir of peace and unconditional love for yourself and others around you. Because of this, you will continue to grow and evolve, to feel and be in love with yourself and your life while moving continuously towards your destiny on your life path. You can celebrate in the circle of life with peace, love and joy in your essence. Celebrate life. You can be at peace and be free just by being authentic.

In this way, you are living in love as you allow yourself to give and receive love freely. You invite true love into your life as you get to experience the intimacy and spiritual connection with your soul mate. Your creativity is free-flowing as your soul is nourished by all the love, support, and encouragement you need. Your fulfilment comes from living your higher calling.

In fulfilling your life purpose, you are making a meaningful contribution to the world around you. Also, when you are fulfilled and happy, you have created an authentic community of like-minded people around you. In this collective field of consciousness, evolutionary partnerships are cultivated which support you in becoming an agent of change in the world. You can celebrate in this circle of life with peace, love, and joy in your essence. Celebrate your life. You can be at peace and be free just by being authentic. Surround yourself with a loving and happy environment. This is what will provide you with the right conditions to grow and prosper. In this way, you allow your true nature of happiness and bliss to emerge.

The circle of love is the circle of light. Forgive and let go. Love is all there is. Anything else is less than that. Love is all. Love all. Just love. By expressing your authentic self, you are already free. Freedom is love. When you are free, you are happy to express your love both in words and actions. Happiness and fulfilment are yours already. Focus on happiness to bring it forth. True happiness does not come from the outside, but from the inside. True happiness and fulfilment come from being in service to others, and this is what will return to you in turn, according to the law of attraction. You attract like a magnet as you are already, by feeling happy and fulfilled. As you focus on your vision and dream, you create the circumstances in the universe to bring this about. When you expect something to happen, it will. Never worry about the how. Just detach and leave that up to the universe and know it is coming. That is why you can be happy and fulfilled right now. You have a knowing that it is so, and so it is. Your thoughts have the ability to co-create with the universe in this way when you know something to be the case. When you know, you can just let it go.

Exercise: Meditation

It is good and expansive for you to meditate on a daily basis. When you are preparing to meditate, make sure you are in a comfortable position, either sitting or lying down. You can listen to a guided meditation on a CD, or just to relaxing music, when you are meditating. Have your palms face upwards so that you are ready to receive. Sit quietly in a place that you know you will not be disturbed. Make sure you are warm and that your clothes are not restrictive. Have both feet placed firmly on the ground. Imagine that you have roots from your feet connecting you to the earth that spread out twelve feet in diameter around you and twelve feet deep, spreading all the way down to the centre of the earth. Picture in your mind the earth-centre like a glowing crystal, from where light travels up through the roots into your being to give you grounding. This "crystalline" light energy grounds you in your being and travels all the way up into your heart. Know that your connection to your "h-earth-centre" also links you to your divine source. During meditation, you become aware of being in the moment as you connect to something greater than yourself through your heart centre. That greater something is the source through which all becomes possible in your life. Meditation gives you access to the universal realm from where you bring magic into your life. You need to be patient and persist in this routine on a daily basis. It is best if you stick to the same time each day. During meditation, you empty your mind. Do not resist any thoughts that may pop into your head; just observe them in a non-attached way and focus on your breathing. Allow all that occurs, no matter what it is. Just let any thoughts that arise to drift over and away out of your mind like waves over the top of the ocean.

Now imagine yourself floating down into the depths of the ocean below, where all is peace and calm. As you look up, you can see the waves of thought passing overhead, and you can also see the reflection of your higher light from above. The light of the sun pierces the ocean of your consciousness from above as you inhale its love and light. As you do so, your whole being becomes filled with the essence of your divine being. The light travels down through the crown of your head into your body. As you exhale, you let go of tension. You can feel your body becoming lighter as it fills with light. Imagine your heart filling with the light from the crystal earth below and from your higher light above. Open your heart to radiate this love and light into the world. As you project your light outside you, imagine a cocoon of light surrounding you that is covered with a gold colour on the surface. Wherever you go, your shield of golden white light surrounds you. Each time you meditate, you are reinforcing your own shield of loving light that becomes your very being. Each time you meditate, you are also raising your vibration, as you connect more and more with your divine essence. As your vibration rises, so does your impact on the material world. Your higher vibration has the ability to transform how you view the world and how others see it also. Others are indirectly affected by who you are in the world. They are automatically affected by the example you set at an unconscious level. You can be a catalyst for change in this way, just by being your self. You do not need to do anything. Just be yourself. Just be. All else will follow.

ACKNOWLEDGEMENTS

I would like to thank all of the people who influenced me in many positive ways during my life. I appreciate all that I have learned in hypnotherapy and psychotherapy from my teacher and mentor Dr Joe Keaney. He truly is a great teacher and taught me some great techniques. I am also grateful for the time I spent with the Buddhist monks in Thailand and for their teachings. I would like to thank Mike Obersteiner, who taught me how to "fly with wings" when I took up paragliding in 2006. I have had many paragliding adventures with Mike since, and he showed me how to overcome fear while living a life of adventure. I would also like to acknowledge the book coach Christine Kloser. Christine has taught me a lot about creative writing and expressing my message into the world in the best possible way. Chris Howard has had a huge impact on me also in terms of what I have learned from his courses and seminars, as well as from him personally. I would also like to acknowledge all the great writers and inspirational leaders in the world we live in. I have been influenced by writers such as Wayne Dyer, Deepak Chopra, and many others. I have also been inspired by leaders of the present and the past, such as Nelson Mandela, Mother Teresa, Martin Luther King, and many others. Lastly, I acknowledge you for reading this book. In doing so, you allow yourself to expand and move forward with more power and choice in your life. I am grateful to be able to serve you in this way.

AFTERWORD

Writing this book has been a journey in itself that has deepened my road to self-discovery. I trust it has done the same for you. The main theme of this book is self-empowerment. When you realize who you truly are, you realize the true power that lies within you. It is in expressing the truth of your authentic self that you can transform your own world, as well as the world around you. You are living your life with authenticity when you can express yourself with freedom. When you take this journey inwards towards your core, you move towards your authentic self. It is a process that takes time as you remove what you don't need while keeping what is valuable. Use what you now know to move forward in your life. Build on the momentum as you become a force of strength for good. Follow your inner guidance and know that you are never alone. Follow your bliss and your heart's desire. You are a child of the universe, and you are loved more than you can ever possibly know. You have everything you need already, including your own truth. Your inner truth sets you free. Express your truth and unleash your authentic self now! When you do, you can live your life with authenticity because you are free. May the source be with you! Go forth in peace, love, and happiness.

ABOUT THE AUTHOR

 Elaine Mc Guinness is passionately dedicated to leading you on your own journey of personal and spiritual development, as well as self-empowerment. As a certified clinical hypnotherapist, hypno-psychotherapist, co-active life coach, reiki master, master NLP practitioner, and nurse, Elaine's mission is to inspire and empower you to live your life on purpose with freedom and fulfilment in expressing and "real-izing" your authentic self. As a black belt in tae kwon do, she uses her own personal experience of how true empowerment comes from within.

Elaine has always been on a spiritual path seeking deeper answers to life's mysteries. Her innate curiosity has allowed her to question people's beliefs about themselves and how these are based on their conditioning and experiences in life. While teaching people how to release their layers of conditioning, Elaine is also dedicated to helping them to live a life on purpose towards fulfilling their highest potential, while remaining true to their authentic self. Elaine's love and passion for inspiring and empowering people to express and live life with authenticity drives her in her ongoing exploration of consciousness and human behaviour. Elaine's stance is that when you come to know who you really are, your self-belief evolves also, as does your consciousness and your ability to create your best life yet!

Elaine is passionate about waking people up to stand more powerfully alive to their own magnificence in realizing their purpose and mission in life.

...perience of the spiritual realm has set her on this path and mis-
...ot helping people to consciously evolve and shape their lives through
focused intention, self-awareness, and self-knowledge. Elaine currently lives
in Kilkenny city, Kilkenny, Ireland, and practises yoga in her spare time.

RESOURCES

www.drdavidhamilton.com (for information on brain studies and research carried out by Dr. David R. Hamilton)

www.glcoherence.org "The Global Coherence Initiative is a science-based, co-creative project to unite people in heart-focused care and intention, to facilitate the shift in global consciousness from instability and discord to balance, cooperation and enduring peace." The project has been launched by the Institute of Heartmath, a non-profit organization and global leader in researching emotional physiology, heart-brain interactions and the physiology of optimal health and performance. The Global Coherence Project is designed to help individuals and groups work together in a synchronized way that increases the impact of their efforts to create positive global change.

www.hayhouse.com (for subliminal messages on Louise L. Hay's CD *Stress Free*)

www.healyourlife.com (Louise L. Hay's website for reading about affirmations, healing, intuition, emotional support, health, meditation, prosperity and spirituality)

www.heartmath.org The Institute of Heartmath has been researching heart intelligence and stress management for over nineteen years. It was founded by Doc Childre in 1991 to help individuals, organizations and the global community incorporate the heart's intelligence into their day-to-day experience of life. Heartmath connects heart and science in a way that empowers people to reduce stress, build resilience, and unlock their natural intuitive

...making better choices. The goal of Heartmath is to create a heart-connected world.

www.mindpowermp3.com (for CDs that use the Solfeggio frequencies)

www.youwealthrevolution.com (for teleseminars hosted by Darius Barazandah, which are inspiring and informative on all aspects of your being)

REFERENCES

1. De Mello, A., *Awareness* (Michigan, USA, 1990).
2. Dyer, W., *The Power of Intention* (London, 2004).
3. Emoto, M., *The Healing Power of Water* (Carlsbad, CA, USA: 2007).
4. Grossman, E.D., Blake, R. *Brain Activity Evoked by Inverted and Imagined Biological Motion*, Vision Research (41) 1475 – 1482 (Vanderbilt University, Nashville, TN, 2001).
5. Hamilton, D.R., *How Your Mind Can Heal Your Body* (London, 2008)
6. Keaney, J., *Lesson 1. Advanced Diploma in Hypnotherapy & Psychotherapy* (Cork, Ireland, 1999).
7. Keaney, J., *Lesson 2. Advanced Diploma in Hypnotherapy & Psychotherapy* (Cork, Ireland, 1999).
8. Lipton, B., *The Biology of Belief* (London, 2005).
9. Morison, J., *Analytical Hypnotherapy*, i: *Theoretical Principles* (Carmarthen, Wales, 2004).
10. Morison, J., *Analytical Hypnotherapy*, ii: *Practical Applications* (Carmarthen, Wales, 2009).
11. O' Connor, J. and Lages, A., *Coaching With NLP* (London, 2004).
12. Schucman, H. and Thetford, W. N. *A Course in Miracles* (New York, USA, 1975).
13. Tolle, E. *The Power of Now*, (London, 1999).
14. Whitworth, et al., *Co-Active Coaching* (California, USA, 2007).